FREEING
DAVID
McCALLUM

FREEING
DAVID
McCALLUM

THE LAST MIRACLE OF
RUBIN "HURRICANE" CARTER

KEN KLONSKY

Lawrence Hill Books
Chicago

Published by Lawrence Hill Books
An imprint of Chicago Review Press Incorporated
814 North Franklin Street
Chicago, Illinois 60610
ISBN 978-1-61373-793-4

Library of Congress Cataloging-in-Publication Data
Names: Klonsky, Kenneth, author.
Title: Freeing David McCallum : the last miracle of Rubin Hurricane Carter /
    Ken Klonsky.
Description: Chicago, Illinois : Lawrence Hill Books, [2018] | Includes
    index.
Identifiers: LCCN 2016057950 (print) | LCCN 2017032104 (ebook) | ISBN
    9781613737941 (pdf) | ISBN 9781613737965 (epub) | ISBN 9781613737958
    (kindle) | ISBN 9781613737934 (cloth : alk. paper)
Subjects: LCSH: McCallum, David, 1969– | Klonsky, Kenneth. | Carter, Rubin,
    1937–2014. | Prisoners—United States—Biography. | Judicial error—United
    States. | Criminal justice, Administration of—United States.
Classification: LCC HV9468.M31 (ebook) | LCC HV9468.M31 K56 2018 (print) |
    DDC 365/.6092 [B]—dc23
LC record available at https://lccn.loc.gov/2016057950

Cover design: John Yates at Stealworks
Front cover photo courtesy of Marc Lamy/Markham Street Films
Typesetting: Nord Compo

This book is dedicated to the memories of Rubin Carter,
Ken Thompson, Larry Hoffman, and Willie Stuckey,
David's coconvicted, who died in prison in 2001.

CONTENTS

INTRODUCTION

If you're giving up on something, what you're really giving up on is yourself.

—Rubin "Hurricane" Carter (1937–2014)

MY CHILDHOOD WAS ENCOMPASSED by a history of segregation and unmasked brutality that has abated but by no means disappeared. Most of my family and friends disapproved of segregation in the United States, but, as some of us northerners later discovered, we were scapegoating the South to cover our own sins of exclusion.

In Rockville Centre, Long Island, where I lived as a child and adolescent, the African American population lived in Lakeview, a census-designated place (CDP) located adjacent to our town, that few white people ever saw. Back then, its inhabitants provided a workforce for menial jobs and domestic help for the white families of our town. My family and many of my friends' families had black maids throughout the time I lived there. Most of the maids came to work via a local bus that made its way up Hempstead Avenue; the only other passengers on this bus were young people who had yet to receive driver's licenses.

Rockville Centre was divided into three religious groups that had minimal contact with each other: descendants of the original Protestant inhabitants who founded the village; Long Island's largest Catholic diocese, with a Catholic hospital and a Catholic school; and a sizeable contingent of upwardly mobile Jewish families to which I belonged. The main property in the village was a golf course, the Rockville Centre Country Club (now Rockville Links Club), an immense fenced-in area that sat in the center of the town's upper-middle-class neighborhoods. My father's generation did not seem to mind that Jews were excluded from membership; the situation was accepted as a fact of life and the cost of residing in a privileged community with highly respected schools and artesian well water. Kids, myself included, used to climb over the very high surrounding fence and damage the greens and fairways. We resented the exclusion even if our parents did not.

One summer in the mid-1960s, I worked as a security guard and was dispatched to various places in Nassau County. My second assignment, for $1.79 an hour, was at a small public housing development in Lakeview. I wore a dark blue uniform and carried a nightstick, my outfit closely resembling that of the local police force, which was viewed unfavorably by the black population. Given all I knew about policing, I might as well have been wearing a Halloween costume. No one threatened me, but I don't doubt now that the uniform made me a potential target. One hot afternoon, two kids were having a serious argument; a long knife was drawn by one and sunk into the shoulder of the other, passing through the skin with no more resistance than through a stick of butter. Appalled and extremely frightened, I left the premises, billy club in tow. I called in the incident to the police but never bothered to find out how the wounded boy had fared. Soon after, I tried to convince a local reporter to investigate what I presumed was a volatile situation in Lakeview. He expressed interest in the story but dropped it soon after. I suspected that the paper didn't want to stir up a hornet's nest.

I requested that the security guard agency find me a new location, resulting in a two-week stint in a bone-chilling supermarket in Long Beach, where one day I confronted a woman for stealing a pack of chewing gum. For some reason, maybe a growing consciousness of social inequalities, witnessing the petty theft and intervening in it felt almost as bad as witnessing the knifing.

In 1967, when I moved up to Toronto to attend graduate school, I came to an understanding of who I had been all those years: a white liberal whose actions failed to match his words. Reading Eldridge Cleaver's famous quote from *Soul on Ice* produced no small amount of discomfort: "If you're not part of the solution, you're part of the problem." Perhaps the phrase, like so much in those turbulent times, was too categorical.

Doris Kearns Goodwin, the famous historian and biographer, wrote an autobiographical book in the 1990s, *Wait Till Next Year*, about growing up in Brooklyn and Rockville Centre. Goodwin, then Doris Kearns, had gone to the same high school as my siblings and me. She made the village sound like *Happy Days*, and compared to many other places in the world, it *was* idyllic. However, I wrote to remind her of both the Rockville Centre Country Club and an incident involving Floyd Patterson, the heavyweight champion of the world. Patterson had bought a house in Rockville Centre in the early 1950s only to find a cross burning on his lawn the next day. She acknowledged the memory and regretted the omission, while emphasizing that the story would have been at odds with the intention of the book. A selective forgetting, even while we were young and living there, a blindness to our privilege and the reasons we prospered, was as much a part of my youth as sexual frustration. I believed that the real problem was in the South: murdered civil rights workers, Selma, Birmingham, dogs, whips, fire hoses. While the bodies of African Americans in the North may not have been maimed, their souls were damaged by the indignity of their situation. As a teenager, both in high school and college, I read every book I could find by great black writers such as James Baldwin, Ralph Ellison, and Richard Wright. My interest in their plight coincided with my voracious appetite for Holocaust books. Even then I was obsessed by victimhood and passionately opposed injustice.

I certainly knew about exceptionality. My parents were divorced in 1961, a shocking embarrassment for me in a state where divorce was outlawed. My mother disappeared one day and flew to Mexico with her soon-to-be new husband to have the divorce granted. She left behind a maid to care for me and my father; my brother and sister were away at college. My father was a personable and hardworking businessman and was helpless around the house. He purchased a toolbox when I was a baby, but I never saw him even hammer a nail. The washing machine bewildered him. My mother leaving devastated us both. At the age of fifteen, I was being mothered, in effect, by an African American woman who had to leave her own children in Lakeview and reside in a spare room in our house. I was happy to know that she was able to spend Sundays going to church with her family. Her dislocation and the puniness of her salary produced anger that she could only half conceal.

In *Soul on Ice*, Eldridge Cleaver compared Floyd Patterson to two other heavyweight champions: Sonny Liston and Muhammad Ali. Oddly enough, from the standpoint of black history, Cleaver's insight produced the most telling comparison of the decade. Patterson was a humble sort of man who helped his defeated challengers off the canvas. With respect to his fights with Liston and Ali, the mannerly Patterson became, ironically, the Great White Hope. In a time of upheaval, Cleaver saw these three men as representatives of competing images and roles in the black communities. Patterson was characterized, rightly or wrongly, as the soon-to-be extinct remnant of slavery. Liston was the thug and rapist. And Ali was the rising of a new black consciousness: "Black is beautiful," the Black Power movement, the Black Panthers, Malcolm X—the defiance of a system that had heaped atrocities on a whole race of people. Patterson refused to acknowledge Ali's adopted name, continuing to refer to him as Cassius Clay. And yet, despite the supposed love white people had for Patterson, he and his family were not welcomed into one of their choice middle-class communities. Patterson moved out.

Where does Rubin Carter belong in this historical context? Although whites were ambivalent toward Muhammad Ali, the personas adopted by Rubin Carter and Sonny Liston, good friends and sparring partners, made them reviled figures. Ali infuriated my father's generation because he converted to Islam and refused the draft, but he was loved by the baby boomers who opposed the Vietnam War. His incredible good looks did him no harm either. For a time, Carter embraced Islam as a reaction against Christianity, which he and other black radicals characterized as a slave religion. In combination with his balefulness, his Fu Manchu mustache, and his Jack Johnson–like shaved head, it is doubtful that any boxer, indeed any person, had a worse image among white Americans than Rubin Carter. I hated him too.

How is it then that I became enmeshed with Carter for the last twelve years of his life? What forces drove the two of us together to accomplish a singular enterprise: freeing David McCallum? And how was it that a dedicated group of professionals from inside and outside the legal profession came to share in this successful undertaking? The title of Rubin Carter's favorite book, *In Search of the Miraculous* by P. D. Ouspensky (G. I. Gurdjieff's interpreter to the Western world), provides a partial answer. David McCallum, incarcerated for decades for a heinous crime he did not commit, had his life frozen in time. The fight for his freedom was ennobling and transformative for every one of us who was involved and his miraculous release is, hopefully, an inspiration for those who believe that diverse groups of people working together to achieve a goal have better odds of success than a single individual.

1

RUBIN CARTER
The Hurricane

IT WAS A WARM, muggy Toronto morning in the summer of 2002. My son, Ray, was at home sleeping off a party that ended after dawn broke. I lay awake the whole night, anticipating how the day would unfold. This summer vacation had a feeling of finality for us both: he was going into his last year of high school, and I was to begin my final year of teaching. I had driven to 155 Delaware Avenue, then the home of Rubin "Hurricane" Carter, to interview him for the *Sun* magazine. I was ridiculously early. Fear and anxiety had me getting caught behind some dump truck or getting a flat tire or losing my way in the city I had lived in for thirty-five years. I got out of the hot car and walked slowly around the block. The interview had been arranged at my home by an intermediary, a dissolute-looking fellow who was to die of alcohol-related illness a few years later. *You are going to interview Rubin Carter*, I kept telling myself, *the famous boxer you hated in your teens; the same Rubin Carter who had been thrown into prison for a triple murder in Paterson, New Jersey, that you were sure he had committed; the same Rubin Carter who was now* *a legend.* I had seen Norman Jewison's searing film *The Hurricane,* about Carter's wrongful conviction, in which the boxer is brilliantly portrayed by Denzel Washington.

I had actually met Rubin Carter previously when he visited the high school English class I taught. I had taken the class on a field trip to see the *The Hurricane,* and they were as overwhelmed as I was by Washington's remarkable portrayal. Knowing that Carter lived in Toronto, I suggested to my students that we write to him and invite him to speak to us. It seemed a good life lesson for them to take the risk of rejection while getting a chance to accomplish something of value. Finding his home was easy because the son of my good friends lived across the street from him. The letters from the class moved Carter to call my home. In an act of inexplicable generosity—his speaking engagements in those years earned him minimally ten thousand dollars—he agreed to speak to us for no fee.

What happened that day at school was magical. Carter and I met with the principal in her office, where I first witnessed a part of his repertoire that became familiar to me over the years: glowing charm. He was the most charismatic individual I've ever known. He entered my classroom and spent an hour and a half "running off at the mouth," as he later described it, talking about Og Mandino, spiritual awakenings, and life lessons that neither the students nor I could comprehend. But what he said was secondary to his presence. The fact that he was there made the moment memorable and life changing for those students. He was validating them; they were special that day; they were envied by other students. Many of them went on to become better students and more involved in the school and went on to graduate.

I understood intuitively that his presence was also a gift to me. I wanted to learn where his ideas originated from, what these ideas might mean to others, and what their ultimate meaning might be in my own life. The *Sun* expressed immediate interest in my interview proposal.

Carter's house was red brick and large, one of thousands of sturdy winter-resistant homes in older Toronto neighborhoods. I climbed up the steps of the covered porch and rang the doorbell. My heart migrated to my throat. I rang again. Nothing. I sat on the railing, thinking he must be doing something that temporarily prevented his coming down. Five minutes later, beset by a different sort of anxiety, I rang again. Still nothing. Maybe the dissolute man had neglected to tell Carter about the appointment or had gotten the day wrong? Excitement slowly ebbed and turned into despair and then to humiliation. Briefcase in hand, I walked back to my car. Had I overreached?

Driving north past his house, I stopped and looked at the front door; seeing no one, I continued on. At that moment, a voice inside me said, *You don't spend months setting up an interview and then just go home.* So I parked and walked back to a corner where I had spotted a pay telephone. (Yes, they still had those things at the time.) Still resisting the culture of the cell phone, I hadn't bothered to take Carter's number with me. My hand shaking, I called home and, when my groggy son answered, directed him to where he could find the number. He gave it to me, but I immediately forgot it after hanging up. So I had to call back. This time, in a very deliberate and condescending fashion, Ray read out the numbers . . . three times.

I couldn't find another quarter, so I went into the corner store for change. Back inside the phone booth, the number eluded me yet again. To stop hyperventilating and to still my mind, I summoned up years of fruitless yoga and meditation. Calling Ray again might make him think that his father was on the verge of dementia. Concentrating fiercely, I heard his patronizing voice: 4 . . . 1 . . . 6 . . . 6 . . . 0 . . . I dropped in the quarter and punched in the number, and the phone rang at the other end.

A deep and authoritative voice answered: "Rubin Carter speaking. How may I help you?"

A deep breath. "Rubin?"

"Ken?"

"I'm calling from Bloor Street. You didn't answer the door."

He let loose the genuine laugh I was to hear hundreds of times during the course of our friendship. "That was you? I never answer the door. You have to call first."

"But M—— never told me that."

"M—— don't know to say shit. Now come on up, my man."

When I went back to Carter's house, the door was open, but no one was there to greet me, aside from a giant fluffy gray cat that brushed past. I rang the bell again, then ventured inside. Carter came down the stairs smoking a cigarette, dressed in casual dark slacks and a dashiki with a gorgeous African print, his skin a darker shade of black. The house reeked of cigarette smoke and an additional annoyance: a very strong cologne. Whenever I returned home from seeing him, I would open a vial of eucalyptus in my car and throw my clothes in the washing machine.

It didn't occur to me until later why he would splash on such a powerful fragrance, why, as I discovered, he would even bathe in it. For ten years in total, he had been in solitary confinement down in a dark hole at ancient Trenton State Prison. Given that he was only allowed to shower every fourteen days, the smell of his own body was repugnant to him. His preparations for being in public, in addition to the cologne baths, included the insertion of a custom-made glass eye—he had lost one eye after a botched retinal operation in the ill-equipped prison hospital—and a set of glistening false teeth. When male pattern baldness set in, he bought an Akubra, a wide-brimmed Australian hat, to wear at public events and speaking engagements and on television. But it wasn't just vanity that motivated him. Since the justice system had stolen his youth and middle years, he was determined to take them back: he told his friends that his date of birth was now November 8, 1985, the year, month, and day he emerged from prison. An odd but compelling mixture of a man, he died at age twenty-nine—or seventy-seven, if you insist on being conventional.

"Phoenix, get on in here." The cat obeyed. It had a beautiful face and less separation from its master than most of its breed. "Come on up, my man." Carter waved at me to follow him.

On the stairway walls hung many photos, all of Carter with well-known people—Nelson Mandela, Denzel Washington, Norman Jewison, Ellen Burstyn, and Sugar Ray Robinson—and one iconic photo of Bob Dylan in a flop hat staring in at Rubin through a prison door.

Inside his office, he sat down in front of a well-ordered desk and motioned for me to sit a short distance across from him. He blew out a cloud of smoke, the kind of billow wherein the smoker actually disappears for a second. I began to cough. This did not bode well for my image, or for my allergies.

"Well, well, well, well, well." He butted out. Fiercely, frighteningly, he asked, "What is this about?"

Just then I knew that he hadn't bothered to read the numerous *Sun* magazine copies I had sent him.

When a person is falling, his brain subdivides time in much the same way the seconds tick down at the end of a basketball game. While seconds are the only measurement for twenty-three minutes, the final minute of each half is measured in tenths of a second. Those tenths suddenly take on significance. In just the same way, my mind subdivided tenths of a second into thousandths. I knew I needed to say something perfect to avoid getting thrown out the door.

"Posterity." Yes, that bought me time for a full sentence. "Posterity, Rubin. People are going to know what you think, not just that you were a boxer and a wrongly convicted man." He didn't stop me, so I kept going. "The *Sun* gives the longest interviews of any magazine; they let you have your say."

From the look on his face, whether by chance, luck, or intuition, I knew I had appealed to something inside him, his innermost need for serious recognition (having not yet received his two treasured honorary doctorates). He smiled and lit another cigarette. I took out my tape recorder and my writing pad. *Suck it up*, I thought. *Wait until next time to ask him to stop smoking.*

Carter then stood up, broad and powerful despite his smallish stature, and, with a mischievous look, walked out the door, closing it behind him. Ten seconds passed, the door opened, and he peered inside.

"Turn that thing on." He pointed to the recorder. From the hallway, he boomed, "There are four kinds of knowing, Ken. The first kind of knowing is not knowing, or ignorance. You listening, my brother?"—Rubin Carter had just called me "brother"!—"Anybody can guess there's a desk and a chair and the normal stuff you find inside an office. But what's that person gonna know about the other contents in the office? Nothing! He can only guess, and he's gonna be wrong most of the time. That's ignorance. Spouting off when you don't know a damn thing."

Then he stuck his head inside the door. "The second kind of knowing is what I see from the door. I can't know everything that's in the office, but at least I have some facts in front of me. The desk is there; the window's at the back. My guess about everything else is going to be educated but superficial; that's superficial knowing."

Then he stepped fully inside. "This is the third kind of knowing, Ken. I'm in the room. I see everything that's in here and can name everything I see. It's all in front of me. I'm not guessing anymore. I now know that the other Rubin Carters, the ignorant one behind the door and the superficial one, did not know the full contents of the room. But I do. I know it all . . . don't I, Ken?"

I nodded, quietly assented, "I guess so," while realizing that I was awaiting the kicker.

He laughed. "You guess, but you're wrong. The third Rubin Carter, the one who just walked into the room and thinks he knows everything, is worse off than the other two. He's asleep, but he's convinced he knows what he really can't know. He's the dangerous one, like all people who judge things from what they see on the surface. Like people in a court of law. They can't know the whole truth . . . and you can't know it either. Can you? Damn right you can't." He laughed mockingly, sat down, and lit another cigarette, his body embracing the smoke like a doomed lover. Then he laid the lit cigarette in the ashtray. He liked doing that, keeping a lit cigarette in the ashtray.

"And that brings us to the fourth kind of knowing. I'm in the room, above the room, below the room, inside the drawers and the closets all at once. I don't mean that. No—no—no." He began to stammer. Pointing to the tape recorder, he said, "Turn that thing off! Turn it off!" Rubin had stammered as a child, a speech impediment so terrible that he could not speak a single full sentence before he was thirteen years old. His life was encompassed by ridicule, humiliation, and the meting out of violence to those who laughed. He sat there in front of me but not seeing me, struggling with words. He picked up the cigarette and dragged deeply.

"Turn it on again. These ideas . . . these ideas . . . mmmmmm"—a deep rumble—"It's almost impossible to talk about. What I'm saying, Ken, is that this room doesn't exist for the fourth Rubin Carter. Not at all. On a higher level of life, this room does not exist. That's the level of consciousness. Consciousness. Consciousness." He punctuated the word with his trademark smile, all-embracing and forbidding at the same time, and his laugh, which hinted a bit at self-mockery, but only a very little bit.

He went on. "Those first three Rubin Carters were all sleeping unconscious beings. Not the fourth. The fourth man . . . the fourth man . . . is not even Rubin Carter. This man is awake. This man woke up to this world of infinite possibility. From inside a prison cell, he woke up." He stared into my eyes and held my gaze. Once again, he let out that sonorous laugh, that deep cackle.

"You hearing this, my brother? There are laws that govern this level of life: what goes around, comes around; every action has an equal reaction. These laws don't exist on a higher level, but you don't need to climb up a mountain to reach that higher level. You can even find it in a prison. The day-to-day life in a prison is the lowest level a man can be on this earth and still be alive. Nothing but savagery. Nothing but unconscious human insanity. People acting like machines—robbing, raping, killing one another. But the highest level is right inside you. It's always been there; it will always be there until you die. You can find it anytime and anyplace you want, but you have to do 'the work.'" I could not escape the feeling that he was speaking as much to me as to the readers of the magazine.

"What kind of work?" I asked.

"The work. On your inner self. That work is too difficult for most people. Even outside a prison. I never would have found myself if I *hadn't* been in prison. That's the miracle. A miracle is nothing but higher laws manifested on a lower level." Dragging on the cigarette, he leaned back. This big house that he shared with Phoenix, this office, was his domain.

I began to think of a riddle: What's the hardest thing in the world to find yet is sitting right next to you? I listen now to this first tape of many and remember my initial cynicism. Was he just blowing more smoke?

"You know what I'm talking about, Ken? Let me try and explain it a different way. I work with the law; I'm the founder and CEO of the Association in Defense of the Wrongly Convicted. Wrongly convicted people need a miracle to get them out of prison. The whole system is stacked against them. When one of them goes free, higher laws are acting on a lower level. The fact that you can see me sitting here in front of you is a miracle. This man here, who is Rubin Carter and who is not Rubin Carter, just narrowly escaped the electric chair.

"I don't blame the law for wrongful convictions. I don't blame police. I don't blame prosecutors. I don't blame judges. The law is just what it has to be on this lower level of existence. But don't be mistaking it for the truth, my brother. You have to *fight* for truth against falsehood."

Carter invited me out to his backyard, where on several subsequent occasions I would find him tending his impatiens. His extended family came from the rural South, and he was never happier than during the times he spent in his yard, which he called Summer Garden/Winter Light. A cement pathway wound its way around some venerable trees and earthenware pots and led to a place of meditation underneath a trellis. "This is what I call heaven," he said.

I moved quickly from interviewer to intimate. When we began that day, I had been the man outside the door of the room. He decided to let me inside. He decided to grace me. I knew for certain that my life was going to change irrevocably, but I didn't know, for better or worse, how that was going to happen. I also knew, like Sancho Panza, that I was ready to follow this Don Quixote to wherever he might take me. I was to become a part of his story, he of mine.

Carter had sized me up for two qualities: perseverance and loyalty. He also saw that I was naive and easy to manipulate, but uneven relationships can still serve the needs of both parties. When in 2004 Carter decided to break away from the Association in Defense of the Wrongly Convicted (AIDWYC)—the premier innocence project in Canada, now known as Innocence Canada—because of an ethical dispute that he called a "betrayal of principle," he knew he needed someone like me to accompany him into the wilderness. Considering that AIDWYC had been his life and his living, his decision to leave revealed equal measures of courage, rigidity, and belief. At the time, I tried to get him to reconsider for practical reasons. He would be sacrificing his salary and a base of legal expertise second to none. But practicality was a contemptible consideration to a man who had spent nineteen years in prison protesting his innocence, refusing to wear prison garb, refusing to do prison jobs, refusing to eat prison food, resulting in those ten years of solitary confinement.

Nothing could negate the suffering he felt from the loss of his organization. Carter was as emotionally distraught as I would ever see him and said about losing the baby that he had "swaddled," "I loved it, I nurtured it, I educated it with the love of Truth. The organization stood for Justice and Truth in the face of error, injustice, deliberate falsehood, and state violence."

AIDWYC's loss was almost equal to Carter's. His legal work and considerable oratorical gifts brought the immense problem of wrongful convictions to the forefront of the legal community. His other undying legacy was personal transformation. As he said in the *Sun* interview:

> In my twenty years of unjust imprisonment, I had resisted everything about that foul abomination of the human spirit, but I also needed to resist those things about myself that had put me into prison. I was just as capable as anyone else of hurting people, jailing, enslaving, cursing, disrespecting, and raising hell. I was endowed by nature with all of the weaknesses, frailties and human failings that every other human being possesses. Knowing this allowed me to understand that compassion and forgiveness begin with the self. Before we can forgive anybody for anything, we first have to forgive ourselves for being the very things we hate.

In August 2003, my *Sun* interview with Rubin Carter appeared, distilled from over twenty hours of audiotape. Carter received several copies in the mail before the magazine was sent out to me and to its seventy thousand subscribers. He called me up and, using an uncharacteristically neutral tone, asked me over to see it. This time when

I rang the bell, the door opened within seconds. There stood Qwen Chapman, a thin, tall, and stylish woman with a radiant smile and a black fedora, part of a large cast of characters who came in and out of Carter's life. She extended a hand and welcomed me.

From up the stairs, Carter shouted, "That Ken? Bring him up here, Qwen." At that moment, hearing a lilt in his voice, I knew I could relax. Qwen and I climbed the stairway and entered his office.

From his desk chair, leaning dangerously back, Carter boomed, "I love it, Ken! I love it!" Brandishing the magazine, which had a photo of an intense African American boy on the cover, he crowed, "This is a seed, a seed! You don't know where it's gonna grow, how it's gonna grow, or what it's going to grow into, but it's not just gonna sit there on the page." Then, a very big smile and a hand extended. "I love it. Thank you, my brother. I only wish they hadn't put my prison photo in there. I don't look like that anymore." Giving it another glance, he muttered, "And those bell-bottoms."

When I got a look at the interview that evening, I could understand his elation. It had been brilliantly edited. The ideas were intact, and the reordering of questions and answers made the piece feel completely organic. As I had led Carter to believe, they had taken him seriously; the result revealed the intellectual and spiritual core of a man who had suffered grievously in isolation but had miraculously triumphed.

The concept of a "seed" that Carter referred to was meaningful and yet elusive. It is always difficult to trace the seed of a human endeavor; if you go back far enough, looking for the place to begin, you might wind up in the Garden with Adam and Eve. With an African American, you might trace the origin of a tragedy back to the institution of slavery. But where exactly does the story of freeing David McCallum from prison begin?

McCallum wrote over six hundred letters to every innocence project, every lawyer who worked pro bono, evidence testing labs,

TV and radio outlets—six hundred letters! He even wrote to Rubin Carter while Carter was still at AIDWYC:

August 21, 2002
RE: FALSE JUSTICE
Dear Mr. Carter:

Please be advised that I am writing you in hopes that you and your agency will take an interest in helping me prove my innocence. I have enclosed a copy of a letter from the Prisoner's Legal Service of New York informing me that they could not assist me in my cause, however they indicated that your agency may be in a better position to help me.

I am sure that you and your agency receive an abundance of letters across North America asking for help with them all claiming innocence. I am mature enough to realize that it is simply not possible to do that for everyone.

To some extent, I have adopted a defeated man's mentality when it comes to trying to obtain the help I need to prove my innocence but I cannot give up because I really believe that help is out there. It is just a matter of me continuing to fight for what I believe in.

Since my state appeals have been exhausted, I have commenced a letter writing campaign hoping to bring as much awareness to my case as I possibly can.

Win Wahrer, AIDWYC's executive secretary, sent David McCallum an application, which McCallum filled out and returned soon after. Thus far, as he wrote, his campaign from prison had yielded little in the way of results. I learned from Rubin that the process David was using, seeking all possible avenues of appeal, is known in prisons as "fishing." In my experience, most convicted people who claim innocence actually are innocent, because a claim of innocence might harm them. They will usually be prevented from getting parole since they cannot show the required remorse for crimes they did not commit. Parole boards sometimes treat claims of innocence as indicative of a delusional personality.

For indigent wrongly convicted people, finding an innocence project is the only means of escaping many years of failed pro se appeals. But it takes time for innocence projects to assess whether each person is worthy of support and has a case that might lead to exoneration. Those applying have to be as persistent, patient, and personable as David McCallum. Innocence is only the first requirement. In addition, a project has to be certain that the person, perhaps damaged irrevocably by his or her experience inside a correctional facility, will not go out and commit a crime. While tens of thousands of innocent people sit behind bars, a select few get the help they cannot otherwise afford to pay for.

Once a prisoner has been accepted, an innocence project can provide research, legal assistance, private investigators, financial and emotional support, educational opportunities, and media publicity. David was driven by the knowledge that a project will go to the wall for that prisoner until the day he or she is released. A good thing too, because David and I would learn that once a project accepts a case, it takes ten years on average for the wrongly convicted to be freed.

2

DAVID McCALLUM

The Prisoner

ON FEBRUARY 2, 2004, in the prison library at Eastern Correctional Facility, in Ulster County, New York, David McCallum came across the August 2003 issue *of* the *Sun*. The magazine is distributed for free in many prisons throughout the United States. Prisoners, most guilty of some heinous, thoughtless, or foolish crime, are frequent contributors to the *Sun*'s "Readers Write" section. David's acquaintance Earl Coleman was reading the Carter interview, "Going the Distance: Rubin Carter's Long Journey from Convict to Crusader," and he asked Earl if he could read it next. He knew Rubin Carter had been released after nineteen years and was now the key spokesperson worldwide for the wrongly convicted. He digested the interview like manna. Looking back on the experience after gaining his release, David recalled to me his excitement: "Things get lost or stolen in prison, so I made four different copies. I read it fifteen times."

Carter became another possible means to McCallum's ultimate end. Since I was the interviewer, I was the recipient of David's next letter.

February 16, 2004

Dear Mr. Klonsky,

... I wrote the Sun because I was intrigued by an interview I read recently with Mr. Rubin "Hurricane" Carter in the August 2003 issue. I wanted to write to you personally to thank you for such an inspiring interview because I firmly believe that I got a lot out of that interview that will help my very own situation ...

I have been incarcerated for nearly nineteen years for a crime I did not commit, and it has been a passion to prove my innocence or at least bring some awareness to my case by establishing a letter writing campaign, but no one seems to want to take my letters serious enough to take an interest in. Fortunately, that has not discouraged me at all and I am able to move forward.

My question to you is would it be alright for me to share my story with you in a future letter? I am confident that you would be intrigued and interested by my plight. Like your interview with Mr. Carter, my story would be able to inspire and motivate people to get more involved in advocate work because there are thousands of innocent people languishing in prison with what appears to be no hope at all.

I immediately believed that David McCallum was telling the truth. Granted, I had no prior experience in wrongful convictions or even with the law. When I talked to family and friends about my early correspondence with him, their response was invariably, "How do you know you can trust him?" Even now, with media stories every week of exonerations in North America, the unfounded belief still persists that part of being a prisoner is being a con artist. What could I say? That I felt through McCallum's letter that he was genuine? If that made a sucker of me, so be it. McCallum had found the right person *because* of my inexperience and my recent association with Rubin Carter. While ignorant of the law, my experience as a teacher of English made me an expert in gauging the sincerity of writing. Coming to the law from the outside would involve a steep learning curve, but it was also advantageous. I was able to see things that others within the legal profession might miss or discredit, things born of elementary intuition or shaped by Rubin's unique perspective.

I learned from Rubin that the strengths of the legal system also point to its weaknesses. Its use of logic and precedent allows a lawyer to reasonably argue either side of a case. The law subjugates emotion in favor of logical argument, leading from subjectivity to objectivity. But every person brings intuition, common sense, and feelings to the courtroom. The court makes witnesses "swear to tell the truth, the whole truth, and nothing but the truth," but that oath is a chimera. Witnesses are unreliable because memory is unreliable and because what a witness sees and hears is subject to individual interpretation. What Carter made me understand was that a verdict—a word that implies truth—*might* be the truth or is usually the truth, but it should not be mistaken for the truth. I was to learn this fact many times over.

My impression of the legal system at that time—and when I look back, it's almost impossible to imagine such naïveté—was that its ultimate aim was justice. I believed that as soon as a wrongful conviction was recognized, the wrongly convicted person would be on the verge of freedom. This sense of belief explains my enthusiasm in my response to McCallum, dated February 24:

> I would be honored to read your story and I would be happy to pass your story on to Rubin and AIDWYC (Association in Defense of the Wrongly Convicted) to see if something cannot be done to help you. . . . If, as you allege, you have been wrongly convicted and served nineteen years for a crime you

did not commit, it is a testament to your strength that you are still alive and have not abandoned hope.

Remembering this moment after his release, David said, "Your letter represented hope, an opportunity. I was ecstatic. The mail itself may have been my lifeline, but in nineteen years [from October 1985 to February 2004] I had never received a good vibe from the six hundred other letters. . . . Every time someone said 'no,' you felt they didn't believe you. Tears flowed with every rejection. By 2004, I decided that my letters were too long. I had to stick to facts and minimal details then offer to tell them the full story."

He hooked me at the end of a line that was growing frayed after nineteen years. McCallum, of course, was using me to bait the big fish, Rubin Carter. On March 23, he sent me a response along with a synopsis of his case.

I cannot say enough about the encouraging and reassuring words that you mentioned in your letter. . . . I enclosed a brief synopsis of my story for you to read and to forward on to Rubin Carter and AIDWYC. Mr. Klonsky, with the strength and determination that I have displayed throughout my years of incarceration, it saddens me to say that there were also tragic events that I have endured along the way . . . which I have used for motivation nevertheless.

In my story, you will read about Willie Stuckey. . . . Mr. Stuckey passed away on December 3, 2001, from an undisclosed illness.

David McCallum's story actually began with an incident in Ozone Park, Queens, on October 20, 1985, in which a young woman, according to a police interview, was washing a red Buick Regal in her driveway. As this woman told a police investigator, two twenty-year-old men of noticeably different heights, one with braided hair, stopped on the sidewalk and turned to speak to her. In 1985, when murder and theft were rampant in New York City, one might assume that this was no casual encounter.

"Nice car," one of the men said.

Her answer: "If it's not here in the morning, I'll know where to look."

The two men moved on. Shortly thereafter, around the corner, a young man named Nathan Blenner was entering a black Buick Regal. Two African American men, or two "brown men," as they were described by two child witnesses, accosted Blenner and carjacked the vehicle, taking Blenner along with them. Blenner was found dead the next day in the rear of Aberdeen Park, Brooklyn, a bullet in the back of his head. The car was found a day later in a warehouse parking lot, doused with kerosene and half-burned.

David McCallum and Willie Stuckey, both sixteen, identical in height, and neither with braided hair, were arrested on Sunday, October 27, charged with and ultimately convicted of the murder. Since they rejected a plea bargain of fifteen years to life, opting for trial against legal advice, they received sentences of twenty-five years to life. This case is still mystifying. Why, despite having no concrete connection to any aspect of this killing, despite never being seen in Queens by anyone or having ever driven a car, were McCallum and Stuckey questioned in the first place? How could they have been convicted of murder? Why were two different suspects fitting the woman's description, one of them working at the hardware store where the kerosene can originated, questioned and ultimately ignored? Some of the *whys* will never be known with certainty, especially when one follows the steps of the investigation and attempts to get inside the head of a deceased police detective. The *how* is far easier: David's case, in every aspect, is a template for wrongful convictions, including false confessions and ineffective assistance of counsel. Permeating this case from the start, along with an amoral cruelty, is the smell of corruption and collusion.

I assured McCallum that I would pass on his letter to Carter and AIDWYC. After that, the least I could do would be to learn more about him, while hoping that the AIDWYC lawyers would pick up his case. One of the early revelations in David's letters was that he also drew inspiration from the Jewison film about Carter, albeit for different reasons. While my initial identification with Carter was rooted in my past, David's was very much in the present:

> I had the opportunity to watch the movie "The Hurricane" a few years ago and I must admit it was very emotional. . . . There were so many instances in that movie that reminded me of my own circumstances that I actually cried in front of my fellow inmates. Seeing the movie and then reading afterwards what Mr. Carter had to contend with during his young life, and what he has become, is enough motivation for me to never abandon hope.
>
> I have learned through the years that when they give you a life sentence they just figure you will rot quietly in prison. And they are not far from right. Nobody really cares about you. . . . There's no urgency or sympathy. You are just behind these walls sending out S.O.S.'s.

Upon seeing this letter, Rubin was taken with David McCallum. Showing vulnerability like that inside a prison, especially by someone who had been there for such a long time, spoke to David's strength and inviolability.

In late July, I wrote to the office of Governor George Pataki to request a pardon for McCallum. The reply I received assured me that since McCallum had a perfect disciplinary record, he was eligible for clemency. How simple! Here I was, an amateur, and I had broken through the system on the first try! A good thing too, because Rubin, at this same moment, was splitting up with AIDWYC. He had a falling-out with them over the appointment of a judge in Ontario who, as a prosecutor, had manufactured the wrongful conviction of Guy Paul Morin, AIDWYC's founding case. The organization refused to back Rubin when he demanded that they come out against the appointment.

Dear David,

I have some not so good news and some perhaps very good news. I'll start with the first. The delay in visiting you has been precipitated by a disagreement between Rubin, an extremely principled man, and the organization he heads. . . . Rubin has resigned (I hope temporarily) from AIDWYC . . .

The "perhaps very good news" is that you are being encouraged by Pataki's office to apply for clemency and I believe that you will get it. I hope and pray that your time of incarceration will soon be ending.

David did not read these developments with the same enthusiasm.

To say that I am disappointed would be an understate-ment. . . . It is extremely unfortunate what has transpired between Mr. Carter and AIDWYC. I cannot imagine the effect their disagreement will have on so many people. However, I am cautiously optimistic that a compromise will be reached between them.

Seeing the word "compromise" now, I realize that both of us knew one thing that the other did not. David knew the system, but he did not know that "compromise" was not a word in Rubin Carter's lexicon; I had already seen the way Carter jettisoned former friends when they disappointed him. This disagreement between him and the organization he founded, seen through David's eyes, was suddenly more worrisome.

In fact, AIDWYC did try to propose a compromise. Rubin was welcome to call a press conference, and the members of the board would attend. He could speak out against the judicial appointment, but if they were asked, they would make it clear that he was speaking for only himself. An outraged Carter stepped down, issuing a characteristic condemnation: "In my mind's eye, the passion for Truth, the spirit that drove AIDWYC, was gone!"

As to my enthusiasm for Pataki's office, David also put a damper on that. He thanked me for the "wonderfully written letter" I had sent them but cautioned that "Mr. Pataki is not a popular person amongst the prison population because of his hard-line approach toward non-violent crimes resulting in unfair sentences." As I read David's letter further, I sank even lower.

> Hopefully my application will be given serious consideration for a pardon, but I have to caution you that my chances may not be very good considering that inmates typically have to wait several years due to the many applications. . . . I am sure you can sense by the tone of my words that I am approaching this pessimistically.

So for the first time I was confronted by my ignorance of the legal system, especially the postconviction system. Sobering realities would counter unrealistic expectations. Many times I was elated by a supposed breakthrough only to face cruel disappointment. Since David was inured to stalling and duplicity, my disappointment would be greater than his, but he was the one whose suffering would continue. While I could go off and do other things, he had to face the razor wire. People in authority talk a lot about justice, but they won't often go out of their way to right injustice. Wrongful convictions are anathema to judges and prosecutors because of the inevitable damage inflicted on their reputations. Some of them go to great lengths to avoid taking personal responsibility for the suffering of the innocent. Some are concerned with protecting their departments. Some make sure that one layer of the justice system covers up for another.

When I asked David how he kept hope after coming up against all these obstacles, he said that his innocence gave him no choice: "When I saw prison guards come in the next morning or outside workers leave the building, that motivated me. I knew there was a world outside the door. When I was taken by bus for physical check-ups outside the prison, I saw some of the world, children, dogs, trees, outside the window. That world was waiting for me."

Hope turned up in unexpected places. Rubin was given an honorary doctorate of laws by Griffiths University (Brisbane, Australia) during a graduation ceremony held in Toronto for their teachers' college. Before he addressed the graduates, he introduced me to his old friend, Sam Leslie, a tall drink of water whom he'd flown up from Georgia for the occasion. Rubin explained, "I met Sam at Trenton State. I've never been as close to anyone in my life, man or woman." They both laughed, considering how that remark might go down inside a prison. "I promised Sam that when we got out of prison I'd take him to the Blue Lagoon in Jamaica and we'd put our feet in the water. I haven't paid off yet, have I, Sam?"

"Rubin is always good for his debts," Sam remarked.

"Damn right I am."

Rubin was introduced with fanfare and stood behind the lectern on the stage, resplendent as a cardinal in scarlet cap and gown. He spoke with pride and unfettered joy at being honored by an academic institution. For twenty-five minutes, he spoke about himself, his ordeal, and his triumph, saying nothing to the graduates about the hard work they had done to get a degree or the challenges they might face on the road ahead. Rubin sometimes forgot that these ceremonies were about the students, and no one, including me, ever reminded him. He finished each such speech with "Dare to dream!" And since the graduates felt blessed simply by having this dynamic speaker address them, I think that was sufficient.

At that time, Griffiths had committed to establishing a new innocence project with Rubin as the CEO. The rift with AIDWYC would not be healed, and Innocence International was born in its stead. In my next letter to David, I was over the top again. What miracles could Rubin not perform? David would be Rubin's first case.

This time my enthusiasm was reciprocated. Rubin's reputation alone made anything possible, both to those inside and outside the prison walls.

Dear Ken,

After receiving the great news, I am finding it extremely difficult to contain my enthusiasm. I have taken your advice and am enjoying this news because for the first time in years, I genuinely believe I am on the right path. I am really looking forward to receiving the help of Innocence International.

Mr. Carter's words, "Tell him we are going to come get him," were very profound and encouraging. They even elicited tears of hope and belief from me. My spirits have been uplifted considerably, and I have no intention of allowing doubt to seep into my thought process . . .

I sent a copy of your letter to my Mom and Dad because I like to keep them abreast of what is going on with me. I am sure they are going to be overwhelmed with happiness.

Whoa! What had I committed myself to? I never even thought about his family: aged mother, father at home and unemployed because of a work-related accident, three brothers, and three sisters. Like Rubin, David was the middle child in a family of seven siblings. They now had expectations as well. None of them knew how unqualified I was for this work. But, I told myself, with money coming from Griffiths University and Rubin's reputation, we could get secretarial and legal help, even hire a private investigator. I would be an emotional support for David until his inevitable release. But then I discovered, during a dismaying phone call, that Rubin was not quite ready to commit. "We got to visit the brother, Ken. Go down there. See what he's like. If I think he's going to leave the prison and do something foolish, I won't represent him." Given Rubin's promise about "coming to get" David, this caveat weighed on me. David and I had thought that Rubin's impending visit from Toronto was to say hello and meet our new client, not to assess his character.

Most of the prisoners had seen Jewison's film, so even the youngest inmates were aware of Rubin Carter. At his first restaurant dinner after his release, David recalled, "For lots of us, *The Hurricane* had a deeper meaning: what you can accomplish inside the prison walls. He had stood up for himself while inside the prison. He was held in high esteem because of his time in SHU [solitary confinement] for going up against the system."

I had only been to a prison on one occasion, to visit a former student who had been incarcerated for sexual assault. I still remember the smell of stale cigarette smoke permeating every square inch of every wall. Before leaving Toronto for our first visit to David McCallum, Rubin appointed Alonzo Starling, a big bear of a man with a sunny disposition, his chief of staff and me his director of media relations. I wondered if Alonzo was as bemused as I was when taking on a role for which I had no experience aside from writing. Alonzo drove us in his red SUV along rural back roads in upstate New York, roads with small restaurants where a brief time ago African Americans would not have been served. Rubin also faced segregation in the South with the armed forces and on the New Jersey Turnpike, where his family could not use the washrooms in the gas stations. On long trips, he always rode in the back seat with an empty coffee cup. (I discovered later that this was not a holdover from segregation days but a way of dealing with an enlarged prostate.)

This trip was filled with coincidence. We were going to visit an African American prisoner, who, like Rubin, had been wrongly convicted of murder and who had been incarcerated eleven days before Rubin was released. Rubin exited and David entered prison in the same year (1985), and by 2004 David had been in prison for nineteen years. Rubin spent a total of nineteen years in prison as a wrongly convicted man. For Rubin, who believed that everything in the universe is connected, there was transcendental significance to these details. "Of course there is, Ken!" he said then and countless times thereafter.

I discovered that David McCallum is an unusual person. When confronted by emotional situations—and we were to have no shortage of them before and after his release—he draws in his breath and goes silent, as if needing to consider how to respond. I think the nineteen years of prison he had endured by 2004 had forced him to repress emotions for his survival. And yet, paradoxically, he is a deeply empathetic and compassionate person. That he was able to maintain his humanity after twenty-nine years in that "foul abomination of the human spirit," as Rubin referred to prison, is the truest measure of his triumph.

David is small in height but imposing in stature. Some prison inmates, because of depression and bad food, tend toward corpulence, but while David is heavyset, he is as solid as a steel ball. His pained expression from years of injustice is tempered by gentleness. His sense of humor also surprises. He suffers and he laughs, exhibiting a full panoply of emotions that endears him to everyone.

In telling me thirteen years later about our 2004 visit, the experience was still indelible for David: "How would I present myself?

Would I cry? Would I be too nervous? This was my opportunity. I spent a lot of time in the bathroom. I went through my daily ritual focused on the clock. By afternoon I wondered, *When are they coming?* I'd have to go put on different clothes, my newer state greens. I started to doubt. Everyone knew I was waiting. At the mattress shop where I worked, a couple of guys went past the door and pointed at me. They knew something. They looked very happy and moved on. I knew then that the Hurricane was in the building. Other prisoners are happy for you; they have seen you suffering. Of course, the front room guards, the first stage in the grapevine, sent word around to their buddies."

David entered the visitor's room, actually the prison cafeteria, with an uncertain smile. One of the corrections officers had told him to take a deep breath. Conquering his hesitation, "I walked over and hugged everyone," he told me, "including you."

David and Rubin's first meeting appeared to be love at first sight. They hugged for longer than the allowed ten seconds. Then they sat on opposite sides of the table, staring silently into each other's eyes for perhaps five minutes. Remembering these moments, David continued, "I would not be the one to start the conversation. It was eerie. I didn't realize that Rubin was reading me, looking for my spiritual core. I had no solid religious beliefs, but Rubin was looking beyond religion. I thought that Alonzo was just Rubin's bodyguard. But he was so friendly, I felt comforted by him." At a certain point, David began to feel puzzled by this man staring at him. He thought, *Who is this guy?* Alonzo and I could only look on with bewilderment and awe.

All subsequent visits with McCallum by us or by anyone I knew—and I knew almost everyone who visited him—suspended time. I think this phenomenon was the result of David's unshakeable integrity, his readiness to learn, and his genuine interest in other people. Like Rubin, he commanded respect by his very being. The prison cafeteria was drab, the plastic chairs small and uncomfortable, the food from vending machines (although David called it filet mignon), and yet some force transcended the banal circumstances. You could tell that the other prisoners sitting with families and friends—that minority of prisoners who have any level of support in the outside world—knew that *the* Rubin Carter was talking to David McCallum.

Finally, Rubin spoke to David. "I don't know how long this is gonna take, my brother, but we are going to get you out of here. Guaranteed." My doubts about Rubin's commitment dissolved.

David tried to focus the conversation exclusively on his case, mentioning variously: "I was handcuffed." "The detective slapped me." "He held a chair over my head." "He tricked me into believing that I was a witness to the crime and not a suspect." "My lawyer did nothing to protect me."

Rubin stopped him short. "The law put you in prison, my brother. The law is there to keep you in prison." David sat back as Rubin went on. "The law won't help you all by itself to get you out of here. It never does. Now stop talking about your case and tell me about yourself."

David related how he grew up in Dillon, South Carolina, in a large family. Upon coming to Brooklyn in the late stages of the Great Migration, he had to earn respect in the streets. "I had no goals or future. Just hung out in the street. The street provided a refuge from my home. I had to escape from the horror of my father abusing my mother. Still, it's no excuse. I abused my freedom and allowed myself to be influenced in the wrong direction." David committed a serious crime, exactly the same crime for which Rubin was justly convicted, the robbery of an older woman. David had used a toy gun to frighten the woman, who, he said, reminded him of his own mother. Rubin had snatched a purse, knocking the woman down in the process. Both men were humiliated and regretful by simply recalling the episode. David's father told him that if he continued this way of life, he would wind up in one of two places: a prison or a coffin. He was on probation for the robbery when Nathan Blenner was murdered.

Now thirty-five, he had known the insides of four separate prisons. The first, as for many New York City–area offenders, was Rikers Island, where he was placed in remand for the Blenner killing. "I was in C-74 for adolescents," he said. "These kids were violent and wild, and the guards were just as violent and wild. When there were fights or race riots in the yard, a guard would push an emergency button and the goon squad came out swinging batons. They'd hit anybody they saw. I was scared to death. You never saw that stuff in the adult section of the prison, all the way on the other side of the complex. For me, adults represented safety. They invited me to the law library just to talk. It was a way for me to survive.

"But to survive in the adolescent wing was pretty much predicated on my making a name for myself, because I had seen if you didn't stand up for yourself, you were subjected to being taken advantage of in many ways, including sexually. What I am saying is that I had to actually be someone other than myself in order to make it through the madness."

After his 1986 conviction, he was evaluated for two months at the Elmira Correctional Facility reception center and sent to Coxsackie Correctional Facility (in Greene County): "While it was very crowded, it was peacefully run and violence was at a minimum. I guess they saw me as low risk. I started working on my case at Coxsackie. I wanted to be like the prisoners going into the law library. I wanted to learn as much as I could so that I could get myself out. I saw people get their cases reversed. I read about prosecutorial misconduct. I learned how to file an appeal."

Prison number three, Eastern, where David was when we first saw him, was "an honor jail with good counselors and where inmates got along." The warden set the tone there. He was a progressive and believed in the transformative power of education in the broadest sense, making sure that prisoners had adequate resources and opportunities to interact with invited guests from the legal and educational professions. Unlike some prison authorities whose only concern is preventing overt violence, this warden wanted prisoners to leave prison capable of functioning in society. How novel that now seems.

David elaborated: "We had tutors. We had a debating club where university law students debated prisoners, and the prisoners usually won. The mattress shop—where we stuffed mattresses with cotton batting and stapled them, two hundred mattresses a day for use in hospitals and institutions—that was a plum job. We made forty-two cents an hour, Park Avenue wages at a prison. We used the money mostly in the commissary and for extra stamps."

The major problem with Eastern was not obvious to an outsider. Rubin alerted me to the danger that David, serving a life sentence, would become so inured to prison that he would no longer care about leaving. "Never get comfortable in a prison if you are wrongly convicted!" Rubin warned. David admitted years later that he had become institutionalized: "I accepted myself as a prisoner. I didn't see that making prisoners comfortable was the prison's method of keeping peace. I fell asleep." Even though he doggedly continued to pursue his case, he was "heartbroken" to leave the maximum-security prison where he had spent eighteen years. "And the officers were sad to see me go!"

When Rubin spoke to him during our first meeting, David had been unaware of his institutionalization. His eyes were opened by Rubin's metaphysical message. "Before you walk out of here, the first thing you need to do is to free your spirit," Rubin told him. "It may take a lot of time because you're too used to being in here. You're too used to the rhythms of the prison, to being told what to do, when you can eat, when you can sleep, when you can use the phone, when you can shower. And you're told to do these things under threat of sanctions or violence from the guards. Prison closes down the will and destroys your spirit."

A long pause indicated that David was awaiting a prescription. Rubin continued, "I was able to free my spirit. I got beyond the walls while I was still inside. One day, in the heat and dust of the prison yard, I just started staring at the brick wall, thirty-six feet high topped by barbed wire." Alonzo and I had heard this story before, and yet, like most of Rubin's stories, the pleasure was in the retelling.

I stared at that wall, and something strange began to happen. A pinprick of light was coming through that solid wall. As I stared at the light, it began to quiver and grow bigger and bigger. Eventually, I could see through that hole in the wall! I could see children coming home from school. I could see cars in the street, people going about their lives. Maybe it was the heat? I asked myself. Maybe someone had slipped a pill into my glass of water? Maybe I was going insane? The moment I began to think about it, as suddenly as the hole appeared, it disappeared. Maybe that hole in the wall was my avenue of escape? I was determined to find it again and to walk right through it even if it deposited me somewhere in infinity, even if it seared the flesh off my bones. That's when I threw out my law books and my papers: words, nothing more than words.

David was not about to travel to these outer realms or throw away his legal papers. He was too polite to cross the Hurricane at this juncture, knowing how lucky he was to have attracted Rubin's advocacy. Rubin perceived David's frame of mind. "You have to think outside of these walls, David. Train yourself. What's inside the prison, the guards, the cells, the yard, the law library, is all for the prison. That's not for you, at least not if you're going to get out of here. You've got to get yourself out of the universal prison of sleep before you can get out of the prison of bricks and mortar. Become educated."

Turning to me and placing a hand on my shoulder, he continued, "This man here is going to help you with that." In an instant, I became educational director as well! Then Rubin turned toward David and put a hand on his arm. "David, you have to break through that hole in the wall just like I did." Rubin's solutions to wrongful incarceration were usually self-referential; he believed in miracles, in higher laws manifested on lower levels. He believed that if such a thing could happen to him, it could happen to anyone.

Once again, a silence descended, silence and staring, and once again, Rubin broke it.

"We're going to get you out of here, David. It may take time, but we're going to get you out of here. One hundred percent. But you have to do your part. You can't leave this place with the prison inside you and go out and do something foolish. You have a responsibility to every wrongly convicted person in this entire country to live a pristine life."

I left the prison in a daze and tried to regroup with Rubin and Alonzo out in the parking lot. Innocence International, lacking manpower and as yet without a reliable funding source, was as insubstantial as the Wizard of Oz behind his curtain. We just gave our word to a fine young man, but we had only ourselves to throw against the considerable weight of the Brooklyn District Attorney's Office and the judicial systems of the City and State of New York. I was unaware at the time that Rubin Carter had helped to fund and raise millions of dollars for more than a score of innocence projects in North America and several others around the world. I was also unaware of the good karma attached to his name, which would result in assistance coming to us from distinguished people in the field of wrongful convictions. That assistance would not carry a price tag and would be worth far more over the next ten years than any grant we might have gotten from Griffiths.

Inside Eastern Correctional Facility, David began to be seen in a different light. Before, he had been an industrious and well-behaved prisoner. With Rubin Carter fighting for him, he said later, "guards and prisoners spoke to me with great respect. I was given celebrity status."

When I entered the prison in a state of high anxiety, I had barely looked at the building. From outside, I gazed at the massive front-age of Eastern, a maximum-security prison that appeared more like a medieval castle. I have learned since that prisons are not uniform in construction; some are former sanatoriums, some army barracks sites, some modernist and cold. But all of them—maximum, medium, and minimum—are soul destroying.

"How can you stand going back to these places?" I asked Rubin.

"Doesn't bother me one bit. I know I can leave any time I want."

Looking at the stone walls chilled me. After McCallum's bogus trial, the hanging judge had written and underlined "Court opposes any release, ever" at the bottom of the sentencing report. Thinking of it then felt like a noose around my own neck. McCallum was all of seventeen at the time. A teenager sentenced to a living death. I looked at Rubin and asked, "Who the hell is going to get David out of here?"

Dressed in his signature black suit, gold tie, and gold handkerchief pyramiding from his front pocket, he looked straight at me with his infectious grin. "You are, Ken. You are."

Right, Rubin, I thought. *Sure thing.*

———————

On our way to the motel from the Eastern visit, Carter asked me to turn on the tape recorder; the same recorder that I used for the *Sun* interview was now being used to prepare our book. He spoke:

We just visited David McCallum at Eastern Correctional prison. It brought to my mind a visit I made to Mumia

Abu-Jamal just before the Academy Awards in 2000. I was amazed with the energy that I felt on death row visiting Mumia, compared with being flown to Beverley Hills on a private jet, changing into a tuxedo, and walking down the red carpet into the auditorium. I sat there watching all the gowns and jewelry, and it struck me as strange that I would find more energy, laughter, and goodness on death row. David McCallum had that same energy and goodness I found in Mumia.

We pulled into a motel outside of Kingston, New York, where I had reserved a couple of rooms for an overnight stay. Alonzo and I went inside to check on the reservation. When we returned to the SUV, Rubin appeared disconsolate. He held his new cell phone as if ready to drop it out the car window.

"What's wrong, Rubin?"

"I just got a call from Win Wahrer. Mo Carter died."

Maurice Carter (no relation) had been wrongly convicted of killing an off-duty police officer and developed liver disease near the end of a very long incarceration. He lived sixty years, but to look at him, you would have thought he was well over seventy. He had been released by Jennifer Granholm, the governor of Michigan, as a humanitarian gesture. Of course the State of Michigan contended that Maurice had a fair trial, as if all trials were inherently fair.

"They let him out to die like some old cat." Rubin said.

Rubin collected himself and got out of the car. While Alonzo drove the SUV to the parking lot, we went inside to pay for the rooms. When Rubin handed his credit card to the desk clerk, she ran it and sadly relayed to him that it had been rejected. He asked the clerk to try again, which she did, but to no avail. His card had been maxed out. He blamed a woman for taking advantage of him and using his card without his knowledge. I was dubious about that story but found out since that it was true.

I wound up paying for the rooms that night. The following day, we visited Rubin's alma mater, the New Jersey State Home for Boys in Jamesburg. Rubin spent almost seven years there for the stabbing of a child molester, and now he was returning as a celebrity hero to address the current population. He said a thousand times he would never return to New Jersey—"I wouldn't even fly over New Jersey"— but made an exception. It began to dawn on me that my responsibilities would be far greater than originally anticipated. This luminous figure who made over ten thousand dollars per speaking engagement appeared to be broke. I was doing some substitute teaching, but my income was insufficient to run an innocence project. Alonzo was also working for free, taking time off from his work in security, sacrificing income that his wife and two young children badly needed. I still had hope that Griffiths University would be picking up the tab, so I saved all the receipts from the trip.

Along the way, Rubin told story after story, which I was able to record. With reference to Jamesburg, he related how the students used to put on skits in the surrounding community. Their favorites were from *Amos 'n' Andy*, the TV show they watched before dinner. I was shocked, remembering how the show was replete with stereotypes.

"*Amos 'n' Andy*? Didn't you think that was racist?"

"Hell no! That was the only place on TV you could see a brother. We *loved* it! Algonquin J. Calhoun! Honorary lawyer of New York City! We were furious at the NAACP for having it banned."

Rubin was unimpressed, actually depressed, by the State Home for Boys, once a model farm that was now a fenced-in prison for mostly black youth. A few of the inmates in the audience behaved disrespectfully. He couldn't wait to leave the place.

The trip home was not without incident. After crossing the border in Niagara Falls, the SUV started to show signs of distress. By the time we reached Hamilton, Alonzo was in the right lane, anticipating that we'd have to go onto the shoulder. At some point farther up the QEW, he shifted the car into neutral and brought it to a halt by the side of the road. It was dark, but Alonzo and I got out of the car. Rubin relieved himself inside the SUV, came out, and threw the piss on the road. We laughed, even if I was a little frightened by our proximity to speeding traffic. Rubin, having faced far greater adversities, was good humored.

Alonzo phoned the automobile association, and the dispatcher sent out a truck. We hoped the problem was the battery, which could easily be replaced. Alas, it was the alternator. The driver would tow us only to the closest affiliated station, which would have left us somewhere in Oakville, Ontario. We wanted to get home, so I offered him a hundred dollars if he'd tow us to a gas station in Toronto. While we were driven to Toronto at a severe tilt, Rubin held forth from the back seat of the SUV.

The subject turned to George W. Bush's reelection. We had stopped that afternoon at a pizzeria in Niagara Falls, New York, and the restaurant patrons were in a state of mourning.

I turned on the tape recorder. "Why do you think Bush was reelected?" I asked.

"Because the people in the United States are crazy. They're crazy!" Rubin said. Alonzo and I laughed, uncertain if he was being disingenuous. But then he launched into one of his many parables: "It reminds me of this very wealthy man and woman who had a young son and they began to find things missing. They thought that something very wrong was going on with their son, so they took him to a top psychiatrist. They paid this psychiatrist five or six hundred dollars an hour for nine sessions. Then he called them in. The parents were sure that he was about to tell them something terrible about their son. 'Sir, ma'am, from my analysis, your son is a thief. Plain and simple. Your son is a thief.'

"You ask why Bush was reelected after causing a savage war that was completely unnecessary. People are crazy. They are asleep. When people are asleep, they can be controlled by fear. The United States is fighting a war over oil because people are still afraid of 9/11 and Bush knows that."

"So . . . what you're saying . . ."

"I'm saying call it for what it is. You don't need to look for something complicated. Someone who steals is a thief. Someone who doesn't tell the truth is a liar."

"Hey, Rubin," I said, "I may have to borrow that cup."

"You just have to hold on, my brother. We ain't too far from home."

"But I'm tilted; there's pressure."

"We're all tilted. Ain't you tilted, Zo?"

Alonzo laughed, a great laugh with a little click inside it. Rubin laughed too.

"Now, what was I running off at the mouth about?"

"Bush," said Alonzo.

"George W. Death Bush. There is nothing we can do about George W. Bush or about the Senate or the House of Representatives. But we can do something about ourselves. That's the magic of it. Since everything in this universe is connected and everything is doing the job it was created to do, the only thing we are capable of changing is ourselves, and once we make a change in ourselves, just a minor change, put some resistance against a particular habit, for example, the world around us changes."

A week after we came back from New York, I got a call from Rubin. Since his credit card was still frozen, he wanted me to help him book airplane tickets to Montego Bay, Jamaica.

"I'm taking Sam to the Blue Lagoon. You know I promised him a long time ago, my brother. We're going to dip our feet in the Blue

Lagoon. We've been dreaming about this." He assured me that, since he had a speaking gig coming up, I'd get the money back.

While in Jamaica, a friend called Rubin with some terrible news: Rubin's house had burned down. Rubin was devastated, but he decided to finish the trip. Why lose that as well? When, upon returning, Rubin went to the house and saw the damage, the charred mess, his response was "It's only stuff."

Somehow Phoenix the cat had risen from the ashes and survived, not a display of symbolic fiction but a Carter-like miracle.

———

David wrote to me some time after our visit about his idea of transcending prison walls: "[It's] putting myself back into society around family and real friends who have my best interest at heart; . . . doing things that we sometimes take for granted." While it was easy to appreciate our new client's down-to-earth realism, I now sensed that the idealism at the core of Rubin's message would have to play a significant role in freeing David McCallum.

3

OSCAR MICHELEN
The Lawyer

RUBIN'S RETURN FROM JAMAICA forced him to deal with the material fact and the practical implications of his burned-down house. When I asked him about insurance, my first discovery was that he had none. My second discovery was equally disillusioning: he was renting the house on Delaware Avenue. Aside from the cat, he had lost all his worldly possessions. Although the landlord may have been found negligent for failing to repair a faulty electrical outlet, Rubin decided against a lawsuit.

I helped him find a living space in a basement apartment on a dead-end street off Lawrence Avenue. It was a cheap and decent place in a good neighborhood, and he was content with it as a temporary home. "After where I've been, I could live in a matchbox," he said. Never one to observe niceties, Rubin cut a hole in a screen where Phoenix could go out and in as he wished.

Trying not to dwell on his own misfortune, Rubin doggedly pursued legal representation for David. The powers that be in the legal system in Brooklyn could safely ignore outside interventions, even in

Rubin's name. Since we lived in Canada, we needed someone with inside access.

Rubin contacted Myron Beldock, his former attorney in New York City, who, along with Leon Friedman and Lew Steel, represented him on the appeal of his murder conviction and later against the State of New Jersey's attempt to return him to prison. The ruling by H. Lee Sarokin to vacate the convictions of Rubin Carter and John Artis went all the way to the US Supreme Court in 1987, making the case the longest litigated in New Jersey's history, testing the endurance of Beldock's pro bono team. While still in practice at seventy-five, Beldock was unable to take on David's case.

But then it happened—our single most significant piece of good fortune in the history of our involvement with David's case: finding that attorney. In looking at the letters that David sent out over the past decade, I noticed one written to a lawyer, Oscar Michelen, in which David asked for pro bono legal assistance. Oscar had responded, telling David he would become involved in the case if David were to find new evidence he could use. Given the limitations of a prisoner, the task of finding new evidence was all but impossible. Yet Oscar, who successfully helped to exonerate Angelo Martinez in 2002, had taken the time to answer. A quick check revealed that he was a busy lawyer, one of three partners in the firm Sandback, Birnbaum & Michelen. Originally a criminal lawyer, he switched to commercial law when, as he told us, the crime rate declined. Still, he never lost touch with his specialty.

From his long experience working on wrongful convictions, Rubin knew that Oscar was a possible lifeline. As per his instructions, I wrote to Oscar explaining our involvement and asked him to call Rubin. After a long conversation with the Hurricane, Oscar sent a letter to David. As any wrongly convicted prisoner would tell you, this letter was priceless.

Dear Mr. McCallum,

I heard today from the folks in Toronto who are helping you out with your case. They have asked if I would be willing to provide the legal services on a pro bono basis to try and make the necessary motions to reverse your conviction.

I have informed them that I would be willing to do so and I look forward to working with them and yourself on this matter. If you would like to contact me, you can call my office collect so we can speak. I will let you know as soon as I get the necessary material from them and begin the motion process. If I can I will try to make a visit to you before to go over the details.

Very truly yours,
OSCAR MICHELEN

When I spoke years later to Oscar, he said that one factor motivated him beyond all others: "If Rubin Carter asks you to do something, you just don't say no." We had to cultivate Oscar just as David had cultivated us. Oscar is straightforward in manner and deceptively easygoing. There's also a bit of the kid left in him that is equally disarming. What makes Oscar special is his streak of unabashed idealism. He was raising three sons who were later to go to expensive universities, and yet he was committing himself to an unknown number of years of unpaid labor. At the start, he told me that his whole practice meant less to him than seeing the face of one innocent prisoner as he emerged from a courtroom a free man. His remarkable grasp of legal issues, his canniness, and his tenacity would carry us through the long years to follow.

Oscar's willingness opened the gates that David had been pounding on for twenty years. David recognized the gift for what it was, telling me later, "*Wow!* I thought. *This is the same guy that turned me down a couple of years ago.* He was going to work for me pro bono. I could now stop writing letters and focus on my case. I was elated and shared the news again with my parents. With Rubin and Oscar helping me, I thought it would be easy from there. As soon as people saw my case, the truth of my wrongful conviction would be obvious. But I was still cynical about the system, and it's a good thing too. Otherwise, the disappointments would have crushed me."

Writing back to Oscar, I laid out the case as succinctly as possible. I had been through the trial transcripts a second time and begun to see the daunting problems that David and Willie faced from the outset: they were out of their depth during the trial. Easiest to spot and most damaging to them at the time was an ineffective and thoroughly incompetent lawyer. I further wrote:

> We have numerous examples of incompetence by David McCallum's lawyer (likely deceased since he was seventy-one in 1986). We have also found near the beginning of the trial a sidebar conversation amongst the judge and the two defense lawyers where one of the lawyer's relates having told his client "I don't believe that there is any possibility of coming out victorious in this trial." . . . It indicates that despite the complete absence of forensic evidence and the refusal of their clients to cop a plea that neither attorney was seriously considering a defense.

Over the years, Oscar would say repeatedly that a first-year law student could have gotten David off.

We were now in a position to acquire David's and Willie's video-taped confessions. From everything we'd read thus far, the tapes were the major piece of evidence against them. At trial David claimed his interrogator slapped, threatened, and deceived him into making the videotaped statement implicating Willie Stuckey as both kidnapper and killer of Nathan Blenner. Stuckey, also alleging physical abuse, fingered David for the same two crimes. The police detective, Joseph Butta, from what we could surmise, had played one off the other with the promise that each could go home if he came clean about what he had witnessed. In other words, each boy was set up as a witness to a crime and a helpless victim of the other boy. Neither understood that he only needed to admit being at the scene to be implicated. What would these videotapes tell us twenty years later? Would we see bruises on their faces? Would the suspects give information about the crime that the police could not have known? Would the tapes point to innocence or guilt? Years later when David saw the video, he was shocked at how brief his statement was: "Looking back, I say to myself: *How could I have confessed? What if I had stayed silent?* I was young and scared. I figured if Willie said that I killed Nathan Blenner, then I'd say that he did it. Butta knew we'd say anything just to go home."

Our first visit with David had resulted in a full shopping list. After the videotapes and the trial transcripts (which David provided), we needed to find physical evidence mentioned in the police reports, have it tested, and attempt to find and interview witnesses. The most important of these witnesses was the woman living around the corner from the Blenners who was accosted right before the kidnapping. Other witnesses included two children (now thirty years old) who saw the kidnapping across the street and got a neighbor to phone 911. David wanted a copy of the "sprint report," a transcription of the 911 call. Petitioning the court for these items was impossible without Oscar's assistance.

We spent the summer of 2005 going over the transcripts again and again for anything we missed. I discovered that trial transcripts reveal facts in very small doses. One needs context and tone to fully understand testimony, and, even then, readings are subject to mis-interpretation.

From David's point of view, this was a difficult time, even more so than usual. My wife, Mary Ellen, and I decided to spend a few months in Vancouver, British Columbia, to see if we wanted to live there (which we did in 2006). David put on a brave face in a letter he wrote me, trying to downplay the enormous physical distance:

> It is funny how you mentioned the constant rain you are experiencing in Vancouver because every time it rains here I am often reminded of my ambitions in life, which is to visit Seattle and Portland. . . . I was once told that Vancouver is one of the most beautiful cities in North America. Do you agree? The most important thing is that you are settled and have space in which to work.

In retrospect, I believe that David was trying to maintain and cultivate our relationship so as not to endanger his precious link to the outside world. I had no intention of abandoning him, but how was he to know that? Rubin and I were then not fully aware of his degree of isolation from the outside world, something he later mentioned to me: "When you told me about your living in Vancouver, I was extremely sad. My family didn't visit much. My mom was getting older, and I didn't want her to come to the prison. My sister Mattie came from time to time. I was afraid that communication would break down. But I got a letter from you that said I could call whenever I wanted. I also had faith because I knew that Rubin was involved with my case."

Earlier in 2005 my father died in Boynton Beach, Florida. Two days previous, his specialist had said that he was no longer able to take dialysis. The whole family, leaving from different cities, went down immediately. Our son, Ray, who was studying at Concordia University in Montreal, met us there to see his grandfather ("Poppi") for the final time. My father had been the glue that held the family together; for my brother, my sister, and me, all roads led to Boynton Beach. Sam Klonsky was respected and charismatic, a man who loved life and lived it without complaint, even as he suffered through two years of debilitating kidney treatments. At the age of fifty-nine, I became an orphan. I was luckier than most, however, because in Rubin I had a second father, albeit one more directional and opinionated.

Because people from outside cannot call a prison, I was unable tell him about my father, and David had no idea why he couldn't reach me. When I returned home to Vancouver, I saw he'd been trying to phone every day. When he called again, I told him about my father's death. His written response to the news moved me, coming as it did from an incarcerated man:

> I am deeply sorry to hear about the passing of your father. I would like to think that one could only aspire to live the life he had the privilege of living. I guess in some way your father's passing can also be a cause for celebration for the good that he represented. I pray that your family members are coping as best they can. I wish your father the very best during his journey and may God bless his soul.

For the next few months, I dealt with the agonizing issues around my father's estate and watched my family split apart in the wake of his death.

Without the anticipated help from Griffiths University, my portion of my father's estate funded Innocence International for the next nine years. I wonder if my dad would have been happy with that. He was so down-to-earth that an idealistic and expensive pursuit might have seemed like folly. But then I was who I was partly because of him and my mother (who died in 1988), two Roosevelt-era Democrats. Their warmth to strangers and lack of racial prejudice were a good example to my siblings and me.

We first used the money to help David enroll in a college course for the incarcerated offered by Ohio University. These courses, restricted to inmates who had access to outside resources, would be something constructive for him to do apart from working incessantly on his case. Since he was sent to prison at the age of sixteen, his knowledge base about anything outside the law and prisons was limited to what he learned on television. He took full advantage of the opportunity to learn from the university teachers who provided feedback for the correspondence courses. In the following years, my sister, Joan Ustin, shared the cost with me and became another of the many people helping David.

Solace was available in other forms too. For nine years I sent food packages to David every single month. Prisons are tied to a variety of outside companies that maintain monopolies in particular states. Most people think that only privately run prisons are the moneymaking operations, but they don't understand that state-run prisons are also huge commercial enterprises. A New Jersey company called Bust the Move has a monopoly on care packages of much-needed warm clothing and food that people can send to New York State prisoners. Prison inmates with access to these goods are envied and often must share them or sell them to other inmates. David shared the food out of generosity. "Many guys had no money, no visits from anyone. The thirty-five pounds of food a month was a blessing," he told me later. "Near the end of every single month, one of them would remind me to check the mail room for the package I always knew would be there."

David, of course, had to call us collect from the prison telephone. Once again, outside companies such as Global Tel Link or Value-Added Communications were ceded control of the service during the time we became involved in the case. The cost of phone calls to friends or relatives of the prisoner now varies wildly from state to state. Collect calls from New York to Vancouver, British Columbia, cost less than two dollars for thirty minutes. Calls from Washington State to Vancouver, British Columbia, cost twenty-five dollars for twenty minutes.

A company called Swintec, operating out of New Jersey, may be the last company in North America producing electric typewriters. These overpriced, see-through (so that inmates cannot hide contraband) typewriters are used exclusively by prisoners. When David was arbitrarily moved from his job in the prison library, he no longer had access to a computer. Since he needed to type his own legal work and his letters, I ordered him one of Swintec's typewriters and stacks of overpriced ribbons.

Prisoners are cash cows in every sense, foremost as workers. They perform the menial jobs of the prison—cooking, mopping, cleaning—for as low as fourteen cents an hour, and that money, measly as it is, is quickly rerouted to the commissary. The prison also hires them to do contract work—for example, making mattresses, military helmets, and other army gear. Those who are in minimum security get to do landscaping jobs and roadwork in the community. While the wages are almost comically exploitative, most inmates thirst to get out of the confines of the prison and into the natural world. One of David's most plaintive letters described this longing with pathos:

> Over the years, I have hidden away my suffering. I smile when I feel like crying. I laugh when I feel like dying. I often stare at pictures of my nieces and nephews to see them grow up. I miss the simplest things of ordinary life, such as having dinner with my family, taking walks in the park. I miss dogs barking. I miss the feel of rain on my face. In a strange way, the feel of rain in prison is totally different from raindrops out there. I miss the sound of birds singing and women laughing. I miss

winter and summer and spring and fall. I miss my freedom. So would anyone in my predicament. I will never forget the taste of freedom.

Late that summer, Thomas Allen & Son, a small but successful Toronto publisher, called Rubin and asked if he would be interested in writing an up-to-date book about his life. They were unaware that we had already begun to write such a book together based on the *Sun* interview. The publisher's call seemed fortuitous. Their main editor asked to see what we'd already produced. The writing was a literal transcription of Rubin's words, my role to that point being nothing more than amanuensis. Because Rubin's authorial voice was raw and unfiltered, I was reluctant to show the excerpt. Still, I gave it to the editor, hoping he would understand that the work was preliminary.

Returning to Thomas Allen a week later, we met with the editor and the publisher. The editor laid the manuscript on the table, his body language communicating his distaste. In a businesslike manner, the publisher told us that they really wanted to do a book, they could see it doing well, but it was obvious that no one in that office wanted me to be involved as cowriter or ghostwriter. It was a moment of truth, and the decision fell to Rubin. I girded myself for disappointment. I remember him, dressed resplendently, this time in a silvery suit with a red handkerchief in the front pocket, looking me in the eye and laughing a small laugh.

"Well, gentlemen," he said, standing up and holding out his hand, "I'm sorry we can't do this book with you, but I can see you won't be persuaded. Thank you for your time." He shook the proffered hands, motioned me to leave, and followed me out the door. At that moment, I was both stunned and grateful. Here he was being offered a contract by a respected publisher, but he had chosen to stay with me. I had no doubt that the chief editor at Thomas Allen could do a better job on the book.

We took the elevator down, went out into the street, and got into his old blue Mercedes, the "Blue Goose." "Thanks, Rubin. I appreciate what you just did. But you didn't have to. Those people know their stuff."

He turned to me and gripped my shoulder. "Ken, don't you ever let people tell you what you can and cannot do! You are a good writer, and you know what needs saying in this book. This is just one publisher. I never trust anything that comes that easy." Over the next year, with help from a writers' group, we finished a draft of the book.

Knowing Rubin's impracticality and the ease with which some people took advantage of him, I offered to find an agent to sell the book for us. I thought about an old friend from the University of Toronto graduate school in the late 1960s, Larry Hoffman. I knew that he was a literary agent sometime back, so I looked him up and called on the chance that he might be interested. Larry told me he had been battling kidney cancer for the past five years and had left the business, needing time to recover from an operation. My telephone call was apparently the elixir he needed to restart his career. He was ecstatic. The intervening years dissolved, as sometimes happens with old friends. Rubin had a separate conversation with Larry and liked his feistiness and irreverence. He could also relate to the fact that Larry had had some past trouble with the law. As it turned out, the kidney operation was only fifty percent of the reason Larry had been away from his business. "We are both former felons," he told Rubin.

Larry's first act was to pull off a miracle. In 2000 Rubin met Nelson Mandela at World Reconciliation Day in Sydney, Australia. The agent suggested that we get Mandela to write a foreword. I laughed out loud at the chutzpah, expecting nothing. But Mandela's people sent back a letter with a positive response. Nelson Mandela!

With the foreword in tow, Larry threw himself into the project, playing one publishing house against another, dreaming of great sums of money. A bidding war as such did not materialize. One publisher,

Key Porter Books, made an offer that two others were not prepared to match. The contract that Larry eventually negotiated was substantial for a nonfiction book in Canada. Key Porter also seemed to be a natural fit because they had recently put out an autobiography of Norman Jewison, the director of *The Hurricane*. We were to receive three increments of $18,000, the first on signing, the second on delivery of the manuscript, and the remainder of the $54,000 on approval of the manuscript. We went out and celebrated. The book was to be titled *The Rest of My Story*, a reference to Rubin's first book, *The Sixteenth Round*, which ended while he was still inside the prison. The final lines of that book, to this day a staple of the black consciousness movement, still resonate:

> Now the only chance I have is in appealing directly to you, the people, and showing you the wrongs that have yet to be righted—the injustice that has been done to me. For the first time in my entire existence I am saying that I need some help. Otherwise, there will be no more tomorrow for me, no more freedom, no more injustice, no more State Prison, no more Mae Thelma, no more Theodora, no more Rubin, no more Carter. Only the Hurricane.
>
> And after him, there is no more.

Rubin was to experience another ending beside oblivion. This new book would tell of Rubin's life after his release, how the lessons he learned as a prisoner shaped the man he had become.

David was elated because he knew we were committed to writing a full chapter about his case, hoping to get *his* wrongful conviction the publicity it so badly needed.

> I am keeping my fingers crossed that everyone will continue to support the idea of putting my story in the final chapter

of the book. I have provided you with more details about
my childhood. Coming to prison at such a young age, prison
became a part of my childhood as well. . . . I congratulate you
and Rubin for reaching a contract agreement for the book. I
am confident it will generate a lot of interest.

I wrote to David in August after a memorable dream. Was it wish
fulfillment or prophecy or both?

I had an unusually long nap during which I had the most
amazing dream. I dreamt that I was reading an official document declaring that you had been released from prison. I felt
so wonderful. Tears were in my eyes. When I awakened I
was truly disappointed. No dream has ever felt so real to me.

The dream made me understand that I identified with David's
predicament. Most other people who assist prisoners, sometimes
labeled "rescuers," have the same kind of unconscious connection to
the horror of unjust incarceration. Some aspect of our lives is stuck
in the past or imprisoned; hence, getting a wrongly convicted person
out of prison is akin to liberating the self.

One other such rescuer is Gary Dolin, a psychiatric social worker
in Bellingham, Washington, who agreed to help David on a voluntary
basis. Gary had also seen *The Hurricane*, read the interview in the *Sun*,
and become obsessed with Rubin Carter. We maintained a friendship
via e-mail until Mary Ellen and I came out to Vancouver for the first
five months of 2005. We met Gary and his wife, Martha, at a bayside
restaurant in Bellingham. Gary is a big man with a big pair of shoulders, but in retrospect it wasn't fair of me to saddle him with David
McCallum's emotional needs. Gary works at the VA with homeless
veterans suffering from PTSD and other mental disorders. Almost all
wrongly convicted people, and I have never seen an exception, suffer

from PTSD. Were it not for Gary's generosity of spirit—and generosity of every sort—I am sure that David would have died of despair. No one else could have given David the kind of support he most needed while slogging through the grinding legal process. I wrote to David, celebrating the connection:

> I am so happy that you have struck up a relationship with Gary and his family. They are, as you already know, wonderful people. They feel strongly about your innocence and it's best that you have support from as many human beings on the outside as possible. We all believe in you and we want you to hang on.

David's gratitude toward Gary has only increased over the years. "I trusted him right away. I didn't realize that he would become a lifelong friend," he told me. "We talked on the phone about things outside the prison, how to have relationships with the opposite sex, stuff like that. Things I had never experienced as a sixteen-year-old. His wife and his kids took me into their family. When I spoke to them, I felt like I was inside their home, but I couldn't visualize it—the small farm where they lived that I only saw years later. Their chickens were my chickens; their dogs were my dogs. I sometimes spoke to Gary three times a week. I would call when I felt beaten down or frustrated, and he let me vent." When the Dolins acquired another golden retriever, they asked David to name him. The name he chose was Freedom.

When my wife and I returned from our temporary stay in Vancouver, I asked Gary to fly to Toronto in October and join Rubin and me for a visit to David at Eastern. For Gary, the trip would be a dream come true. When David heard from him about coming to the prison, he responded in his typically self-effacing way:

I informed him that it would be a wonderful experience for
me to meet him, and I could not thank him enough for showing a genuine interest in my well-being. For someone to want
to travel thousands of miles to visit me, [gives me] a feeling
that is difficult to comprehend. I believe it says more about
that person, than it does for me. I thank God for the opportunity He has given me to meet people.

For Gary, the days he spent in Toronto and his visit with David at
the prison in New York were euphoric. He remembers Rubin driving
him around the city in the Blue Goose. The visit to Eastern assured
Rubin and me that Gary would be an emotional and psychological
support to David for as long we needed him. As a bonus, Alonzo's
SUV made it all the way back without assistance.

––––––––––––

Rubin received his second honorary doctorate from Toronto's York
University in October during a graduation ceremony. That afternoon,
he spoke to thousands of people in a massive white tent about his
ordeal and the miracle it took to overcome the brutal circumstances of
his wrongful conviction. Once again, he did not speak to the particular
occasion, ad-libbing around the speech I wrote for him honoring the
graduates. He went with the crowd-pleasing anecdotes that always
worked for him. He introduced Larry, Mary Ellen, and me as part of
Innocence International to that huge audience. It was embarrassing
for us since we were irrelevant to the moment.

After the second honorary degree, Rubin became Dr. Rubin
Carter, LLD. Many people thought his insistence that he be addressed
as Dr. Carter pretentious, but I discovered that some people from the
black communities in the United States and Canada were proud that
he had been so honored. Rubin, a self-taught jailhouse lawyer, had
become a doctor of law without ever graduating from high school.

Later, when I pointed out to him that he didn't need his name to be sandwiched between the Dr. and the LLD, he was adamant. He would be both a doctor of law and a doctor!

———————————

What happened soon after set off a series of events that no one could have possibly foreseen. Mary Ellen and I had become increasingly concerned with Ray, who at the age of twenty began to show behavior that one could charitably regard as brainless and less charitably as reckless. We made an emergency visit to Montreal to look into an incident wherein Ray had been arrested for throwing a rock through his landlord's car window. Forced to stay in jail for three hours, he was filled with self-justification and anger. We had hired a lawyer in Toronto to settle another incident when he had fallen for a scam. Now we had to hire a lawyer in Quebec. Our relationship was already frayed by the usual father-son adolescent conflicts, but now I barely knew who he was. The visit turned out to be valuable simply by demonstrating our concern, but the long-term issues remained unresolved.

When we returned home from Montreal, Gary called to tell us that David's father had died. As Rubin explained to me, when a parent or immediate relative is dying, the prison gives the inmate a choice: either go to the hospital before the death or go to the funeral and the wake. In general, only minimum-security prisoners can go to the cemetery. David went to his father's wake shackled, just as Rubin had gone shackled from prison to see his own father right before he died. In a letter, David described his complex feelings:

> Considering the circumstances of the last few days, I am doing
> as well as can be expected. God blessed me and allowed me
> to go down to the city to see and talk with my father and to
> spend some time with my family. To say it was tough would

be an understatement. . . . Upon first hearing the devastating news, I was in a very difficult state. However, life is strange, in that after speaking to my father as he rest in peace, I felt a little better as if he was actually listening to me, and reassuring me that everything would be fine. Besides, I had to be strong, because my mother, nieces and nephews were all on hand, along with my sisters and brothers.

I repeatedly assured my father that I will continue to make him proud of me, and that I will never quit on him or myself in anything that I do. My quest for justice is no exception. I told him that I did not come there to say goodbye, rather I let him know emphatically that I will see him again in Dillon, South Carolina, the birthplace of the McCallum family. The shackles prevented me from giving him a hug before I was taken away.

David went on about his biggest worry of all, his mother's chronic diabetes. I feared that if she were also to die, David would lose the strength to continue. Because of his father's death, her condition made him more determined to gain his freedom.

I could tell that I had been gone far too long and that I have to do everything I can to get out of this place to be with her. There will be constant work ahead for me; no more rest time.

. . . The sudden passing of my father has only reinforced the importance of my freedom because there are a lot of people out there who could use my help right now.

What a pair of bookends! My father died in January and David's in November. What could I say to someone who had already suffered so much? Not much more than platitudes:

I want to send you words of comfort and words of encouragement to keep on going. . . . You were a good son to him
and it's only too tragic that you were not able to show him
the fine person that he brought into this world.

As I was writing this letter, I had a selfish inspiration. Mary Ellen
and I had been helping David nonstop for over a year and a half. Why
not ask him to help us and in so doing find a way to get him out of
his mental confinement? After all, a wrongly convicted prisoner has
little he can do for anyone on the outside. So I shared with him some
of the scrapes Ray had gotten into and how my attempts to intervene
had been met with resistance.

I'm going to ask you a favor, David, when and if you feel
you can do it. I want you to write to Ray and tell him about
bad friends, useless anger and bad judgment. Maybe you can
share a little about what you are going through, because I tell
you that as much as he tried to reassure us that he's learned
something, we are just as worried that he hasn't. I know of
no one better qualified to write this letter than yourself.

David was honored to be asked. It was a perfect moment for
him to reach out, because he had, for the usual arbitrary reasons,
lost his job in the law library helping disabled prisoners and become
a porter, which he said required him "to sweep and mop corridors
in the mornings and evenings." One of his previous letters gave me
confidence that he would be effective in a counseling role:

I have always been sensitive toward others, and I do not
see any reason why I should change that approach, because
there have been too many instances in my life when I cried
out for help, or that others have cried out for me to help

them, and I was unable to. Why? Because I simply did not know how. Over the course of my incarceration, I had to learn how to help other people and I found that by just listening to someone, and issuing sound advice when appropriate can be conducive to helping an individual.

He reflected on his checkered past, demonstrating the primary quality that would, we thought, influence Ray in a positive direction:

My troubles began when I started to think of ways to make easy money to supplement the income I received from my parents. . . . I made poor choices by robbing people in my community and, as a result, I was arrested four times. . . . The truth is that I chose to live a destructive lifestyle.

David never blamed his upbringing for his crimes, admitting that his parents had done their best for him. Sociologists say that the range of choices for African American youth is limited; nevertheless, within that range are opportunities for those who would seek them out, for those who, unlike David, did not need to establish reputations for toughness in order to fit in. While Ray, craving respect, was never guilty of robbing people, David set him straight about where his poor choices might lead him.

Following his father's death, when he wrote me and said, "The last week has been the toughest of my life," David also wrote Ray a carefully worded letter:

Dear Ray,

I want to give you a synopsis of who I am, and what are my intentions of writing you. I met your dad nearly two years ago by reading an interview he conducted with Rubin "Hurricane"

Carter. Me and your dad have become really good friends, and I was hoping that we too can become friends, because ironically, I was around your age when I came to prison. I believe that you can help me by simply lending me your ear for a little while.

You see Ray, I have never been to college before, nor has anyone in my family so I am hoping that you share some of your college experiences with me, because I lost my teenage years, and all of my young adult life to this place because I was simply at the wrong place at the wrong time.

I was not an angel out there, and even at the age of fourteen, I found my way to crime, and I'd be lying to you if I tried to put it on someone else. I had a lot of terrible so-called friends, who did horrible things to people, but I was just as guilty as they were because I had a choice to walk away but I didn't. Most of my friends that I hung around with are dead and in prison. But me, well, I have a chance, because I am more than confident that when I am eventually released from this place, I will be ready to live a productive life. I even have plans to attend college.

David had the intuition to ask for Ray's help in understanding the world outside prison. From my experience with young people, I knew that they were far more motivated to help others than to receive unsolicited advice. David's restricted life conveyed to Ray that his own life had limitless opportunities. The immediacy of this message, coming from a man inside a prison, woke Ray up. A relationship was born between David and him and became a bond between brothers. Ray and his friend Marc Lamy launched a project that would eventually result in *Fight for Justice: David & Me*, a film that began as an analysis of a wrongful conviction and morphed into a story of this burgeoning relationship. The film and the young men themselves became another part of the network that we hoped would eventually free David McCallum.

At the year's end, David reached his thirty-sixth birthday and his twentieth year in prison. He had experienced twenty years of noise, unpalatable food, gross odors, extreme heat and cold, and daily violence; twenty years of rigid emotional repression; twenty years of Thanksgivings spent away from home; twenty years of joyless Christmases. Speaking to him during holidays was always dark, somber, and depressing. This year, however, he took comfort in knowing he had a growing family of supporters outside the prison walls.

Mary Ellen and I were equally comforted by the quality of Ray's mentor. It would not have been possible to find one better than David McCallum. David wrote to tell me about his progress with my son:

> I received a letter from Ray yesterday, and I must say that he is a very impressive young man. What I was most fond of . . . was the contriteness that he repeatedly displayed. I am fully aware that it is possible that he could be attempting to pull the wool over my eyes, but I am choosing to give him the benefit of the doubt. Ray is a young man who really wants to not only please himself, but he also wants to make his parents proud of him . . .
>
> I actually felt bad for the young man in the sense that he is in a constant battle with himself, and I, for one, know exactly what that feels like. One thing I will mention to him in my next letter is that it would be wrong for him to acknowledge his mistakes to me, or anyone else, but yet continuously fall back into the same situation. . . . I will say to him that eventually he is going to run out of "my faults" every time he gets into trouble. That stuff adds up. . . . He spoke about his

little hiatus in jail, and made it clear that he was going to do everything that he could not to allow that to happen again. I will explain to him that how can anyone take him seriously, because I am sure they have all heard it before.

4

STEVE DRIZIN
The False Confessions Expert

IN JANUARY 2006 we moved to Vancouver permanently. Despite the very long distance, David now knew we would never desert him. Confident that he would soon be exonerated, he continued to write to me about the importance of keeping his focus outside the prison, planning to visit Gary and me in Washington and Vancouver. But none of us can control the unexpected, least of all a prisoner whose helplessness is magnified by random events.

An elderly woman driving the wrong way on a one-way street crashed into Ernestine McCallum's car head-on. David's mother suffered a stress fracture of her right hip. Ernestine's health, including her diabetic condition, and her age (approaching seventy), were still David's most pressing issues; to be face-to-face with a close call like this made being in prison even more intolerable. She was hospitalized for several weeks.

His older sister, Ella, was another grave concern. Born without a spine and also suffering from cerebral palsy, Ella is as disabled as a person can be. She was not expected to live past the age of thirteen and was now approaching fifty. Her will to live in her bodily prison forged a link between her four brothers and two sisters. She was David's hero and a huge motivational force, but her health now seemed to be failing. A letter to me from David reflected desperation:

> I feel absolutely helpless right now. I am angry and I'm not sure who I should be angry with. . . . My sister Ella was not feeling too good a couple of weeks ago, because her stomach was shrinking and no one knew why she was crying all the time. The doctors discovered the problem. They said my sister is getting older, and considering her condition, it was not abnormal. My mind has been racing furiously because I cannot understand why my family is being tested in this way. . . . I am capable of saying anything that I may regret down the road.

The danger here was the hint at possible reckless behavior, defying a guard or mouthing off to another prisoner. In my mind were Rubin's words, always Rubin's words, defining the moments. As he later wrote in *Eye of the Hurricane: My Path From Darkness to Freedom*:

> Prison is the easiest place on earth to hurt others and to be hurt. Behind those walls, prisoners are always engaged in life-and-death struggles. Any altercation or show of disrespect can be fatal, particularly in the morning. . . . When those cell doors open, the place becomes a pit of poisonous vipers.

Rubin worried that were David to explode—and that is always a possibility when a person holds himself under control for so long—he could easily be killed by guards or other inmates. It happens all the time.

David's close supporters—Gary, my sister, Ray, Marc Lamy, and me—became his pressure valve. He called me twice a week to ask about the progress of his case, forgetting that Oscar, with a very busy practice, had only so much time for pro bono work. Every letter would remind us that he wanted Oscar to petition for the videotaped confessions or that he wanted Oscar to interview the two child witnesses or whatever else needed to be done that was taking too long. I could not counsel a man who had been incarcerated all these years to show patience.

Another of his coping mechanisms was to read and copy everything he could find about wrongful convictions. David sent me an article from the *New York Times* about the case of Marty Tankleff, from Suffolk County, Long Island, who in 1988 at the age of seventeen was charged with murdering his parents in their bed. At the end of a very long interrogation, the police convinced him that he may have blacked out and killed his parents in some kind of trance. Although he immediately retracted it, he was convicted on the strength of his initial statement. Tankleff, now thirty-four, wanted a new trial based on new evidence, but an appeal judge denied his petition for procedural reasons.

An American innocence network composed of noted defense lawyers and an expert on false confessions weighed in negatively on the appeal judge's decision; their statements were contained in an amicus brief attached to a motion (known as a 440 in New York State) filed in the Appellate Division of the State Supreme Court in Brooklyn. The judge appeared to have ignored the new evidence gathered by Tankleff's private investigator, Jay Salpeter, a former NYPD officer, that purportedly identified the killers and the man who hired them. The expert witness on false confessions, Steve Drizin of Northwestern University, wrote the following in the amicus brief: "Juries convict innocent people because false confessions are counterintuitive; most jurors simply cannot imagine that that they would ever confess to a crime they did not commit."

I later learned something else from the Tankleff case but chose not to tell David. Oscar said that people who falsely confessed in New York State were not entitled to compensation upon release. They were seen as the authors of their own misfortunes. The injustice of this self-serving rule was galling.

By the end of February, the Brooklyn District Attorney's Office located the videotaped confessions, but we were told that Oscar would have to wait sixty days to get access. David's previous dealings with that office made him cynical about the delay. For him, it was an unnecessary roadblock.

By 1985 the use of videotaped confessions by police and prosecutors had been around for a decade. Since confessions, but not the interrogations that led to them, had to be taped, the purpose of taping was to solidify the state's case against the defendant. Even today, only twenty-one states require interrogations to be taped. The method of extracting the confession, the possible use of violence, threats, and deceit that occurred in David's situation, can be far more revealing than the confession itself. Videotaped interrogations, while no panacea, at least prevent the use of overt coercion. A videotaped confession back in 1985 meant an almost automatic conviction, there being no scientific literature on false confessions at the time. Whenever we received the tape, we would need to have it analyzed by an expert in the field.

Oscar did not respond to David's letters about expediting the delivery of the tapes. Rubin wrote me that "waiting sixty days should not be a problem at all, considering that he has already been in prison for over twenty years." Relaying Rubin's words only made David angry. In his usual way, David was able to express his impatience in the context of patience:

> Knowing how this system works here in New York regarding the requesting of evidence—I would not be shocked if those sixty days turn into four months. . . . I am going to consider Rubin's advice by sitting here waiting on Oscar to do what he has to do. Just know that I am not going to sit on my hands if I sense that nothing is getting done in a reasonable fashion.

David's strategy was to light a fire under me so that I would continue to hound Oscar. He understood me better than I understood myself. He knew that I would be on the phone to New York as soon as I read his letter. My overworked imagination would continually place myself in his position: the twenty-one years, the gnawing injustice, the confines of the prison, the steel doors sliding open and shut like diving chambers, the harassment by the guards. Whatever the element of the torture, I tasted his pain and misery.

I warned him about the possible consequences of importuning Oscar and the situation we would find ourselves in if Oscar chose to quit. Without a pro bono attorney, we would lose our ability to make motions to the court and our access to documents. After years of trying, David had finally gotten legal representation. Given the situation at home with his mother, I could understand his urgency, but continued patience was his only option. David's next letter indicated that he understood:

> You can be sure that I will never do anything to mess up such a good situation because I realize that I have a very supportive and caring group of people out there on my side. To sabotage this is simply something that is not going to happen.

In the end, Oscar did as his client asked, even more than he asked, albeit a bit later than his client would have desired. It was a display of caring that this attorney repeated throughout the years. In his next letter, David was exhilarated:

I was absolutely floored when you informed me that Oscar had [gone] to Ozone Park, Queens, to speak to people that live on the block where Nathan Blenner was allegedly abducted. . . . I know of investigators who would not go into certain communities to interview prospective witnesses. In other words, good lawyers are extremely difficult to find. It is surely a blessing that Oscar has agreed to help me.

Later that month, Oscar received the 1985 videotaped confessions. He sent copies to Rubin and me. Ignorant of the law as I was, I could still see that David McCallum and Willie Stuckey were two frightened teens whose sole desire was to go home, where each of them falsely believed he was going, as quickly as possible. The interview was conducted by a youthful-looking assistant district attorney, David Rappaport, whose mustache, tight-fitting sport jacket, and bell-bottom pants make him appear very 1970s. During both confessions, a smiling detective, Joseph Butta, muscular arms protruding from his rolled-up shirtsleeves, was sitting close by. His imposing presence ensures that neither boy will suddenly reverse himself. Willie's videotaped confession takes only five minutes and David's only four. David wrote, expressing surprise at this revelation:

Because I never saw them, I just assumed that they were long and drawn out. You would think that I should never forget such an experience that occurred at the precinct, but I have managed to do exactly that. . . . You would think Mr. Mirto as my lawyer would have scheduled a visit with me at the courthouse to go over the tapes, but he never did.

Rubin called me from the house he was now renting in Toronto's High Park area. "Ken, I'm sending the tape to Rob Warden and asking him to take a look at it. I'm not going to make any comment; I just want to see what he thinks." Warden is the head of the Bluhm Legal Clinic at Northwestern University, specializing in false confessions. Warden and Larry Marshall, also of Northwestern, met Rubin through the failed attempt to gain Maurice Carter's freedom and through the successful exoneration of former death row prisoner Rolando Cruz. It took no time for Warden to label the confessions "dubious." He gave them to his colleague Steve Drizin, the expert on false confessions in the Tankleff case. Drizin's subsequent involvement in David's case, along with the work of Northwestern students, would prove invaluable. The willingness of people from a highly regarded innocence project to take up our case was a tribute to Rubin's name and reputation.

David knew about Steve from his own research into false confessions. "I never thought I'd be able to connect with the Bluhm Clinic, and I couldn't have done it by myself," he said a year after his release. "I mean I saw him [Steve] as LeBron James in the false confession field. I just couldn't believe he was now a part of this team. I guess I'd just become used to things falling apart." While a wrongly convicted person, out of the many thousands in the United States, is very lucky to get one project interested in his or her case, David now had two innocence projects working for him, Innocence International joined by Northwestern.

Steve and Oscar then began to coordinate their efforts. Both of them assigned law students to the case, Steve's from Northwestern and Oscar's from New York Law, where he taught night school. The plan was for Steve to issue a report so that Oscar could make a motion, based on Steve's findings, to reopen the case in court. Steve has the virtue of brilliant people: he can make complex ideas understandable to a layperson. He is also a dogged researcher; he sent us the locations of witnesses who might be able to provide us with information about who murdered Nathan Blenner and why.

One of the witnesses, James Johnson, was a police informant who testified against Willie and David at the trial in exchange for being let off on a serious charge. With the address Steve provided, Oscar found a James Johnson and interviewed him in David's old neighborhood. It turned out that this James Johnson had been in prison at the time of the trial. In fact, there was a long list of James Johnsons on the Department of Corrections website, the name being a common alias. Neither the police reports nor the court transcripts identified him in any other way but by that name. (We knew he was twenty years old because David told us.) Were they trying to protect him or maybe themselves?

Steve felt that the right James Johnson would be a significant find. Johnson had attempted to rob a bodega at gunpoint and shot off his gun when the store owner attacked him with a baseball bat. Johnson told a story that would protect him from future criminal prosecution and from neighborhood retribution. After the abortive robbery, he went to the hospital to get stitches in his scalp. On the way to the hospital, he dropped off the gun with his Aunt Lottie. Aunt Lottie, he testified, gave the gun to someone named Jaime. Jaime gave the gun to Willie Stuckey. None of us could locate Jaime or find his family name. We never even tried to find Lottie, as no last name was given for her either since, for some strange reason, she was never interviewed by police.

Steve Drizin's report came out that November. The observations and conclusions, based on police reports, trial records, and previous witness testimony, stood up right until the end. To make a solid case for an appeal and to back up his report, he suggested that we now hire a private investigator. The investigator needed to find the material evidence mentioned in the police reports so that it could be sent for testing. We also needed the investigator to find and interview key witnesses, and even held out hope that he or she could find James Johnson.

Drizin's analysis hinged on unshakeable facts from 1985 police notes and interviews that district attorney Charles Hynes's office stubbornly refused to acknowledge. When the police canvassed the Queens neighborhood where Nathan Blenner was abducted, they spoke to Chrissie Owens (pseudonym), the woman washing her red car around the corner from the Blenner home. The notes told Drizin what we already knew. Owens said that two black males, age twenty, one five ten and one five four, one with braided hair, accosted her as she washed her Buick Regal in the driveway. One said, "Nice car," to which she responded, "If it's not here in the morning, I'll know where to look." She also said she was willing to identify photos down at the station house.

Three days later, the Queens police arrested two men, Jake Prince (pseudonym) and Murray Howard (pseudonym), fitting Owens's description. They were implicated in eight separate carjackings in a forty-eight-hour period right before the Blenner incident. All the carjackings occurred in Queens; all descriptions of the perpetrators matched Prince and Howard. The Queens police, having received an all-points bulletin from Brooklyn with regard to Nathan Blenner's murder, notified Joseph Butta, the detective in charge, about Prince and Howard. These two possible suspects had been arrested and detained on an unrelated charge of theft. One of them had "snatched a chain" from around a woman's neck on the subway.

When Blenner's auto was found, it had been badly burned. The kerosene can used to douse the car came from Pop's Hardware Store, where Jake Prince worked. The 1985 investigation to this point represented solid police work. It was within reason that the two men Owens saw were the men who kidnapped Blenner, whose car, like

Owens's, was a Buick Regal. Buick Regals were a car of choice during those crime-ridden days in the greater New York area. In fact,
Owens's car was stolen four days after Blenner's body was discovered.
Drizin's educated guess was that a car theft ring was operating out
of the hardware store.

Indisputably, the two men Owens saw were not Willie Stuckey
and David McCallum, both sixteen and both five foot five. Though
it did not jump out at us immediately, because Willie's videotaped
confession differed from Detective Butta's notes during the interrogation, there was another piece of exculpatory evidence. In the notes,
Willie confessed to Butta that he had seen a woman washing a red
car and that David said, "Nice car." Since it was evident, even to
the prosecutor, that Owens did not see Willie and David, Stuckey's
statement contained what Drizin characterized as a false fed fact.
The fact was that two black males had accosted Owens. The falsity
was that Willie and David were those two men. The only way, aside
from being there, that Willie could have known about this encounter
was if the detective fed him the information forcefully. Whether a
judge would consider it new evidence (i.e., evidence that would have
changed a jury's original verdict) depended on a technicality. Could
David's original lawyer, Peter Mirto, using due diligence, have discovered the false fed fact? If so, we were procedurally barred from
using it. The law governing appeals of jury verdicts, as I perpetually
discovered, was designed to sustain convictions, not to acknowledge
obvious truths.

While we had always been convinced of David's innocence, Steve
had provided a structure on which we could hang our theories. We
also had a compelling case for actual innocence if a judge would allow
it. The confessions provided the foundation for David's and Willie's
convictions; Willie's confession was demonstrably false.

For the jobs of locating the physical evidence in New York's vast
criminal investigations warehouses, interviewing Chrissie and the two

child witnesses, and finding the prime suspects, Steve suggested two possible private investigators: Jay Salpeter of the Marty Tankleff case or Louis Scarcella, another former police officer. Luckily, we did not hire Scarcella; we would have taken a fox into our henhouse. Scarcella told Drizin that Brooklyn never had a wrongful conviction based on a false confession. Years later, he was implicated in up to fifty wrongful convictions gained through the use of forced confessions and fraudulent witnesses. Jay Salpeter, with a reputation for toughness and an endorsement from Tankleff's lawyers, was our choice.

Rubin was happy. "We need someone to kick some ass. David's buried right now under two tons of bullshit," he said. Barry Scheck of the Innocence Project warned Drizin that former cops make the worst private investigators. Still, we were confident about Salpeter, a curt man with a barrel chest who believed that young people under interrogation invariably confess to crimes. He was certain that the only way David could emerge from prison would be if he solved the case. His self-confidence in the wake of Tankleff's case was limitless.

———————

With respect to his burgeoning relationship with my son, David gave me as much and more than I was able to give to him. Ray had found a mature adult, a mentor figure, with whom he felt safe enough to unburden himself. David also became a conduit of information between father and son. Our move to Vancouver not only affected David but was also a source of grief and mourning for Ray, who loved Toronto and the anchor that our house afforded. David wrote to me:

> Ray explained to me how disappointed he is to have moved from Toronto. He had become so attached to that house and the friends he has there. My guess is that it is going to be awhile before he gets over it, which, quite frankly, is understandable. I basically explained that there is no timetable for him to erase

his memories of that house from his thoughts. . . . In fact, it may be best that he never forgets, because some memories are destined to be with us forever, which is the beauty of it. I explained to him that his memories from his childhood will help to shape him as he matures.

Whenever I read things like this from David, I wonder how a man from the streets of Bushwick, with little formal education, and who entered adult prison at the age of sixteen could have developed such wisdom, maturity, and consideration. His letters were frank yet worded with delicacy:

Not once, since we started to correspond did I get the impression that he feels resentment toward his parents. . . . What I can say is that he feels he let you down by getting himself into some things he wish[es] he had not. . . . He can sound like a young man who is carrying an entire nation on his shoulders. I come to suspect that nation may be some of his friends.

Ray, in gratitude for David's role as mentor and honorary older brother, promised David that he would make a documentary film about his wrongful conviction and the broken criminal justice system in the United States. He saw it as a way to free David from prison, while his mother and I, knowing how long the process would take, saw the project as a way to free himself from impulsive behavior.

Ray and his friend at Concordia University Marc Lamy, the codirector and cameraman for *David & Me*, are a dogged and resourceful pair. They borrowed equipment from the school in the early stages of filming and went down to New York, Cambridge, and Chicago to do on-site interviews with legal experts. We understood that they would need substantial funding upon graduation to complete the film. That funding would be contingent upon shooting enough professional-looking film to make the idea compelling to a producer. Until then, Mary Ellen and I and our generous friends footed the bill.

That June, Mary Ellen and I met Ray in Toronto to visit David at Eastern. I don't think David was overstating the importance of this meeting when he wrote, "I was thrilled to death for the opportunity of meeting your family for the first time." We had to wait forty-five minutes for David because the visiting room guards, with typical insouciance, forgot to tell the inside guards that we were there. We were annoyed at the loss of precious time, because Mary Ellen and I had previously decided to leave Ray with David for the second half of the visit. Later, David wrote to thank us for coming:

> I was appreciative that the both of you allowed me ample time to talk with Ray. . . . You once said that you and your wife [have] always given Ray his space, which I was able to see, especially with the fact that you allowed us to spend time alone—to talk about things maybe he didn't want to express in your presence. . . . He appeared to be a mature enough young man, who would now take responsibility for his own actions. I thought it was telling that he was glad you were able to come to Toronto, because he needed to take the initiative to work on his relationship with you. He said he was going to start by being honest with you.

As parents, we knew we were lucky. The relationship between Ray and me would have continued to be dysfunctional, maybe forever, without David McCallum as intermediary.

In early September, Ray and Marc shot interviews with Steve and Rubin. They also sought out witnesses in Queens and Brooklyn and tried, with some success, to get them to speak on camera. We were concerned about Ray roaming the streets of Bushwick looking to talk to people with criminal pasts. But the quest to free David was the kind of risk he needed to take, a test of his courage and compassion. They tried to find people from Steve's contact list, anyone whose name was associated with police and trial records, or people whom David remembered from the neighborhood. Although most of them recalled the murder, concrete details were forgotten. Not a single one of them thought that David had been involved in any way with the murder of Nathan Blenner.

Ray and Marc interviewed Nathan Blenner's family. His still-bereaved mother and the rest of the family refused to appear on camera, but Mrs. Blenner had been interviewed in an earlier TV news broadcast. The footage is still painful to watch. Rather than concede even the possibility that David McCallum was wrongly convicted and that justice had not been served, she threw up unyielding resistance. She was certain that the two boys received a fair trial, just as certain as she was, when she looked at Willie Stuckey during the 1986 court proceedings, that he killed her son. Her mistaken beliefs are understandable to any parent, considering what the loss of closure at that late date would mean to her and her family.

Thus far, the most important step for the filmmakers was blocked. They needed to gain access to the prison to interview David. Ray complained that the prison even refused to allow a telephone interview. I could not imagine how this faceless bureaucracy would be forced to yield to Rubin's higher power. It appeared that there were no miracles in prison, just the mundane quotidian grind.

———

Among the many variables that had been put into play, the one most immediately controllable, Rubin's book, hit a snag. The publisher of *The Rest of My Story*, now called *The Way of the One-Eyed Man*, sent our manuscript for the customary legal vetting before acceptance and payment of the final advance. We received word that a controversial section of the book would have to be deleted. The section dealt with the aforementioned wrongly convicted Canadian Guy Paul Morin and his prosecutor, Susan MacLean, just appointed to a judgeship by Ontario's attorney general, Michael Bryant. Rubin believed that her pursuit of a conviction in a murder case for which the defendant had already been acquitted (utilizing a rare form of double jeopardy allowed in Canada), amounted to criminal harassment. Since MacLean's appointment to the judgeship was the reason Rubin quit AIDWYC, he was outraged by the demand to alter the text. The publisher was frightened by the possibility of a lawsuit.

Given the stubbornness of both sides and Rubin's belief that "the truth is not actionable," the book would likely go unpublished, the work wasted, the money repaid, and David's story would not garner the publicity it needed. A book by Rubin would be read by thousands of people, many of them in the legal community. Its publication, with a full fifty pages on David's case, was part of the overall effort to free him from prison. David wrote to me with the usual wisdom, hiding his extreme disappointment behind a cloak of rationality:

> Like any other potential relationship, once trust has become an issue, there might not be another alternative. Given the publisher's apparent stubbornness, it is highly unlikely that he will see the light. I guess anything is possible at this point, but, realistically, it might not be feasible or in the best interests of you and Rubin to deal with them. Indeed, it is very unfortunate—to say the least.

Talking about this impasse after his release, he owned how deflating it was to have lost this opportunity. "I was upset with Rubin because he wouldn't compromise, but I've learned to live and let live. He was who he was, and I had to take his bad side along with all the good that he did for me. I wasn't about to sit around and feel sorry for myself."

———————

In the summer of 2006, David was transferred to Arthur Kill Correctional Facility on Staten Island, a short distance in miles from Brooklyn. We thought that visits from his mother and the family could now be regular. The problem was that the transit time between Bushwick and the prison on Staten Island was two and a half to three hours, double the time that it took to drive all the way up to Eastern. After one exhausting visit involving poorly scheduled buses and the Staten Island ferry, David would not see his mother again until he left prison. She could not bear the physical and emotional costs, nor did he want her to. Even the visit that day produced an infuriating moment:

> I cannot tell you what a wonderful experience it was to see my Mother and my brother Rufus. Unfortunately, I did not get the opportunity to see my four year old Niece and nine year old nephew, because they did not have their birth certificate and social security number cards. I am proud of myself from the standpoint that I was able to have restraint, and not allow my emotions getting away from me. Make no mistake about it—I was definitely pissed off, but I realized that nothing good would come of any of this. . . . I took the high road.

The prison was medium security, a less restrictive environment than Eastern. Convinced that the state was recognizing David's good behavioral record, I read this development as a step toward freedom but failed to appreciate how bad things were in a different way. David was out of an individual cell but now living in a dormitory with fifty other prisoners sharing communal washrooms and tight spaces. The risk of violence in this setting, especially when the weather was hot, was far greater than anything he encountered at Eastern. He wrote that sleep was also a problem with all those people in the same place: "The first night was the worst. . . . However, things got a little better, mainly because I adopted a plan that was better for me." The plan was to get out of bed at 5:30 AM and work on his course; the early waking hour made him more tired at night and able to sleep better.

One change from maximum security was that this prison had windows. He could now see the sky, birds, and the tops of trees in the distance. Yet David told me that he was much happier at the maximum-security prison. Looking out the window only reminded him of the world from which he was being unjustly excluded. Rubin thought it was good that David was no longer comfortable and told him that he *should* look out the window. "That's where you want to be, my brother." In a letter to David, I echoed Rubin:

> David, how can you leave the prison unless your soul is focused outside the prison? . . . Your most important job is to heal your soul; that's what you do by staring out at the beauty of this planet, the birds, the grass, whatever you can see.

This advice was a bit of a joke, given that Arthur Kill was more wasteland than forest. I also sympathized with him, but Rubin said that "*sympathy* falls between *shit* and *syphilis* in the dictionary." The weekly telephone calls from David became excruciating. I felt the weight of his life on my shoulders and thanked God that Gary Dolin was able to share the load from his Washington farm, because whenever David got this way, Rubin would refuse to talk to him.

Arthur Kill was even worse than David let on at the time, but he told me about it later: "I didn't like the lack of programming. If it weren't for the college courses, I'd have had nothing to do. I was surprised that the black and Hispanic guards had terrible attitudes. Some came from our neighborhoods in Bushwick and Bed-Stuy, but they had no respect for us. One female guard played two inmates off against each other. She seduced one to make the other jealous. Some of the male guards cursed at the prisoners. During searches, they attempted to humiliate guys, made them squat and spread themselves more than usual. Guys came out to family visits very upset.

"It was a sadistic atmosphere. They would bait prisoners into violence, then put them in solitary when they took the bait. Like on Rikers, I was lucky. First I had my support system, you and the legal team and Ray and Marc. I got a job again in the law library, away from the general population, helping handicapped prisoners with their briefs. My day had a routine. I stayed out of the yard. The yard is a dangerous place; you can get shanked, especially during night yards. I was also fortunate to have a great counselor, Ms. Henderson. The other counselors did next to nothing. They were lazy and spiteful."

David's moods at the prison became mercurial, encouraged by the help he was getting and discouraged in equal measure by the intransigence of the Brooklyn DA's Office and his family's problems. Money was always an issue at home, so Gary and I sent the occasional check to Ernestine. Our gesture caused an unforeseen problem. Two of David's brothers needed money to buy a car, so they pressured his mother to call one of us. Ernestine was conflicted but afraid to alienate me, so she asked Gary. When Gary told me about her call, we realized that sending money to David's mother, as much as she needed it, could only create further difficulties. David, who wanted to set his brothers straight, felt helpless from inside the prison. He knew that his mother would never have done such a thing on her own:

> You see, Ken, my mother has always been very sensitive to the feelings of others, so I know what it would do to her, because it would give the impression that she has done something

wrong. From this point forward, I appreciate the fact that we
do not have to mention this whole thing again.

Gary, my sister Joan, and I decided to focus our financial support
solely on David, helping him buy clothing, food, and electronic equipment. We also invested in his future, continuing to pay for tuition
fees and textbooks.

Building for the future was necessary inside the limbo that was
Arthur Kill prison. Most of the prisoners there, guilty or innocent, had
little hope, at best awaiting a parole hearing that might be scheduled
many years down the road. The lack of programming presented David
with dangers that we feared the entire time he was at that prison. "I
am definitely being cautious in this place, because it really appears
to me that because nothing goes on here, the officers look for things
to harp on," he wrote to me. "I have no choice but to do whatever I
have to do to stay out of trouble."

5

RAY KLONSKY

The Brother and the Son

RUBIN WAS ELATED that so many highly regarded professionals were now involved in David's life and the quest for his
exoneration. How gratifying that he could still attract this level of
support despite his break with AIDWYC! With the irregularity of
income and his reduced public exposure resulting from his AIDWYC
departure, I worried about his future. The following e-mail bolstered
me, because his personal sacrifices—his leadership of AIDWYC and
his loss of the book—suddenly seemed worth it to him:

> It's wonderful what's going on! I see doors opening. People
> communicating—important people! That's what I'd envi-
> sioned Innocence International to be: bringing the neces-
> sary components together to look at and solve a wrongful
> conviction. Plain and simple. That's working the system
> and not letting the system work you! We'll talk soon, Ken.
> Great work!

Jay Salpeter, our first hire, was to figure prominently in 2007. Salpeter exploited a previous contact at *MY9 News*, a show broadcast from a local TV station in New York. David's appearance from prison on this show and the story of his wrongful conviction were his first shot at media exposure. The interviewer, Barbara Nevins Taylor, sensing his unmistakable integrity, was sympathetic to his plight. The taped confessions figured prominently in the segment. Salpeter hoped that the exposure might jog the memories of witnesses who remembered the case and that those witnesses would come forward. Instead, Oscar received an e-mail from John O'Mara, an assistant DA in Charles Hynes's office, chiding us for calling into question the work of Detective Butta, who had died several years before. O'Mara also laid on a guilt trip for disturbing Nathan Blenner's bereaved mother, even though the news station made that decision.

Mrs. Blenner's assertion that the boys had a fair trial helped me understand that the average person views a jury's verdict as equivalent to the truth. Even in the press, a man found guilty is labeled a murderer, not a convicted murderer. The difference between the two is greater than it first appears, since the word "convicted" allows room for "wrongly" convicted.

Rubin warned us that media is of little use unless it is part of a concerted and well-coordinated campaign, like the outpouring of support that gained him his second trial. In addition, because of O'Mara's response to the *MY9* segment, David, Rubin, and I believed that the district attorney's office was hostile to our case and would try to undermine us. On the positive side, Ray and Marc discovered a way to gain media access to the prison; interviews with prisoners on camera were possible if the filmmakers were part of a recognized network, media company, or organization. Subsequently, they were able to interview David by getting a small Quebec-based company to provide bridge financing for the film.

Our legal goals remained the same: interviewing witnesses, retriev-
ing the old evidence, and finding new evidence, all of which could
throw the state's case into disrepute and prompt a sympathetic judge
to allow us a hearing, which we were certain to win. My old beliefs—
that reason would prevail, that judges are impartial arbiters, that the
primary goal of the law is to arrive at the truth, the whole truth, and
nothing but the truth—were delusionary. It was one thing to hear
Rubin talk about the postconviction process, another to experience
it directly.

One of the infuriating elements of appeals, from the point of
view of a defendant, is the definition of *new evidence*. The prosecutor at trial, Eric Bjorneby, distorted the time that Chrissie Owens saw
the two men whom we assumed to be Prince and Howard. Owens
had told the police interviewer it was "around 2 PM," but despite
Stuckey's lawyer's objection, the jury heard Bjorneby's distortion:
twelve noon. Reasonable doubt would very likely have arisen if the
jury knew that Owens had seen Prince and Howard right before the
carjacking took place around the corner. Would revealing Bjorneby's
deliberate deception, this unethical attempt to win at all costs, constitute new evidence? The trial transcripts also showed that Butta
interviewed Chrissie Owens, but in a violation of protocol, no police
report existed to corroborate the visit. He gave three different accounts
of this interview during the trial, including one where he claimed that
she couldn't remember the encounter with the suspected carjackers
because she was preoccupied with washing her car. This was a lie told
under oath. Did the suppression of the visit constitute what is known
as a Brady violation? Did Butta ask her to identify photos of Willie
and David? We needed written confirmation from Chrissie Owens.

Because of my inexperience, I had also missed subtleties about
the law that Steve and Oscar later pointed out. "Justice is a game," as
Dylan sang in "Hurricane." In practice, the laws governing appeals
are there to keep the courts from getting clogged and to protect the

conviction. One dispiriting rule, alluded to previously, is that new evidence must be evidence a defense lawyer could not have accessed before or during the course of the trial. What we discovered was contained in the very police reports to which both Willie's and David's attorneys had easy access; even Bjorneby's attempts to suppress or obfuscate testimony happened in the courtroom. Our insights did not comprise new evidence in this technical sense. So while Peter Mirto was an unbelievably inept, harried, and dishonest lawyer—right after the trial, he was disbarred for stealing from and lying to clients—we might not be allowed to make use of the things he overlooked. Oscar threw on the wet blanket: "The question is whether David or his lawyer raised the issue previously. One improper interference by the prosecutor (if we can establish it was improper) is not going to be enough."

While his primary focus was the false confessions, Steve also looked in a different direction: DNA testing. In a Texas case, Gregory Wallis had been exonerated based on DNA evidence found on a cigarette inside the house of a rape victim over twenty years later. We knew that the box of vouchered evidence in the McCallum case contained cigarettes, a cigar, and a roach clip; we also confirmed, through a relative of the Blenners, that smoking was not allowed inside the Blenner car. I was astonished to learn that cigarette butts could maintain a DNA profile for such a long period. "Good ole DNA," Rubin wrote in an e-mail.

We would have to wait for the actual evidence for who knew how long, so in the meantime, Steve prompted a dialogue with the Brooklyn DA's Office that had begun on the *Dr. Phil Show*.

As some of you may know, I was on the Dr. Phil show with Jay Salpeter last week. On the show, there was a retired detective from Brooklyn named Louis Scarcella (Jay knew him from a case). . . . Det. Scarcella said that he had "never ever" taken a false confession in his career. I responded by saying that this was hard to believe and that I had seen some false confessions at the Brooklyn DA's office. John O'Mara, a Brooklyn ADA, called me out on my blog and asked me to back-up what I had said. The point in making this exchange public is that I've made a connection with John which may help us down the road when we present David's case to him.

Scarcella's reputation in 2007 was stellar. In a crime-riddled era, he was the model detective who put the "bad guys" behind bars. It wasn't until the case of David Ranta, who was convicted of murdering a rabbi in the course of a robbery, that his modus operandi for producing false confessions was uncovered. By use of intimidation, brutality, falsification of facts, and endless cajoling of suspects to accept his made-up scenarios, he would get the confessor, usually a young African American, to follow his script. What eventually called his tactics into question, as in the Ranta case, was the use of the same drug-addicted female witness in several cases. The attitude inside the police department was extremely cynical: *The defendant may not have committed this crime, but he would have done something sooner or later.*

Drizin tried to set the record straight with John O'Mara about Brooklyn:

John, I am at home sick and unable to access my research files but I can tell you 1) that I am working on a false confession case [McCallum] right now from Brooklyn in the 1980s which I hope will be brought to the DA in the near future; 2) that the most infamous false confession case in history (before the CP Jogger case) hailed from Brooklyn; 3) more recently, a jury acquitted a young man by the name of Frank Esposito in a case based solely on a confession that he set fire to a stable in Brooklyn. I remember speaking with the defense attorney at the time and reviewing some documents and coming to the conclusion that the confession was not a proven false confession but was a "probable" or a "highly probable" false confession.

John O'Mara, an aging but crafty veteran, engaged Drizin in a collegial argument. The amount of trust accorded to O'Mara was a bone of contention between Steve and David. Since I represented David's view to the larger group, O'Mara caused dissension between Steve and me as well. To read the tone of O'Mara's words, you might think he was working with us to achieve a common goal. But he was a company man, a prime candidate for tunnel vision.

We switched to videotaping in the 1970s and continue to record all defendant statements—although this is generally not the interrogation but rather the product of earlier police interrogations. As to the case you are reviewing, David McCallum, we take such assertions seriously, which is why your expression on national TV relating to your review of numerous false confessions from Brooklyn was quite troubling. Like all responsible prosecutors, I recognize that false confessions can and do occur—and there is nothing unique about Brooklyn that would prevent one from occurring here. We review each case on an individual basis and attempt to screen out any false confessions, but would never claim that a mistake was impossible. However, advocates of mandatory recording of interrogations, and especially some of the self declared experts, often overstate the prevalence of false confessions . . .

District Attorney Hynes, while not supporting mandatory recording, has (with some encouragement) remained open to consideration of both the costs and benefits of recording. . . . I have read at least some of your writings on the subject and appreciate the time you have taken in reading and responding to my e-mail.

Sincerely,
John O'Mara

Steve accepted O'Mara's intentions at face value. Although David had deep reservations about a DA's office that continued to place barriers in front of him, I wanted to give the ADA the benefit of the doubt. Steve felt that through reasonable argument and persuasion, he could bring O'Mara around on the McCallum case.

John:
When the case is ready, I'd like to schedule a meeting with you and your superiors to present the case and to seek your agreement to do some DNA testing which could answer the question once and for all as to whether a false confession occurred. I am just assisting on the case—there is local NY counsel—but it is generally my practice to meet with prosecutors before filing anything in court . . .

Lastly, if Chicago, which is home to more false confessions than any other city, and which is arguably the birthplace of the modern psychological interrogation (the Reid technique), can go to electronic recording of interrogations in homicide cases, there is no reason why Brooklyn and NYC, can't make the move. The resistance here was tremendous (in fact, the recording legislation took five years to get through) but now the police are promoting their model plan and nary a complaint has been heard from the [front] line officers.

Both men conducted this extensive exchange with a subtext. David and I thought that O'Mara was attempting to neutralize Steve. Hynes's office was concerned about the McCallum case for two related reasons: First, Willie Stuckey died in prison; Rubin, because he tended to view the work of rogue prosecutors as criminal, publicly labeled Stuckey's arrest and conviction "kidnapping and forcible confinement causing death." Second, Rubin Carter's involvement alone and his public statements created pressure to get beyond legal technicalities and deal with the facts of the case.

While Rubin had immense respect for Steve, he also saw him as an academic, a man who might not appreciate the degree to which DA's offices manipulate people and disrespect the truth. Given Steve's impressive track record in Chicago and his reputation for doggedness, I began to question Rubin's judgment for the first time. Steve had related David's case to that of the Central Park jogger, suggesting to O'Mara that David and Willie could not have murdered Nathan Blenner without leaving behind a trace of evidence. How could two sixteen-year-olds have been so meticulous in covering up the crime yet so readily confess to it during interrogation? Their flimsy, wildly differing confessions, gained through intimidation and, according to both boys, physical abuse, were also the subtext of Steve's advocacy for the videotaping of interrogations.

O'Mara held the choice cards: he had the confessions and the quickness with which they had been elicited, a bought-and-sold witness who said he'd indirectly supplied a gun to Stuckey, the two convictions, and all the legal machinery at his disposal. Steve had prestige and an upcoming book, *True Stories of False Confessions*, written with Rob Warden, detailing one wretched case after another in over five hundred pages. The back-and-forth with O'Mara was a practical necessity. He knew that without the cooperation of the DA's office in the retrieval of evidence, especially the cigarette butts, David's chance at exoneration was slim.

The trouble with Steve's position with respect to courting O'Mara had nothing to do with his being an academic. Steve could assume there had been more false confessions and wrongful convictions in Brooklyn than Hynes's office would admit to, but neither he nor any other outsider had the remotest idea about the extent. Brooklyn, even before Scarcella and Charles Hynes, was a cesspool. Michael Race, a former police officer in East New York and a highly regarded private investigator, said that a high percentage of Brooklyn convictions in the 1980s, even a majority of them, were "fixed or improper." Because of the terrible crime wave and daily murders at the time, a deliberate policy of clearing the streets had eclipsed any legal niceties. Rights were routinely violated. I had written earlier to the previous DA, Elizabeth Holtzman, about McCallum's innocence; her hostile and dismissive reply began to make sense. Career police officers and prosecutors under her administration would have been implicated. Joseph Butta's and Louis Scarcella's unethical practices were symptoms of an epidemic illness.

Sometimes, particularly after a grim phone call with David, I began to feel as if the forces arrayed against us were overwhelming. Of course Rubin's credo was "Go the distance," but Rubin had fought in fifteen-round fights and even wrote about the sixteenth round in his book of that title. We were still in the early stages of the fight and had taken some body blows. What kept me from giving in to inertia, aside from Rubin's long shadow, was David and his family. Even if I was tired or discouraged, I was incapable of turning away. Some force in my psyche, engendered, I think, by an emotionally abusive upbringing, made me identify with wrongly convicted people. I too was a victim of circumstances beyond my control. At the time, this realization had not surfaced but troubled me inwardly, like distant thunder.

David McCallum was experiencing his own spiritual crisis:

I need to do some soul searching. I am still growing as a
person and I understand that there are things I have to let go
of in order to truly find myself. . . . Being scarred in the way
I have is a psychological barrier that I daily wrestle with to
overcome. . . . When I mentioned overcoming psychological
barriers, looking out the window is certainly one of them.
When I look out the window, I see an entirely different world;
a world I have not been a part of for nearly twenty-two years.
I get upset because I know that it is a place I should be a part
of and cannot, because they said I did something that I know
in my heart I did not do.

During a subsequent phone call, his tone became so negative, it
was all I could do not to hang up. I chided him for unloading all his
negativity on Gary and me. I no more wanted the weight of the prison
than he did. Criticizing David made me feel terrible, but I had to do
it, just like I had to criticize my son, even if every word I said sounded
hypocritical. My own weaknesses aside, I needed to let him know that
the force of the gravity of the prison itself that he was unloading on
us, could discourage those who wanted to help him. My words had
the desired effect, yet his response provided no satisfaction:

It is not my intention to drag you down as though you were
drowning. I did not realize that I was sending off that sort of
vibe. By no means do you have to feel that your efforts are
in vain. I cannot disagree with you that I may be identifying
with the role the state has given me; it goes back to that psychological barrier I talked about. But I will not submit that
prison has totally consumed me to the point where I can no
longer identify with the outside world, because I fight these
emotions on a daily basis and, for the most part, I believe
that I am succeeding.

Such openness and honesty could not fail to touch anyone. Rather than take the risk of losing our support, he would use two opposing tactics, often within the same sentence: First there would be an attempt to mollify that, for me, was unnecessary but was a way of ensuring that we would stay in his corner. Second, because he was unfailingly honest, he would be true to himself. "I am optimistic about everything that is happening although there are times when it certainly does not seem like I am feeling good about my prospects."

I also tried to make him aware that what he did in his life, even his incarcerated life, was of importance to other people, that his struggle had meaning and was not placed upon him randomly. Surrounded by ugliness and facing the daily denial of his humanity, his life was circumscribed in the most awful way. He tried to deal with this reality in such a way as to not offend my beliefs:

> Ken, at times, I am finding it difficult to fathom that I am actually doing a wonderful thing, mainly because I feel as though I have no other choice to do what I am doing. Sadly, I do not see it as some special thing, rather I feel that my adaptation to these circumstances is being instinctively dealt with. I am glad that I am able to touch other people in the way that I have. I just have to focus on finding more of myself.

David's literature course from Ohio University pushed him toward the self-knowledge he was seeking. "[The work] is inspiring me to want more from an educational perspective," he wrote. "If I plan to have children someday, or if I mentor young people when I get out of here, it would be awfully hypocritical for me to suggest that they do something that I did not do for myself." His embrace of education, in this and future courses, was a godsend and, from a selfish point of view, just what we hoped for. The constant demands of dealing with the intricacies of his case and getting a court hearing created too much pressure on everyone, especially people like Steve and Oscar who had much else going on in their professional lives.

After reading Sophocles's *Oedipus Rex*, David was struck by the idea that a person's tragedy is predestined. Along with his grasp of the power of fate in the life of ancient Greece, he made another and quite opposite point in his response:

> I guess in a sense all of our lives are preordained. If so, there is nothing we can do to change our path. In other words, if I understand Oedipus correctly, I was destined to come to prison, not because I killed someone, but for all the other transgressions that I thought I had gotten away with. While I had a difficult time accepting that logic, I have realized there is truth to that.

Here David was responding to a lesson from Rubin from the *Sun* interview. His imprisonment was as much about karma as it was about fate. One's life is predetermined if one stays unconscious and continues along a self-destructive path. Transformation is only possible, Rubin told me during the *Sun* interview, if you wake up:

> Anybody who is in prison has to say, "OK, whatever I've done in life has led me to where I am today. Therefore, if I want to get out of prison and stay out of prison, I've got to turn around and go back up." You've got to use this time to learn how to read if you don't know how to read, to learn to write if you don't know how to write, to learn a skill. . . . Use this time to better yourself. Maybe on the outside you didn't have time to go to school. . . . Now you've got time. This time is imposed upon you. Use it to look at yourself. Use it to become a useful person.

David's openness to education marked a turning point in his long incarceration. Seeing himself as a victim was keeping him in a metaphorical prison, as he indicated in a letter to me:

> Not too long ago, if I asked myself why I am in prison, I would have given the response of someone who saw himself as a victim. And, on some level, there is truth to that, but I learned that I was only keeping myself in bondage with that train of thought. . . . I am coming to the realization that I am paying a price not for what they CLAIM I did, but I believe for what I actually did and got away with. Believe me, Ken, it was difficult to come to grips with this, because I felt as though I was giving up something very valuable to me. I am careful not to place too much blame on myself in accepting this truth, but I clearly understand my part. It goes back to, in my opinion, that everything in the universe is connected.

In arranging the relationship between Ray and David, I was fully conscious of something that I'd learned while participating in a men's group in Toronto. The role of a father is limited; fathers can teach their sons life lessons mainly by example. Parental preaching produces an automatic response in most children: a dismissive gesture and some phrase that is the equivalent of "You don't know what you're talking about." There are exceptions, of course, but I knew that David McCallum, as a mentor, was far likelier to make headway with my son than I was. Both of them, as it turned out, were hungering for just such a relationship:

> Ray and I have established a bond. I would be doing Ray a disservice to not give him the credit he deserves for helping me help him. I don't think you have to beat yourself up any longer worrying about where Ray fits in this world because

I sincerely believe that he is on the right path. Is he going to continue to make bad judgments along the way—sure he is, but the reward will be when he recognizes and learns from it. . . . There is no question that he still has some of that adolescent stuff in him, but I believe that he has the right to have that child in him.

Ray decided, from gratitude and love, that he would work for David's release and that this work would become the centerpiece of the film. He fastened on to David as the big brother he never had and one he was going to defend. I attribute the positive change that followed in my relationship with Ray to seeing him less critically and more acceptingly, through David's eyes. (The opposite was true as well: Ray saw *me* differently through David's eyes.) David also helped me value my relationship with Ray, however flawed. The film was the counterpart to Rubin's book. Both were now pieces of the puzzle in the larger effort to free David; both, against the odds, had to see the light of day.

That summer, Ray and I began a shared project: writing a film script. The story revolved around a father and son, a police detective and a prosecutor respectively, who become involved in a wrongful conviction. The film was to be called *Conviction*, but the process took so long that another film with the same name came out before we were able to complete the script.

The project, the only creative thing we had done together since his time in elementary school, was a means to further our relationship. We even attended a course given by the late Blake Snyder that summer in Vancouver. Blake and the rest of the class were excited by the possibilities of the script. That *Conviction* was to remain an undone and unpublished project was beside the point. The amount of film know-how that Ray had absorbed from his university courses and my discovery of his talents as a writer made me feel that his education had been worthwhile.

For David, that summer project with Ray was a confirmation of his own ability to make good things happen on the outside:

> I wish I could have been standing there when you wished him off to school. Those kinds of moments are priceless, but filled with sadness as well. I believe that your relationship with your son has in some way helped me deal with the loss of my father, and, I am sure, with the loss of your father as well. Please forgive me, but that is how I feel about it. Like you said, it was special working with your own son.

I wondered why David asked for forgiveness, but it occurred to me that he felt he might be trespassing on my innermost feelings. Of course this was no trespass but the empathy of a close friend. The link he made between the loss of our fathers in the same calendar year was profoundly sad. David had no farewell with his father aside from a wake.

The work on the screenplay foundered while Ray was back at school. David encouraged him to continue, fearing that the gains in our relationship might be jeopardized. When Ray came to visit for the Christmas holiday, working on it became a grind; there never seemed to be a right time to do it. I understood that he was more intent on working through the problems of his life with his mentor, furthering his own film project, and planning for his future than continuing with *Conviction*. My choices were to be hurt or to accept the truth with a sense of humor. David was always careful to foster our father-son relationship, even while the bond between him and Ray grew stronger:

> In talking to Ray, he seemed eager to work with you on the screenplay. I am going to take that as a positive. He also

seemed happy to be home. . . . I am sure he is happy to be with
his parents. . . . I could be totally off base with this, but what
I have picked up from Ray is that you have to take what he
says a little deeper. For instance, when Ray talks about being
home to me, he is really saying how he misses the hell out of
his parents, but feels like he is losing a part of his cockiness
if he admits it. . . . He is really worried about his life after
school. His dilemma is that he knows what he wants to do,
but he is not sure if things are going to materialize.

I often wonder why Mary Ellen and I did not feel some jealousy
that Ray would share so much with David that he clearly was not
sharing with us.

In the summer of 2007, Jay Salpeter was able to get actor James Gandolfini (from *The Sopranos*) to visit Marty Tankleff. It was Tankleff's
seventeenth year in prison. The publicity around the Gandolfini visit
gave Marty's case the final push it needed. Salpeter had met Gandolfini
on the set of the film *Lonely Hearts*, where he had prepared the late
actor for his role as a police detective. Gandolfini was so moved by
Salpeter's account of Tankleff's suffering, he felt compelled to offer
words of solace and encouragement. In Salpeter's words, "We met
over at the prison [Great Meadow Correctional Facility in Comstock,
New York], and I introduced him to Marty and I'll tell you, he gave
someone a very wonderful birthday gift."

On December 21, 2007, Marty Tankleff was granted a new trial.
The vacated conviction put him in the same category as Rubin. The
legal system makes a distinction between exonerations and vacated
convictions. A conviction can be vacated after a trial is found to have
been filled with judicial error or an arrest and interrogation are found
to have violated constitutional norms. A prisoner is considered to

be exonerated only if evidence is found implicating someone else, a body for a body. Exonerations were rare until Barry Scheck and Peter Neufeld of the Innocence Project at the Cardozo School of Law capitalized on the use of DNA testing. A conviction of sexual assault, for example, assuming the availability of a sperm sample, is generally thrown out if the DNA does not match the profile of the defendant. Rubin insisted that there was only one category of innocence: innocent until proven guilty. As far as he was concerned and as many times as he faced questions about it, he would say with fury, "I am exonerated!"

Marty Tankleff's imminent release filled us again with confidence in our private investigator. One day soon Jay Salpeter would produce the same kind of results for David that he had for Marty Tankleff. Didn't both cases hinge on false confessions? In a letter, David summed up what everyone was feeling:

> I really feel connected to Marty. Hearing news of him getting a new trial is as though I am getting a new trial as well. I feel this connection on several levels. One, the pain he has had to endure is a pain I can relate to; secondly, I feel that him getting a new trial is a victory for me in the sense that someone has finally acknowledged the problem of false confessions and steps are being made to do something about it here in the State of New York.
>
> I would be remiss if I did not mention that I am very happy that Jay was very instrumental in helping Marty get a new trial. . . . Obviously, the case is not over, but the foundation has certainly been laid for his eventual exoneration. I believe that.

Because Suffolk County prosecutors stubbornly held to their belief in Tankleff's guilt, Tankleff was never exonerated for his parents' murder. Suffolk County eventually dropped the case for lack of evidence, despite the fact that Salpeter's work pointed to the real perpetrators. Marty's extended family and the public knew the truth, but because the law protects rogue prosecutors and police, this truth contained no consequences. Rubin used to say that, for the wrongly convicted, "truth is your dearest friend and your cruelest enemy." Certainly there is truth out there that can save you; having it deliberately ignored is torture.

Another positive that came out of the Tankleff case was the precedent of providing compensation to people who falsely confessed. By eventually awarding Marty Tankleff a multimillion-dollar settlement, the state made the implicit concession that false confessions could be coerced from an overborne suspect and were not self-inflicted wounds. For David, all the rulings around this landmark case represented personal validation:

> I am particularly glad that not only did the four judge panel rule on the newly discovered issue, I am also elated that they ruled favorably on the false confession issue. . . . As we have talked about for some time, it is my belief that Jay is truly on to something. Subliminally, I get the sense that Jay is, like you said, putting some pressure on whoever he is talking to. . . . I will not allow anyone or anything to interfere with the positive vibe I am getting from the Martin Tankleff case. This is truly a great thing that has occurred.

While all of our hopes around Salpeter were overblown, we could look back on the year and see his three major accomplishments: First, through connections within the police department, he found the evidence voucher. Second, through *MY9 News*, he had set up David's first opportunity for media publicity. Third, and most dramatic, in response to an e-mail I sent to the team wherein I wrote that we absolutely must find Chrissie Owens if she was still alive, Jay responded in his usual curt manner: "I've already interviewed her." For us, it was the equivalent of Stanley finding Livingstone; all roads to David's freedom went through Chrissie Owens. With this revelation, David agreed to a change in strategy, deciding not to push for an immediate court date. He now realized that waiting was in his best interest: "As you said, Jay believes in me; it does not get any more encouraging than that."

Our agent Larry Hoffman's ongoing battle with cancer throughout the year brought about a change in Rubin. He had never been the kind of person who responded to sentiment or to the emotional needs of others, even those who were close to him. Because he felt deserted by his family during his years in prison, Rubin did not attend his own daughter's wedding, nor did he go to his ninety-six-year-old mother's funeral. So when Larry told me that Rubin was driving him to and from Sunnybrook Hospital twice a week for cancer treatments, I was pleasantly surprised.

Rubin had refused to answer his door on a suffocating hot day in Toronto in 2006 when Larry had come over to try to work out a compromise with Key Porter Books. Larry, sick as he was at the time, had walked a considerable distance. While Rubin never regretted his role in Key Porter's cancellation of the book, he did express regret for the way he treated Larry and found a way to show contrition.

Larry's partner, Evelyn Sommers, dealt with the day-to-day difficulties of providing for the needs of a loved one in the latter stages of cancer. She also had a psychotherapy practice to look after. Hence, Rubin's efforts on Larry's behalf were helpful to Evelyn and gave Larry a huge boost in morale. Larry and Rubin had many laughs together as well, not the least of which was during the first trip to the hospital. Larry sat in the rear of the Mercedes, the Black Swan—the Blue Goose had finally given out—in case he experienced nausea. When they reached the driveway at Sunnybrook, Rubin got out to open the back door. An attendant asked Rubin if he was the chauffeur. "Why yes, suh, I am," he said. This anecdote reminded me of a news item from years before. At the wheel of the Blue Goose, Rubin was pulled over by Toronto police for "driving while black."

Larry died in Toronto at the beginning of the following year, on January 28, 2008. Determined to live fully until the end, he and Evelyn managed a trip to Maui two weeks before his death, but they had to cut the trip short. My sorrow was increased by the knowledge that the book still foundered. The fulfillment of Larry's life did not come from his professional success—although there had been some of that—but from his acquaintance with Rubin. The book was to be his crowning achievement as an agent, but being on the receiving end of Rubin Carter's kindness would have to do. David wrote with his usual consideration:

> If you can pass this message on to Larry's family, I would love nothing better at this point th[a]n to send my condolence to his wife. . . . I don't handle these things all that well. I guess I will never get used to them, although passing on is a part of life itself. I have a question, though. Is it remotely possible that I could be provided with a picture of him? I would love to put a face with his name.

6

CHRISSIE OWENS
The Witness

DAVID McCALLUM HAD REASON for optimism at the beginning of 2008. For the first time in the history of the republic, a black man had a shot at becoming president. That possibility constituted real hope, "the audacity of hope," as Obama called it in his autobiography, for the overrepresented segment of African Americans languishing in prison. David's letter at the time reflected the excitement and anticipation many Americans of all races were feeling:

> Much like Oscar, I believe this is going to be a very interesting year for some positive things. Even politically, things are going in a different direction, given the results from the Iowa caucus, where Barack Obama was victorious. However, I cautioned some of the guys here that it would be foolish to look at this process from a racial standpoint, as opposed to looking at this man as someone who will change the political landscape, not only in America, but internationally as well.

"Prisoners feel the changes out in society before anyone else," Rubin had asserted. When he was a jailhouse lawyer at Trenton State Prison in the 1970s, he won the right for him and other prisoners to wear beards and jewelry and have conjugal visits. Although Obama pardoned large numbers of drug offenders in the final year of his second term, his presidency took place during a less revolutionary time. Justice initiatives were met with inaction, public resistance, and congressional opposition. He could do little, aside from deliver empathic speeches, to stop gratuitous police shootings of African Americans or to reach any agreement on effective gun control legislation. Before the 2008 election, though, David and the team were riding the wave of change:

> The profound statement Rubin made after Martin Tankleff's release, that "this will be David's last Christmas in prison" has stuck with me. . . . Hope is a very powerful thing and I am glad that I still have it; without it, I am not sure if I could have survived this long. Now, I think my time in prison is coming to an end.

Oscar's upcoming court motion, and it *was* now imminent, lacked an essential component: the affidavit from Chrissie Owens. That was Jay Salpeter's job, and we were having difficulty maintaining contact with him. When was he going back to see her? Oscar replied to my query about whether to push Jay:

> I think he sees himself as an old fashioned gumshoe—few words, only report when you have something to report. I think he can be trusted to be honest. I do feel, however, that as his employer, you have the right to ask him for more updates. Your nose absolutely belongs in his business because you are paying him. How do you jeopardize the investigation by

asking for regular updates? After all, we are all waiting for Jay to say he's done with Chrissie Owens.

I received the first draft of the 440 motion, our attempt to get an appeal judge to hear David's case, from Oscar. The document pointed to a series of conundrums. How could we know where the emphasis should be: the demonstrably false confessions; the Brady violations, as Steve wanted; or the actual-innocence claim, as Rubin wanted? How could ineffective assistance of counsel be discounted when both defense attorneys failed to interview Chrissie Owens? Why would the prosecution want as witnesses two ten-year-olds who could not identify the carjackers? The preceding question is rhetorical since the implication was clear: accuracy and truth during the trial did not appear to be Bjorneby's goal. I say without irony that I am still disillusioned that officers of the court, knowing that the evidence was tainted, would deliberately railroad two youths into prison.

But what if, for sake of argument, the convictions were not deliberately manufactured? What if they were the product of confusion and error? Error is inevitable after all, not a badge of dishonor. Why then would people in a DA's office looking back over twenty-five years not see what was so obvious to us? Why would they hide behind the technicalities of the legal system? Why keep David McCallum in prison if his conviction was an unfortunate accident? Rubin held that the primary purpose of the appeals and post-conviction system is to protect the system itself, and by that he meant the people who run the system and are employed by the system year after year.

Despite this awareness, nothing could constrain Rubin's intense inner confidence about David's case. His belief was built on his own success, despite tremendous public resistance, in getting Judge Sarokin to release him. The Rubin Carter case was unique. He admitted that in his public speeches: "Even with all those famous people helping me—the Bob Dylans, the Ellen Burstyns, the Muhammad Alis—

I narrowly escaped through the eye of a needle." We *also* needed a friendly judge, along with an airtight 440. After nineteen years in prison and nineteen years in the wrongful convictions business, Rubin knew what it would take. When I told him in a phone conversation that Steve and Oscar thought our case had too many unanswered questions, his e-mailed response showed that, while understanding the misgivings, he felt otherwise:

> Ken, send me all that you've got and tell David that I send my love and respect.
>
> Now, Get the fuck outta here! We do have a strong case! We have a strong case of "factual innocence!" And if WE don't believe that, how in the world are we going to get others to believe what we, ourselves, don't? We must present our case in the strongest possible terms. This is not a one man's show! The very first step in this progress will be our presentation of "the facts." So please tell Oscar not to submit the 440 right now. Give all of us a chance to go through it—that is, David, you, me, Jay (if that's possible) and then back to Oscar for his final review. We've got to give this 440 our best shot. David must be satisfied with it. His life is at stake here! He must approve everything up and down the line. And, right now, if you don't think the Brief sounds strong enough, or misspelt words, or whatever!—then we must fix it—and three or four heads are always much better than only one. Oscar will understand. Our 440 must be the best 440 ever written! And we can do it!

Was Rubin about to be proven right? Had David spent his last Christmas inside prison?

Chrissie Owens was no ordinary witness but the hub of a wheel. David, Rubin, Steve, Oscar, and I played out the same scenario over and over until it became a litany. She was washing her car at the time she saw the likely killers of Nathan Blenner. Her description of the two men did not match David McCallum and Willie Stuckey in age or appearance. "A girl washing a red car" appeared in Stuckey's confession. Willie had no source for this information other than Detective Butta. The confession, slim as it was to start with, was contaminated. The prosecutor and the detective attempted to change Owens's meeting with the two men from 2:00 PM to noon. Why? Because the prosecutor knew as well as we did that Owens didn't see Stuckey or McCallum. If she had seen the two men, whom we surmised were Prince and Howard, at noon, then the meeting could be made irrelevant to the jury. That is precisely what happened during the trial when the prosecutor was able to get the last word on the timing. ("Noon, then.") If an appeal judge looked at this information dispassionately, David was sure we would get a hearing:

> We have made Chrissie Owens become relevant again. This is not newly discovered evidence, but it does present a more than solid claim of ineffective assistance of counsel for not calling Ms. Owens to testify. We can also make a claim of perjury on Detective Butta and make a claim of prosecutorial misconduct, based on the fact that the prosecutor allowed Det. Butta to falsely testify about Chrissie Owens. . . . I am not jumping the gun here, but I do feel that Ms Owens will become an important part of us getting back into court.

I did not need to remind David that the court already disposed of ineffective assistance of counsel in his previous pro se appeal. Oscar guaranteed us that he would try to sneak it through the back door, but he was never convinced the argument would work. Steve still believed that our case was insufficient without evidence testing. But this was 2008, and the "audacity of hope" kept David away from negativity.

We were waiting for Jay. Jay Salpeter's modus operandi continued to be the greatest cause of our frustration. As Oscar had said, Jay was conducting his private investigation in the hope of one day surfacing with the case solved, all tied up in a bow. Just as Rubin judged all cases by his success with his own, Salpeter's underground work on the Tankleff case gave him a recipe. Why expect Jay to be anything other than himself? We discovered, as Barry Scheck had indicated, that the best PIs are not former cops but people who can change, chameleon-like, to fit into their surroundings. Salpeter was no chameleon on the streets of Bushwick. Ray, having filmed him the previous year, said that his very look "screamed cop."

David wrote letter after letter expressing his frustration. He called out "an egregious decision by Jay" and "Jay's non-communicative approach." "We are left to play the guessing game with Jay and, quite frankly, I do not like it." Oscar was finally able to reach Jay on the phone. The PI offered to testify as to what Owens told him already, just in case he was unable to get her to sign an affidavit. Oscar pointed out that such testimony, even by a former police officer, would not pass muster in an appeals court. Jay's offer hinted at the possibility of failure, only serving to further stoke our doubts.

We had another job for Jay that would involve searching for people in Bushwick. The original police reports revealed that a group of boys, now men, were recruited to burn the Blenner car that had been left abandoned in a warehouse parking lot. The boys were caught in the act of setting the fire by a security guard and interviewed by police. The information each gave at the time varied substantively, each attempting to avoid direct responsibility. We knew that a car ring would not attempt to sell a car if its members were aware it had been used in a kidnapping and a murder, and the leaders of the ring would not want to be caught setting it on fire. While the boys were never treated as murder suspects, the initial police interviews were never followed up on. Their testimony would enable us to confirm Steve

Drizin's theory: that the murder of Nathan Blenner was connected to a carjacking ring operated out of Pop's Hardware Store in Bushwick. Since the can of kerosene used to set the fire came from that hardware store, they might tell us who paid them (or ordered them) to torch the car. That vital information would bring us one step closer to disassociating David from the crime, bringing the successful conclusion of the case tantalizingly close. Despite his ongoing frustration with the PI, David felt that we might be on the verge of a breakthrough:

> As far as myself, I am so optimistic at this point that something major is about to happen for me. I don't mean to sound self-serving here, but I deserve some kind of good fortune relating to my legal situation. I like to think that I have done everything a person in my predicament can do with respect to enduring and exercising patience.

My contract with Jay stipulated that I owed him the remainder of $5,000 by the end of one year. Unexpectedly and hearteningly, he refused the money, saying, "You owe me the rest when I get David out of prison."

While Oscar made the false confession and the ineffective assistance of counsel arguments in the 440 draft, he also emphasized the Brady violation at Steve's urging. Our legal experts felt the appeals court would be more convinced by the prosecution's attempts to suppress as evidence Detective Butta's visit to Chrissie Owens's house than an incompetent attorney's bungling the case. We were never able to find a police report of the interview, though it was clearly mentioned in the trial transcript. Oscar insisted that Owens must have been shown photos of David and Willie but been unable to identify them. In September Oscar sent Salpeter an affidavit to take to Owens. According to Jay, she refused to sign it, citing an anxiety disorder. Would we have to subpoena her and risk alienating our most important witness?

Jay went silent once again. Late that fall we reluctantly reached the conclusion that we could expect nothing more from our PI. Oscar decided to seek out the witness on his own; he made a series of phone calls to arrange a meeting and heard something unexpected, which he relayed to the rest of us in an e-mail:

Dear Team:

Just spoke via phone to Chrissie Owens. I have some very bad news. She said that it was not individual photos that were shown to her but rather a series of mugshot books that the detective brought to her house because her Mom would not let her go to the precinct. I even spoke to her Mom who was at the house with her and mom confirmed that and said she remembers it like it was yesterday, it was two or three very large mug books. Chrissie said that she would be willing to sign an affidavit to that effect.

She was also very upset that two days after Jay spoke with her, a reporter from Newsday spoke to her and that she said she has to attribute that to Jay's visit as nobody else knew she was Chrissie Owens from Queens from all those years ago. She told me . . . "This whole thing is killing me." When I stressed the importance of all of this to her, she said "I completely understand. If that was my son or my brother in there, I would want people to do whatever they had to do to get him out, but there was no need to go to the press. I don't want my name in the papers and the papers love these kinds of cases." I told her I understood and that I would do what I could to make sure her name was not in the papers, if necessary proceeding anonymously. I told her I would re-word the affidavit to her liking and mail it to her. That after she read it if she was ok with the wording I would go out to her to have her sign it and notarize it. She said she would agree to do that.

Oscar had concluded that unless Butta had gone to her with specific suspects in mind (i.e., Willie and David), our claim to a Brady violation would have less weight. We knew that David's and Willie's photos were in those mug books, but the range of choices she was given would weaken our case. Rubin insisted that Owens's willingness to sign an affidavit was encouraging. Our client's response to this bit of upbeat news told me that he wasn't quite convinced even that would happen: "An ideal week for me would be my counsellor informing me that you called with some great news; Chrissie Owens signed the affidavit. That is the thought that goes through my mind on a daily basis."

While the eventual outcome of our efforts with Chrissie was unknowable, I continued to emphasize the good news to David—her willingness to sign an affidavit and the proof it would provide of Butta's visit—and spared him the sobering news in Oscar's e-mails. David took the same tack with his mother when trying to spare her unnecessary suffering:

Whenever I update her on the case, I try to be as honest with her as I possibly can. Sometimes, and I am not exactly proud about this, I have to be dishonest with her, especially when I receive some not so favorable news. I have to, Ken, because this is my way of protecting her. We are in store for some good news.

David spotted Marty Tankleff on *The Oprah Winfrey Show* alongside Jay Salpeter and Saul Kassin, another well-known expert on false confessions. Oprah said she could never confess to a crime she did not commit, but Tankleff's case alone demonstrated how easily one could be tricked into self-incrimination. David was happy to know that "a wide audience was watching."

On October 27 a new private investigative company, Fortress Global Investigations Partners, dealing solely with wrongful convictions, was launched at a news conference in New York. The star attraction was Rubin Carter, who spoke on behalf of the three founders: former Manhattan homicide prosecutor Robert Seiden, Marty Tankleff, and, yet again, Jay Salpeter. Rubin was attempting to get a quid pro quo from Jay to refocus his attention on David's case. For David, Oscar, and me, the distraction of a business venture further explained Salpeter's delays.

On November 23, after a full year of waiting, Oscar sent the e-mail we had all been waiting for:

Dear Team:

I am pleased to report that today I convinced Chrissie Owens to sign our affidavit. It took 45 minutes of discussion on her driveway with her Husband and Mom present but it got done. I believe I have also convinced her of the correctness of our position so that we can expect future cooperation. I told her I would be the point person on it. I have attached a copy of the affidavit and I will notarize it on Monday (I didn't bring my stamp home).

Oscar

Oscar's determination and the presence of his ebullient wife, Christine, made the signing possible. Next morning, he picked up a voice message from Rubin on his BlackBerry. He has it to this day: "You did it, Oscar! You did it! Congratulations! You did it! We're almost home now, my brother!"

Although we had Chrissie Owens's signature on an affidavit, our case would still rest on the perception and disposition of a single judge. Oscar was able to submit the full 440 motion on December 23. It was a lengthy and comprehensive document. Its strength was cumulative, counterbalancing our newly discovered evidence with a full history of the case that demonstrated, at every single turn, the absence of evidence against the defendants. Everyone on the team was now quietly confident; surely a judge on a higher-level appeals court would agree to a hearing. But given the vagaries of the system, how could doubts ever cease? David adopted a form of fatalism:

> I have come to a place where I am ready to accept what must be done in the best interest of the case. The bottom line is that none of us has any control. . . . I think the most important thing for me right now is to trust in the process. This is pretty much my last opportunity to get it right. We must leave no stone unturned and we must leave no room for second guessing.

Would we still have to retrieve evidence for DNA testing? What kind of case would the state make against us? Who would be appointed as the judge? Looking at the possibility that the 440 might fail, David hinted at his only other option while simultaneously negating it:

> I often remind myself that I have a parole hearing on the horizon in June, 2010. However, I have no intention of ever appearing before the board. I plan to be exonerated by then. . . . Let's look at it this way. Where was I five years ago and where might I be if I never asked my friend, Earl Coleman, to read his Sun Magazine? I now have an opportunity to regain my liberty.
>
> I am also animated because I am happy with the energy of the people in my circle; the positive energy that's permeating

this entire process, from my education to the legal process that is taking place. Couple that with the project done by Ray and Marc, things are looking good at this point.

As I now know, David's overall confidence was based more on mind-set than reality. Although Ray and Marc had created an allur-ing trailer, the film was a long way from completion. To finish it, they would need considerable financial resources, which none of us possessed. Still the pair pushed on. After Ernestine had recovered from her near-fatal car accident, Ray and Marc visited her and the family to shoot footage inside the home. They also did interviews at Aberdeen Park, where Nathan Blenner's body was discovered, and a school playground where David and his sister Mattie were playing handball when Nathan Blenner was kidnapped.

Ray and Marc, with permission from Albany, came to the prison to interview David for the film. One of the sessions took five hours and was particularly grueling. David was asked for the first time in his life to talk on camera about his personal history. He wrote to me about the experience:

> Friday really was a wonderful day for all of us that includes my entire support team. It was one of the most emotionally draining experiences I endured in a long time. But I must say that it was well worth it . . .
>
> We covered so many areas of my life, that I cannot say for certain that we left anything out. Ray had four full pages of questions, and he was determined to ask all of them. . . . I was emotionally drained and mentally fatigued. The fact that I was able to speak about my past caused me to become emo-tional, not to the point where I cried on camera, but it was just building up.

That the prison even allowed a film interview to go on for this length of time convinced me that David, viewed as a model prisoner, would soon be freed. This belief was based on the erroneous assumption that all levels of the justice system spoke to each other and that their decisions were coordinated.

———————

Ray and Marc had graduated from Concordia that fall, another event, like our overseas trips, that David had to experience vicariously. Now, at the age of forty, he would probably have been a father had he lived on the outside; the system had stolen the prime of his life. David's incalculable loss made him desperate to hear about our lives, to become a part of us, to focus on the good outside the prison—in short, to do exactly as Rubin urged. Paradoxically, our lives reminded him of what he was missing; the pleasure in knowing was counterbalanced by the equivalent pain. He wrote to me about the graduation:

> I would imagine that it was a very proud moment for Mary Ellen and yourself, watching your son graduate from college. I hope it was a wonderful experience, and I also hope that everyone had a good time. A part of me wishes that I could have been present to watch the ceremonies.

David took full advantage of the opportunity he had been given to mentor Ray. It served as practice for actual parenting and the counseling of youth. They had grown close:

> I cannot tell you how my fondness for Ray has grown immeasurably since the time we initially met. He seems to have a good grasp of what is going on around him. He is someone I can trust because I believe he would not betray me. . . . What

has really caught my attention is his desire to move away from some of his friends who might stagnate his growth and development.

He began making concrete plans for the future:

I have now focused a good amount of my time trying to network with various organizations that will become relevant upon my release. The programs that I have in mind are mostly therapeutic and educational. I want to be trained in various programs, although I have become familiar with [the] Alternatives to Violence [Project] (A.V.P.), [Aggression] Replacement Training (A.R.T.) and substance abuse programs that are a staple of prison reform. I am also interested in doing some public speaking, not only about my circumstances, but to also speak about other experiences that I have endured during my youth and incarceration.

I believe all that is left for me to do is to get the hell out of this place.

One of his most painful insights had to do with the problem of having a bad reputation. He knew that because he had a record at the time of his arrest, he was partially to blame for his own suffering. A life of petty crime could put you in police crosshairs—a warning he gave to Ray and repeatedly gives throughout his work with youth outside the prison.

Knowing about the success David had with Ray, Gary gave David the opportunity to become involved with his children—Naton, Dylan, and Sarah—with whom he was experiencing his own set of problems. David tells Ray in the film interview that he wants to have children of his own, but the pathos of his situation and his advancing age predominate. As much as he was deprived of the world, the world was deprived of him. In his role as a counselor, I think he was setting up a challenge for himself. How does a wrongly convicted person leave prison without bitterness and hatred? How does he keep his sense of humanity and connectedness and do good out in the world?

7

LAURA COHEN

The Parole Resource

DAVID'S COLLEGE COURSES WERE A PASTIME, another thing getting him from one day to the next, one month to the next, half a year, and so on. Education was also our investment in his future. Inside prison, time stands still; the future is an act of faith, especially if your life sentence is punctuated by "court opposes any release, ever." By choosing a philosophy course, David was training himself to think as a free man when he was released. Having so little educational background, he was out of his depth, yet he had the innate ability, the drive, and the determination to understand the work. One of David's most attractive qualities is his willingness to ask questions. The opposite is true of most people in prison, because asking questions on the inside can be interpreted as a declaration of weakness. He wrote to me about his choice of course:

> My main reason for taking this course is to gain insight into philosophy and to dispel the misconceptions I have about it.

Ken, I was always one to use certain terms loosely without having any idea what I was talking about. For example, I would use the word "wisdom" without fully understanding what it was.

David had just completed a difficult English course ("It was so hard, I wanted to quit a dozen times") that enhanced his writing skills. After he read off the possibilities from the course catalog, I suggested that Philosophy 1 might be the right course for him to take next; handling abstract ideas and thinking clearly are necessary companions to writing skills. From a more practical standpoint, philosophy taught him to stand at a distance from his personal opinions. From his present perspective, he sees it as a survival mechanism: "Philosophy is about exchanging information," he told me. "You don't want to argue in prison, just make your case without resorting to violence as so often happened in there."

One of the themes of the first-year course was the difference between illusion and reality, as exemplified in Plato's "Allegory of the Cave." Since the Ohio University correspondence course was directed at the prison population, I thought the instructor was gearing the material toward his clientele. The allegory tells of prisoners living in a cave and chained to a wall. The shadows they see on the wall come from people holding puppets who pass by the mouth of the cave. Plato's conscious individual is the philosopher who is able to free himself from the dark confines of the cave and step outside into the light. Consciousness begins when a person becomes aware of the light, the same pinprick of light that Rubin first saw through the wall. When the philosopher understands the importance of what he sees outside the cave, he comes back inside, hoping to enlighten the other prisoners. They reject the philosopher's teachings because after so many years inside the cave, they believe that the shadows themselves are what constitute reality. The allegory was the cornerstone of

Rubin's own philosophy, which he never tired of reiterating. When told that their cherished beliefs are illusory, he would say, "People become downright hostile. They act out. They crucify. That's what sleeping people do. You can't expect anything else from the world of sleeping people."

David picked up on another of Rubin's beliefs closely related to Plato's allegory. The people who operate the legal system are prisoners of illusion who can mistake the processes of the court for the truth. But, as Rubin wrote, "truth would not be recognized in a court of law if she sashayed in and sat in the judge's lap." Justice, then, is an accidental by-product of a closed system. An outsider espousing this heresy to someone within the system (the cave) invites hostility from those still chained to the wall. They hold fast to their illusions because their only other option is cynicism.

Ironically, philosophy itself can also be a closed system, especially through its linguistic demands. David failed the midterm exam and received a D-minus from the professor, Deron Newman. David was disappointed, not as much in the result as in himself. He had a touching exchange with Dr. Newman that spoke to the humanity of both men:

Dear Dr. Newman,

. . . I received my mid-term grade yesterday and I am highly disappointed in myself. I want to take this opportunity to thank you for being honest with me and for also showing confidence in me that I can do much better than my poor grade indicates.

. . . I offer my sincere apology for putting you in a position to have to give me such a grade, which I clearly deserved. I expect a much better performance from myself during the final exam. . . . I offer no excuse for submitting unacceptable work. I prepared for the exam, but elected to take a short cut which cost me a better grade. I have no one to blame but myself and I will use this as a learning experience.

Newman's compassion showed through in his reply letter, written in a flowing cursive. The response was a personal touch that David appreciated in a dehumanizing prison environment. The Ohio University instructor was an experienced prof with a master of divinity and, more recently, a doctorate in philosophy, with a thesis on Plato, at the University of Edinburgh. Working with prisoners was something I was sure he chose to do, stemming from a deep commitment to Christian values.

David,

I sincerely thank you for your letter dated August 18th. Though it was unfortunate on your mid-term, you expressed thoughts and determination characteristic of those who will do great things. Learning from the mistakes we make is the mark of greatness and excellence in life.

I look forward to your continued success and the wonderful contribution you will make.

Dr. D

David took "contribution" to mean contributing something meaningful to the outside world, as opposed to papers and exams in a philosophy course. Even to his philosophy prof, David's life appeared to have some higher purpose.

At this time, a man named Everton Wagstaffe, a Jamaican citizen living in the United States, was also fighting for his freedom in New York. The perplexing catch-22 he found himself in was of concern to us. If a prisoner comes before the parole board and proclaims his innocence, he will be seen as lacking remorse, delusional, or failing to take responsibility for his actions. The board will go on to say that since the prisoner has not taken responsibility for his crime, he would be a danger to the community and likely to commit another crime if released. It doesn't matter how many people attest otherwise. Psychological testing, completion of prison programs, education, a perfect behavioral record—none of it means a thing without remorse, even feigned remorse. In fact, if a person insists on his innocence, he is less likely to get out of prison. Wagstaffe was determined to leave prison with the full public recognition that he was wrongly convicted. Feigned remorse would have destroyed his integrity. What good would it do to gain his freedom if he could not live with himself?

A parole board is the most mechanical part of the closed legal system; the commissioners, many of whom are political hacks and cronies, have the choice to toe the line or be replaced. The members of a parole board are required to believe, no matter what evidence there is to the contrary, that a person convicted of a crime *must* be guilty and therefore *must* show remorse. They know that wrongful convictions take place, yet they cannot admit the possibility in the context of their deliberations. Parole is an object lesson in how people accept illusion for reality in the context of groupthink. In a letter, David drew the parallel to his own situation:

> After reading the article on Everton Wagstaffe I found myself thinking "what courage on his part." Upon further examination of his comments, I began to understand his position. I don't think his position is financially motivated. It has more to do with the truth and the conditions he would be forced to live under. . . . Some would argue that by accepting parole, Mr. Wagstaffe would be better off fighting his case on the outside, where he could access more resources. On the other hand, accepting parole could be seen as an admission of guilt.

Does anyone take into consideration the difficulties Mr. Wagstaffe may incur in terms of searching for employment and/or housing? The prevailing belief for many would probably be—so what, he has his freedom. What else could he possibly want? My feeling is that I will never accept responsibility for something I did not do.

The Wagstaffe case also revealed a pattern of shortcuts taken by Brooklyn police and prosecutors during the 1980s and '90s. Wagstaffe and coaccused Reginald Connor were convicted of the kidnapping and confinement of a sixteen-year-old girl based on fraudulent eyewitness testimony. Wagstaffe, like David, wrote hundreds of letters and received representation in the latter stages of his case. An appeals court judge overturned the trial verdict in the Wagstaffe case in September 2014 after it was discovered that Brooklyn prosecutors buried documents that could have resulted in an acquittal. Unfortunately, Wagstaffe's hope for release was compromised when, previous to the ruling, Connor signed a plea bargain releasing him from prison but forcing him to register as a sex offender. I don't blame Connor for wanting to leave prison under a falsehood; I can only applaud the heroism of Everton Wagstaffe in standing up for his own integrity.

David still speaks of Everton Wagstaffe: "He was confident and strong willed. His stand encouraged me not to compromise my dignity. When I met him at the Innocence Project after we both left prison, we had a spiritual connection. We also had a plan about how to conduct ourselves on the outside and to never forget how important it was to stand on principle."

Back in 2009 I was moved enough by Wagstaffe's plight to write to him, expressing my admiration for his courage and integrity. I received his reply from Greene Correctional Facility in Coxsackie, New York, where he was imprisoned at the time:

Dear Mr. Klonsky:

I would like to take a moment to reply to your letter. Receiving it was a pleasant surprise. Thank you for your concern and know that your reaching out to me is much appreciated.

Although this has been a long, hard 17 plus years, I have never entertained the thought of compromising my fight to prove my innocence. I would rather die in prison than walk out of here without my name fully cleared of this heinous crime. I've always known "that" day is coming. I assure you I will not give in to despair. I have moments when I feel tired and beaten down, but I *always* get right back up again and continue on the fight. This will continue to be my life until my name is *fully cleared*. With the grace of GOD I believe that day is finally coming soon!

In closing, let me thank you for your words of encouragement. GOD Bless, and please give my regards to Dr. Carter.

Sincerely,
Everton Wagstaffe

It takes a special person to survive the ordeal of a wrongful conviction intact. People like David McCallum and Everton Wagstaffe inspire by their determination to hold on to personal integrity in the face of an intransigent and, some might say, vicious system. Like Rubin Carter, they refuse to allow the penal institution and the legal system to define them as "offenders," nor will they give away the one thing the system truly wants from them: their irritating claim of innocence. At the time the above letter was written, Wagstaffe, like David, had five more years of prison ahead of him.

Despite David's misgivings, Steve Drizin was searching for someone to help us get David out of prison quickly, and that could only be done via the parole route. Oscar, who worried that David could be in prison for the remainder of his life, agreed with the strategy. We needed to find a middle ground where the parole board could set David free not because he showed remorse but because he was such an exemplary prisoner. Steve persuaded the highly regarded professor Laura Cohen, head of the Rutgers Law legal clinic, to join our support team. At the same time, he addressed our concerns:

> I know that David is up for parole in May and that it is his first time. I also know that David will not, cannot and should not say he is guilty in order to get paroled. That said, I think it would be helpful for him to have someone who has worked with the Parole Board to represent him at the upcoming hearing as claiming innocence and seeking parole makes for a complicated hearing. A colleague, Laura Cohen, who is the Director of the Rutgers-Newark Law School Clinical Program, is willing to meet with him and take his parole case (assuming that David wants this after they meet) for free. I'd like to make this happen . . .
>
> Steve

While Laura would handle matters relating to parole, a large, bright group of committed and idealistic students would take on an investigative role. Rutgers would be the third innocence project involved with the case.

David met with Laura—finding her knowledgeable, well connected, and judicious—and two of her students, Benjamin Pieh and Sergio Estrada. He managed to maintain a reasonable perspective, saying, "This is merely a process where we want to make preparations for the possibility that things might not go according to plan." The students also indicated their commitment to helping David with the reentry process. Looking back, David was impressed by Laura, telling me that she was "a passionate lawyer." He added, "She cried at first when she met me and infused her students with the same passion to get me out of prison. [In preparing me for parole], she clearly wanted my voice to be heard. After each parole hearing when I was denied, I always told her how much I appreciated all the work done by her and her students. I thought the parole process became a waste of time; I felt bad for the students who worked so hard. But she never gave up on me."

Full exoneration remained our priority. We continued to inquire about the location of evidence listed in the voucher the NYPD had given to Jay Salpeter. Assistant district attorney Ruth Ross was opposing us on several fronts, but she indicated a willingness to allow DNA testing on the cigarette butts from the Blenner car. The butts, the roach, the roach clip, the blanket discovered next to the burned-out car, the kerosene can, a box of cartridges, and several other potentially useful items were in some warehouse, but no one seemed to know which warehouse. Oscar put this problem into some perspective— back in 1986, when the actual trial took place, information about evidence was not stored on computers:

Dear Team:

I called ADA Ruth Ross today and she advised me that the NYPD had still not been able to track down which storage warehouse this voucher went to. She explained the following: After a trial is over, the vouchered property gets sent to one of a half-dozen or so warehouses. A record is made of that. The NYPD is still looking for that record as they have to search manually through volumes and volumes of property receipt books. Once that document is found, that warehouse needs to be searched. It is highly unlikely that the evidence will be in that warehouse as often property on older cases gets transferred to other facilities. So the search then goes on from there and so on and so forth. She is going to ask the court for another long extension 60 days or so to try and locate the material. She said from her point of view there is no need for her to address the non-DNA aspect of the case as the result of the search, and the subsequent DNA search may affect her response to our motion. She told me that in her last case it took just over 6 months to locate the property, a murder victim's clothes. Then it takes about 90 days to do the DNA testing. So you see we are still in for a long haul here.

Long haul. My imagination kept drifting to David's personal circumstances inside the prison, where the temperature and humidity of that summer exceeded the unbearable heat of New York's streets and subways. David's misery was echoed in one of Rubin's descriptions of prison life: "If it's a hundred degrees on the streets, it's a hundred and ten inside the prison." I kept wondering how anyone could live in a dormitory with fifty other prisoners under those conditions and not be driven to violence and insanity. While he maintained his rationality, David's latest letter took on renewed urgency:

The truth is I am getting frustrated, but I have to maintain my focus because, as Rubin said, this is not the time to start slipping or conjuring negative thoughts. [I have to] keep looking through that hole in the wall . . .

Back to the case for a moment. I know, I cannot escape it. I feel like the arguments are so persuasive that we have essentially put the court in a quagmire as evidenced by the delay. However, we have truth on our side, period. I keep hearkening back to the recently decided wrongful conviction cases in which newly discovered evidence and DNA were an issue. These cases have been granted new trials and hearings which made me feel that much better about our motion and impending decision.

Rubin knew the potentially corrosive effects of the waiting and the grinding down of the soul. He referred to the 440 motion as David's Bible. "Read your Bible, David, whenever you start to doubt. Read your Bible!" Rubin also urged David to think about getting a passport when he got out of prison so that he could visit him in Toronto. He was still certain that a decision would be rendered in our favor. Rubin spent hours telepathically "communing with Judge Firetog." We assumed that Judge Neil Jon Firetog was taking such a long time because he was giving our case serious deliberation. Since he was giving our case serious deliberation, we would be sure to get a hearing. When we got the hearing, David's release was inevitable, so confident Rubin was of Oscar's skill and the merits of our case. Hearing all this, David's confidence kept growing:

> I agree that this is an exciting time, especially when you consider where we were five years ago. . . . I am not prepared to make a farewell speech at this time, but too much work has been put into this case not to enjoy the process. . . . I take solace in knowing there is nothing more powerful than having the truth on our side.

Rubin kept encouraging David to imagine a new life outside the prison, to place his concern less on legal matters over which he had no control and more on fitting into a society where he would now be a foreigner. Whenever David was beset by doubts again, Rubin repeated the litany "Tell him to read his Bible."

Horizons for Youth, a shelter for homeless young people in Toronto where I was once a board member, spends a large proportion of its efforts on fund-raising. As a symbolic way of getting David's name out into the world, I made a contribution in his name, which "deeply touched" David, according to a letter he sent me:

> So much so, that I wrote a letter to Horizons in an attempt to establish a dialog. I would love to do some form of social work after my release from prison. I would like to speak to youth homes like Horizons. Not only would I share my experience of being unjustly incarcerated over two decades—I would also let people know that they do not have to give up on themselves because of the hand they have been dealt. . . . I am not suggesting that it is an easy process.
>
> I have made it a point to speak to many young men during my incarceration and they all speak similarly about their anger and hopelessness. Ken, it is really sad to hear some of the things that come out of the mouths of these young men. Fortunately, a lot of them respect me because they see how I conduct myself in light of personal circumstances.

David's vision of himself outside the prison walls would make his reentry less difficult, especially with respect to the challenges that other former prisoners have to face.

Rubin's teachings, while having metaphysical and metaphorical components—the hole in the wall—were also practical, based entirely on what he was lacking when he left the prison. He lived for years in a state of childlike dependence with the Toronto commune that helped to engineer his release. When he was able to stand on his own, he cut them out of his life, including Lisa Peters, the woman he had married to attain legal status in Canada. Likewise,

Rubin urged David to leave Bushwick behind him when he got out of prison: "Family is an anchor. It grounds you but it also weighs you down." David never accepted that kind of ruthless cleansing of the past as something he could do.

David returned to his work with disabled inmates in the Annex Law Library. His salary of seven dollars a week notwithstanding, it was rewarding to assist, as he put it, "people who are not in a position to help themselves." He was now one hundred percent certain that his calling in life was to help others. Instead of turning his experience to darkness and bitterness, he was turning it to the light.

> I enjoy working with these guys because it feels good, knowing that I am helping someone. I help with petitions, legal letters, grievances against the facility when their American Disability Act rights are violated, and their criminal cases. Most of the guys use canes and some of them use wheelchairs. Some of these guys are unable to read or write. . . . Quite frankly, they treat some of these guys badly.

———

As always, during 2009 David would end his letters on an upbeat note: "I look forward to hearing some wonderful news." The longer the judge's deliberations went on, the more certain of a hearing we all became. And yet . . . And yet . . . If the decision were to go against us . . .

> Ray, like everyone else, is waiting for the decision. He told me that he looked forward to hearing some good news. He said that if we are not successful with this motion, he does not think he would ever have faith in the American criminal justice system.

Always acutely aware of the goings-on in Brooklyn and how they would affect our own efforts, we were following another case, that of Emel McDowell, Oscar's other wrongful conviction client. We learned that McDowell was granted a hearing before the Brooklyn Supreme Court.

The result of McDowell's case became a cautionary tale. Oscar had every confidence that McDowell would be exonerated, and so did Hynes's office. Right before the hearing, an ADA came to him and offered a plea deal. These deals, post-conviction plea bargains, usually come about when prosecutors are worried about losing a particular case. They take advantage of the prisoner's vulnerabilities and save themselves the public ignominy of a wrongful conviction. If McDowell were to plead guilty to manslaughter, he would be released on time served. He asked Oscar if he could guarantee his exoneration. As an attorney, Oscar could make no such guarantee. Emel McDowell, like Reginald Connor, was so desperate to leave prison that he took the deal. Oscar was devastated to see most of his work on the case come to naught.

We were concerned that Hynes's office would make the same kind of unconscionable offer to David. It is one thing to say that you won't take plea deals or accept parole, quite another to refuse your freedom in that way.

We need not have worried about that. On October 21, 2009, some ten months after we submitted our 440 motion, Oscar received Judge Neil Firetog's decision:

Dear Team:

It is with a heavy heart that I attach the decision of Judge Firetog totally denying our 440. I would like to set up a conference call for tomorrow so we can all talk. Let me know if you are all available about 4PM NY time.

Oscar

Firetog signed off in the usual curt style of judges who are giving prisoners the shaft: "There being no legal basis for the vacatur of the defendant's conviction, the motion is denied in its entirety."

The full text was only three pages, not a reflection of the voluminous work submitted by Oscar in the 440 and David in his respondent's brief. We felt that the tone of this judge, the apparent arrogance and indifference, bordered on sadistic. The decision was dated August 31 but was not stamped by the county clerk until October 19. Had it been left sitting on someone's desk and belatedly discovered? We had made several inquiries about when the decision was coming down, to the point of being cautioned by Firetog's legal secretary. First she told us that he would complete the work when he returned from his summer vacation. Later she wrote that Firetog was still working on it.

David and his support team suffered a near-death experience. Our course of action at this point—because one does not see many options under such duress—was to submit a reargument to the same judge and to start thinking in terms of parole. David's personal letters ceased until February 1, 2010. He was enervated and humiliated. He became consumed by the decision and the need to refute it. Friends and supporters, including Gary and his family, Joan, Mary Ellen, and me, openly cried. Never had I experienced such disillusionment and disappointment. Even the professionals were distraught. It took Rubin no time to fire off an e-mail:

Dear Oscar and Team Members,

I am shocked! Totally and utterly shocked! How this so-called judge can justify the denial of our 440 with his 3-or-4-pages of bullshit is beyond my understanding. We must immediately go Federal! Firetog's decision will not stand up in Federal Court. And that is why, in my own case, after

19-years of being trapped in the state of New Jersey, I had to seek redress federally. I think the fact that David's parole hearing is imminent may have had a bearing on this judge's decision. What a waste! Let's go to the Feds! I am disgusted with the American people!

Rubin was right about the decision, but Steve, Laura, and Oscar disagreed with him about going to federal court at this time. Unlike Rubin, they worried that our evidence to date might not compel a federal court to grant a writ of habeas corpus, which would automatically entitle David to a hearing. While Rubin spoke often about the attack on habeas rights, especially after 9/11, he seemed to feel that these difficulties would not apply to David's case.

My unschooled belief was that Firetog would reconsider his decision after we pointed out that much of what he'd written was factually wrong. At the outset, he claimed that "any issues relating to the co-defendant are not before the court and will not be discussed, since it is not necessary to do so to resolve this motion." This one sentence alone is still stunning to look at all these years later. Willie and David were tried together; counsel's request that the two be given separate trials was denied. So Willie's issues were David's issues, especially with regard to Chrissie Owens. How many times did we need to say that she had seen two other men that fateful Sunday? Even the DA's office agreed with that. How many ways did we have to demonstrate that Willie's confession was false?

The judge also claimed that no evidence existed to confirm that Detective Butta visited Chrissie with mug books, the main point of the affidavit. He simply denied the validity of the affidavit, despite the fact that her mother and boyfriend also attested to the visit. Firetog could then ignore the issue we raised in this regard, the absence of a police report:

The court is also asked to accept as fact that the police hid the second interview of Ms. Owens, yet this court has not been presented with any evidence of a second interview, other than Ms. Owens's affidavit, created more than 20 years after the incident and subject to the vagaries of memory.

The blindly prejudicial nature of this decision led us to believe that this judge may not have been chosen at random. A member of Hynes's office told us that Firetog was "Hynes's go-to guy." I could not believe—and yet I had to—that a judge would think it preferable to keep an innocent man in prison rather than cast doubt on the work of the Brooklyn DA's Office.

Two days after Firetog's ruling, the DA's office called Oscar to say that the long-lost evidence had been found. Two days after! Firetog, citing his previous decision, denied us the right to DNA testing on the recovered evidence—an almost unheard-of abuse of judicial discretion—but the DA's office, on December 23, agreed to go ahead with it as Ruth Ross had previously promised. Was this an act of good faith, or did they actually think that David and Willie would be proved guilty? I asked Oscar, rhetorically, what would happen if David's and/ or Willie's DNA appeared in the car. He answered nonetheless: "Then it's over. We can all go back to what we were doing."

But how could they possibly think that David and Willie were guilty? They were intelligent enough to see the flimsiness of the confessions. The answer to this question, referred to repeatedly by the DA's office during the time of our involvement with the case, is the key to understanding why David and Willie were wrongly convicted. In New York State, the validity of any confession is tested pretrial in a Huntley hearing. During the Huntley, David claimed that he made up the details of his confession to satisfy Detective Butta. During the trial, David said that the details of the confession were fed to him by the detective. This contradiction was picked up by the trial judge and jumped on by the prosecution. It appeared as if David was lying. Even David's lawyer, Mirto, who had not prepared his client for trial, saw the inevitable disaster. He made matters worse by denying in court that David had ever said he made up the details. Mirto's assertion was a provable fabrication. The Huntley transcript, read out word for word by the prosecutor, confirmed that David's trial testimony was contradictory. Willie's previous testimony, disregarded by the jury, reflected what actually happened to both boys: "I made up some of it and some of it he told me what to say."

Steve focused on the positive: we would be able to test the cigarette butts. For Oscar, the DA's office was conceding reasonable doubt. But the testing came with restrictions: the DNA profiles could only apply to David, Willie, Jake Prince, and Murray Howard; the DA's office maintained that no other individual identified from the database would have relevance to the case. Oscar still saw a major positive here: Prince and Howard were on their radar as viable suspects. Steve argued that this would be a good step. "Some testing is better than none," he said.

I decided to go to New York to visit David, first meeting Rubin at the airport in Toronto and then flying down together. On a cool, sunny day in November, Marc photographed Rubin, Oscar, and me on the steps of the massive US Post Office building across from Penn Station. We headed out to Staten Island to bolster our client's spirits and to quell his fears, Oscar driving as per usual. On our way to the Lincoln Tunnel, Rubin, from the back seat, said he had forgotten to take along a cup and was afraid of getting stuck on the highway. We were already down below Eleventh Avenue, just a block from the tunnel entrance, with nowhere to turn around. At just that moment, I spotted a man standing in the road up ahead. As luck would have it, he was holding out a paper coffee cup, trying to make some money from drivers headed into the tunnel. I asked Oscar to pull over, took out two dollar bills from my wallet, and pointed at the cup. The poor guy stood there in a state of utter confusion. I took the cup from him, poured the change into his hand, and placed the two dollars on top. Rubin now had his insurance.

Seeing us there and hearing Rubin's infectious laughter, David knew that we were not going away. We spoke of the next phase: the reargument of the motion, the upcoming parole hearing, the DNA testing, and more interviews of witnesses. We were hardly out of options, especially with Laura's army of intrepid students ready to fan out over Bushwick. Finally, there was the film, redesigned to garner public sympathy for David. We may have lost a battle, but how could the truth ever be defeated in the long run?

Rubin had phoned me early in 2008 and, after a long prelude in which he explained his financial predicament, finally came to the point. He needed a loan to get through the next unspecified amount of months until his anticipated speaking engagements would provide him with the means to pay it back.

As much as I had urged him to apply for Social Security in the United States and Social Insurance in Canada, Rubin would never get around to it. Although qualified to receive both, he was contemptuous of these benefits, considering them to be handouts. This individualism did not apply to loans.

"How much do you need, Rubin?"

A pause ensued. "Fifteen thousand dollars." That produced another pause. "I hate asking you for this, Ken."

Again, as during the *Sun* interview, I had to consider a myriad of responses in a matter of milliseconds. Fifteen thousand dollars! I had an emergency fund in the bank, but Rubin's solvency was not one of the uses I had imagined for it. His humiliation was palpable, a hero brought low by the root of all evil. If I refused him, the relationship might suffer an irreparable blow. Where would I be without him?

OK, I said to myself, *you're in for a mile and you have to trust his word, but you can never ask him to pay it back.* "OK, Rubin. I'll mail you a check."

"If you go to a bank, they can wire it to my account."

Ah, I thought, *he must need this money to pay the rent and get by from day to day.* "I'll do it as soon as I can."

"Thank you, my brother." I never told anyone, including Mary Ellen and Ray, about the transaction. It was, on some level, as embarrassing for me as it was for Rubin. In conversations with him during the year about other issues, he would bring up his indebtedness and reassure me that the loan would be repaid. I was happy to learn that he started getting speaking gigs again, especially a lucrative one in Australia. Nearly one year to the day of the loan, I received a letter from Rubin with a check inside for fifteen thousand dollars:

Thanks a bunch, my brother! You saved the day. Enclosed please find the return of your generosity. One who tries may fail, indeed, but he who never tries fails more often. We just have to keep on trying!

Again, Thank You,
Rube

Soon after repaying the loan, he received a phone call from Alonzo, who regretfully had to resign from Innocence International. While Rubin had paid Alonzo's travel expenses, he could not afford to pay for his hours. Zo, as he was affectionately known, was raising two daughters and dealing with his own debts. When he quit, Rubin was furious at his chief of staff and even more at Alonzo's wife, who had pressured him into quitting. Alonzo was Rubin's "right eye," the eye he lost while in the prison's so-called hospital. Whenever Rubin appeared in public, Alonzo stood in for his blind eye, protecting his right hand side.

At this point, Rubin did what he always did when people disappointed him: he cut Alonzo off. Alonzo loved Rubin, but the conflict between his wife's demand and his service to Rubin had only one resolution, the one he took to keep his family together. Depressed and devastated, Rubin insisted that he would go alone to the next gig.

After losing Alonzo, Rubin Carter's prostate cancer began to advance though he was sure at the time that his periodic suffering originated from deteriorating spinal discs. He was to last until April 2014. This long final period is fitting for a former boxer who was never knocked out in the ring, losing only one fight by a technical knockout, and that from a head butt by José Torres. When considering the quality and quantity of good middleweights at the time, his was a remarkable record. Dick Tiger, Luis Rodríguez, George Benton, Emile Griffith, and Joey Giardello were just a few of the tough, hard-hitting fighters that Carter had to face. Middleweights in those days were second in glamor only to heavyweights. With my friends, I watched many of Rubin's bouts on the Friday night *Fight of the Week* at Madison Square Garden in the early 1960s, vainly hoping to see him knocked flat on the canvas. As a boxer, Carter's skills were above average, but, as a survivor, both in the ring and in prison, he "coulda been the champion of the world."

In April 2009 Rubin asked me to come down to San Francisco for an event, the Justice for All Awards dinner sponsored by the Santa Clara University School of Law, home of the Northern California Innocence Project (NCIP). He needed a "right eye" on this trip to the coast, having as yet failed to find a steady replacement for Alonzo. On the night of the sixteenth, Judge H. Lee Sarokin, the man who freed Rubin Carter from prison in 1985, was to be presented with the project's highest honor, the Justice Award. Appropriately, Rubin was invited to be the presenter. Every November 8, without fail, Rubin would phone Judge Sarokin to thank him for giving him his freedom and his new date of birth.

That evening at the Four Seasons Hotel was a highlight of Rubin's life. Because of Rubin's veneration for Sarokin, my meeting the judge at our table was akin to meeting a god stepping down from Olympus. Sarokin, warm, bright, and bespectacled, humorously related that he was originally chosen to play himself in *The Hurricane*. While he would love to have freed Denzel Washington from prison, he had to admit that acting in front of a camera, even playing himself, proved beyond his abilities. They found a real actor, Rod Steiger, to replace him. On the surface, Sarokin looked a bit more like Steiger than Carter did like Denzel.

For most of the hundreds gathered at the dinner, the real god was Rubin Carter. I would swear that every person in attendance came up to shake his hand, get photographed with him, and have him autograph their programs. And I'll be damned if he didn't shake every hand and sign every program!

But the glad-handing, the warm smile, the exuberance were all a performance by a consummate performer. The night before, in a Moroccan restaurant, Rubin sat in excruciating pain, unable to eat his dinner. He would wince from time to time as if taking a blow to the liver from Dick Tiger. On his return home, a Toronto chiropractor would diagnose the condition as nerve damage stemming from his career as a boxer. We were later to find that the nerve damage was not the only source of the pain; Carter had lived with that pain for decades. What the chiropractor could not see was that a tumor on Rubin's prostate was impinging on his spine.

The deadly tumor was discovered later, too late, because Rubin could not endure an MRI. As he was slid into the machine, he demanded—he even admitted to screaming—to be let out because the pain in his back was too much to bear. While the hard surface must have produced major discomfort, Rubin could likely have handled it. I always believed that the greater problem was the confinement inside the machine; it would have brought back his years of solitary beneath the ground.

On our way from the hotel on Market Street to the convention center, a couple of young African American men looking for cigarettes stopped Rubin in the street, having no idea who he was. All they saw was a black man in a black suit and a wide-brimmed hat. One of them asked, "Hey, OG, got a cigarette?" Rubin brushed him off, and we continued on our way.

"What did he mean, Rubin? OG? Old Guy?"

"You won't believe this, but I just heard that on TV last night. OG: original gangster. I should have said something to that kid. Original gangster!" He chuckled. "Shit. That's too much. I hear it on TV, and the very next day someone says it to me."

That night in San Francisco, Rubin spoke first about himself. He knew how to warm up an audience. His favorite story involved Denzel Washington, who had absorbed Carter's gestures, voice, and character in his screen portrayal of Rubin. Mary Ellen and I would roll our eyes every time he began it, but the audience in San Francisco lapped it up. Rubin rewrote his speeches with dramatically effective suspensions, marked by ellipses, points of emphasis, and a lot of exclamation points:

> Years after my release from prison . . . I went out to dinner with Denzel Washington. It was MY job to find an actor to play the role of . . . Rubin "Hurricane" Carter in an upcoming film . . . directed by Norman Jewison. After dinner, I left the table for a washroom break, and when I returned . . . the actor had also left the table. I wondered for a second or two if he had walked out on me! But then I noticed him at the front of the restaurant . . . making STRANGE gestures while staring into a mirror. When he returned to the table, we continued

to talk, and something began to happen . . . something I can ONLY describe as falling in love! I LOVED his vocabulary! I LOVED his attitude! I LOVED his stridency! And I just loved his laughter. For another brief moment . . . I wondered if all those years in prison . . . had finally got to me. But then it hit me like a double left hook and a straight right cross! As I had watched him peering into the mirror, he was clearing his canvas, so to speak . . . in preparation for portraying me. And when he returned to the table, he began giving ME back to ME! And I was loving what I saw. I loved ME! Washington was only an actor doing his utmost to sell himself for a role he wanted. But my feelings for my likeness . . . sitting across that table . . . showed me how far I had come . . . from self-hatred to the love of self!

Rubin then came to the subject at hand, Judge Sarokin, whom he referred to as his Solomon. He praised the judge's moral courage in releasing him, reminding his audience how vital it was to locate and publicly support caring and courageous human beings inside the justice system. These people, who made the righting of wrongful convictions possible, were often hated for their liberalism by police, prosecutors, the whole legal hierarchy, and a segment of the public.

Judge H. Lee Sarokin . . . The Honorable Judge H. Lee Sarokin . . . is and was the only Judge in the WHOLE WIDE WORLD who would have made the decision that he did and have that decision upheld unanimously all the way to the United States Supreme Court! If it wasn't for you, Judge, I wouldn't be here standing in front of this distinguished audience.

Judge Sarokin is an old-fashioned lover of liberty, the kind of man Americans USED to love! One man, alone, who speaks the truth, mocking the enemies of freedom, justice, truth, beauty and good. The kind of man who fights for you when you are right and against you if you are wrong! One cannot be for justice without being against injustice! The truth can only hurt a lie!

In the two and a half years following Judge Sarokin's courageous decision to release me, there were 13 . . . VICIOUS . . . attempts by the State of New Jersey to overturn his decision. Judge Sarokin had to pay the price for that! People say they love the right . . . they just hate the one who is right! People say they love the good . . . they just hate the one who is good! People say they love the truth . . . they just hate the one who speaks it!

Rubin picked up a photograph of himself with a king salmon he caught in Alaska; he and the fish, nearly as large as Rubin himself, were projected on an overhead screen to the large gathering.

I sent The Judge this very photo with the inscription: "If it wasn't for you, Judge . . . this fish would still be alive! If it wasn't for YOU! Love you, man."

On November the 8th of 1985—which became my new date of birth—I received the most precious birthday gift that any human being can ever receive on this earth . . . the gift of life itself! My life was given back to me! Judge Sarokin saved my life! I was on my last legs . . . the end of the line for me. . . . I'd have died . . . if it wasn't for YOU, Judge!

He reached into his suit pocket and pulled out a folded piece of paper, slowly unfolding it as one might a biblical scroll.

I hold in my hand here the writ of habeas corpus. Some people in America . . . want to suspend this writ. They are fearful of crime! They are fearful of terrorism! When they suspend the writ, they should know that they're doing what no terrorist could possibly do: they are suspending THE VERY FOUN-DATION OF DEMOCRACY. I'm going to read you what this writ says. This writ says, "I hereby order the release from prison of Rubin Carter and John Artis." It is dated November 8th 1985. It is signed by Judge H. Lee Sarokin. To think I waited all these years to present you with an award! Judge . . . I say again that I owe you my life!

Accepting the award, Sarokin spoke pointedly:

When a judge is responsible for freeing a person wrongly convicted of murder, he worries whether he will live to regret or be proud of that decision. When it comes to Rubin Carter, I have no regrets. He has justified my faith in him, and I am proud of the person he has become. He is a testament to the human spirit.

When I got home, I came across an ad in *Descant*, one of Canada's premier literary magazines that has, unfortunately, gone out of business (although they maintain an online archive). They were soliciting entries for an upcoming prison issue. I suggested to Rubin that we consider entering a chapter from the book. When I phoned Warren Sheffer, our legal counsel in the Key Porter fiasco, to ask about the feasibility of this, he advised us, to our dismay, that in order to get even a single chapter in print, we would have to repay the $36,000 advance we received in 2005. In an act of irrational belief, I told Rubin that paying back the money would be good karma. David and I still felt that the book, with its fifty-page appendix on the Blenner case, would provide needed publicity for David. Rubin agreed that holding on to the money and letting the book founder was against the spirit of the work. While I was able to cash in an investment certificate, what saved the day for Rubin was another speaking tour in Australia. When he returned, he gave me $18,000 and said, "I got to give this to you, Ken, before I go out and spend it."

Descant agreed to publish our chapter, Key Porter was repaid (although they too went out of business), and then something unexpected—I will say miraculous—occurred. Chicago Review Press contacted Rubin, asking to republish *The Sixteenth Round*, then out of print. They were astute enough to see it as a landmark book and a valuable property. We acquired a new agent, Morty Mint of Nelson, British Columbia. Morty then made a deal with Chicago Review Press, packaging *The Sixteenth Round* with our new book, retitled *Eye of the Hurricane: My Path from Darkness to Freedom*. After projecting future royalties, we realized we would not make back the money from the original advance for a long time, if ever, but the loss of money was unimportant. We had begun to move once again in the right direction.

8

I, POLTERGEIST

DAVID WROTE TO ME three months after the rejection of the 440 motion. He was now in the twenty-fifth year of his incarceration. How could one not think of the cruelty of the system in its treatment of young people, especially young African Americans? Had David committed this crime, it was still unconscionable that he be forced to remain in prison after all this time, but that he was innocent and that people outside the system, and some inside, knew this to be true, made his ordeal excruciating. David was, however, a survivor, the single most important trait he shared with Rubin Carter. He would continue finding ways of getting past the recent court decision:

> I need to apologize for my sluggish behavior during our telephone conversation Saturday evening. My voice tone gives away how I feel. . . . I need to pick up my energy level because I could easily sap the energy of other individuals who are affiliated with me. . . . The truth of the matter is that this

process is still a daily struggle. This is where school really helps in the short term.

Speaking of school, I have decided to take the history course.

When Rubin Carter had been imprisoned, his second priority had been education. Rubin was determined not only to get his freedom but also to leave prison a wiser and better man than the scowling, angry boxer who went in there. Through education—Carter was not schooled but an autodidact—he gained the knowledge and respect he never had during his boxing career. After his release, David told me that the study of history resulted in a clearer understanding "about the founding of the country and the civil rights movement"; it also became a means to analyze "the things that are happening right now in society." He could now understand that his incarceration, and the mass incarceration of African Americans, was part of a historical pattern dating back to slavery.

Rubin, wanting David to understand that his freedom was still paramount to us, went once again to the well of his acquaintances and loyal supporters. He asked Judge Sarokin to familiarize himself with our case and then examine Oscar's petition asking Firetog to reconsider his denial of our motion. Sarokin's response to us in an e-mail was heartening for the long term but disheartening for the immediate future:

> Ken and Rubin—I have had the chance to review the draft submitted to me. I think it is excellent, and I have already indicated how I thought the matter should have been decided in the first instance. Motions for reconsideration obviously have the additional hurdle of convincing the judge that his

initial decision was wrong. I think, as I did before, that the motion is very compelling. It is inconceivable to me that a judge would deny you the opportunity to demonstrate through DNA and fingerprint evidence that others committed the crime for which your client had been convicted. I would not be optimistic about success on the motion because of the tone of the earlier opinion, but I would be very optimistic about success on appeal. Good luck. Let me know what happens.

Judge Sarokin

Absorbing the implications of Judge Sarokin's words regarding Firetog, Rubin kept pushing our legal team to file a habeas petition and go to federal court. They were still unconvinced. Personal and professional respect aside, he kept insisting that Steve and Laura were too cautious. As to parole, Rubin remained adamantly opposed, but David had already spent six more years in prison than Rubin. Not offending Rubin while still keeping him engaged was vital, because, in addition to his invaluable experience and connections, he could still call press conferences and garner attention.

Firetog's refusal to permit DNA testing was also "insane," as Steve called it. It took him until May 20—more than six months—to issue his denial of the reargument. The curtness of the denial spoke to his pique. Reading the latest decision made me hate the law itself as much as I hated this judge.

The defendant moves pursuant to CPR 2221 for an order granting renewal and reargument of this court's denial of his previous motion under CPL 440 to vacate his conviction. The People oppose the motion. For the reasons stated below, the court declines to permit reargument of the motion.

The court has reviewed defendant's motion and supporting affirmation pointing out items the defendant states the
court may have overlooked. In fact, the court reviewed each
and every one of defendant's allegations and considered them
carefully. Nevertheless the quantum of evidence adduced *felt*
[italics mine] short of that required of a vacatur.

The court denied a vacatur when it first considered the
motion and finds no rationale warranting a different conclusion, defense counsel's protestations to the contrary.

The motion is denied in its entirety.

I was ready to fire off a poison-pen letter; the only thing that
prevented my doing so was my fear of hurting our client. Any future
legal remedy might still be routed through the same judge. That didn't
stop me from venting my anger by composing the letters, each more
cutting than the last, but not mailing them.

People trained in the law are supposed to be able to separate their
legal responsibilities from their emotional responses. This ability, in my
view, is a fiction. People can no more be separated from their emotions
than separated from their bodies. Judge Firetog and those of his ilk
believe that their rulings stem entirely from legal precedents and that
they are abiding by strict interpretations of the law. They wear masks
of rationality. They do not recognize their animus toward particular
defendants or attorneys, and yet an outsider has no trouble seeing it.
Firetog's Freudian slip—the word "felt" as opposed to "fell"—spoke
to his subjectivity and his underlying hostility. Those judges who are
conscious of their feelings toward a particular defendant are the ones
who can better sort out the merits of a case. Rubin cautioned me that
my own feelings were counterproductive, referring to what was perhaps
his best-known quote: "Anger only consumes the vessel that contains
it; it doesn't hurt another single thing." He added, "And it's not getting David out of prison." David was not an angry person, yet I was.

Facing the implications of Firetog's latest decision, David was forced to seriously consider parole. He would attend the upcoming hearing as required and answer the questions put to him to the best of his ability. Every one of us supported him in his resolve to insist on his innocence. An admission of guilt might only make a liar out of him in the eyes of the parole board. Why, they might ask, would he have insisted on his innocence for twenty-five years? The other problems with parole were equally daunting: David would have to leave prison as a convicted murderer in the eyes of an uncaring world. He would have to report to a parole officer and be subjected to unannounced visits. He would never be able to get anything but the most menial kind of work. His main reasons for considering this unattractive prospect were the indeterminacy of his sentence and his mother's precarious health. The parole process in every aspect, as David wrote about it, was a "joke":

> I just came back from seeing a psychiatrist this morning per the Department of Correctional Services. I was only in there eight to ten minutes. I was asked standard questions: How has my incarceration been after all these years? How was I able to stay out of trouble for such a long period of time? Do I get any support from home? . . . It seems as though it is a big game of chess and the inmates are pawns. . . . A funny thing occurred during my interview with the psychiatrist. He pretended not to know what the prison system is about. Every time he asked a question, he pretended to be perplexed. . . . These people really do have a low opinion of the intelligence of inmates.

I began to be disingenuous with Rubin, a dangerous thing to do with such a perceptive and fearsome man. I believed that his one hundred percent opposition to parole was too categorical. If David wanted to go through with the process, it was not our business to discourage him. Early in the year, I exchanged e-mails with Laura. Her focus and Steve's was still on the shortest road to getting David out of prison. I thought Steve and Laura were being realistic, even though I knew that once a wrongly convicted prisoner is on the outside, his or her case becomes less urgent to the authorities. Laura sensed my ambivalence.

> I also understand your aversion to having David have to live under parole constraints, but even this will be an uphill battle. It's one that we want to help him fight, though my students are forging ahead. We are going to compile a "to do" list for David, which will include obtaining letters of support, offers of employment, and the other components of a re-entry plan. I'm sure that we will be reaching out to you for help with some of these efforts.
>
> Thanks and we'll be in touch soon,
> Laura

My reply to her felt like a betrayal of Rubin. I thanked her for all the work she was doing on David's behalf and conceded that parole, at least in the short term, was our brightest option. In Rubin's defense, I think that outside helpers sometimes desire their client's freedom even more than the client himself. I know that I was becoming tired of the process.

Laura's contacts were inexhaustible. She enlisted the services of a well-known forensic psychologist, Dr. Charles Heller, who would do a separate evaluation of David to present to the parole board as part of our package. As expected, the conclusion of his thoroughgoing report was that David fell into the category of parolees least likely to reoffend. I thanked him for his work just before the hearing:

Dr. Heller,

I wanted you to know how much we at Innocence International appreciate your detailed and insightful psychological report on David McCallum in support of his parole hearing. I'm sure they will treat David and your work with a great deal of respect. They don't often see anything like that. Thank you from Dr. Carter and myself.

For the first time, I simply used Rubin's name. When I told Rubin about Dr. Heller, his response was memorable, very Rubin-like: "Those people don't give a fuck about some psychologist's report!" I was caught among powerful forces. Firetog was an immovable object, but we were not the irresistible force; Steve and Laura were considerable legal minds and scholars; Oscar was a razor-sharp lawyer; crossing Rubin was risky; and David was losing his patience. My first priority was to keep the team together, sometimes doing it in the most cowardly way, agreeing with everyone even when their interests were competing. Sometimes I called telephone conferences during which the differences could be openly aired and strategy mapped out.

David prepared for the parole hearing by writing a required personal statement. Generally, this exercise is meant to be a mea culpa, but of course David could not express remorse for the murder. Still, he deeply regretted the life he lived before his arrest because it was his prior behavior on the street that made him an easy target for the police. He had been on probation at the time Nathan Blenner was murdered.

My troubles began when I started to think of ways to make easy money to supplement my allowance. I made poor choices by robbing people in my community and, as a result, I was arrested four times. I don't want to leave the impression that

I was not accountable for my actions because I clearly understand that my actions were wrong and that I brought harm to
my community. I am not blaming my behavior on the environment I grew up in nor am I making excuses for my actions.
The truth is that I chose to live a destructive lifestyle. . . . My
parents provided for me the best they could, given their circumstances. They instilled in us a very important virtue. "If
we worked hard, we could accomplish anything we wanted."
Unfortunately, I did not listen. Instead I chose to indulge in
activities that went against everything they instilled in me.

Laura and her students coached him for his upcoming appearance.
In both his oral and written responses, they thought the key to his
being granted parole was the balancing act around Nathan Blenner's
death. David's reference to the Blenner family was as genuine as anything else he wrote.

I can imagine the pain and suffering the Blenner family feels
every day. They have lost a member of their family to a violent
death. Not a day passes by when I do not think about them.
While I don't know how it feels to lose a family member to
gun violence, I do know how it feels to lose a family member.
On November 11, 2005, I lost my father, David McCallum II.,
to a heart attack. It has since been four plus years and I am
still feeling the effects of his death. Clearly this is not about
me or my family. It is about the loss of life of Mr. Nathan
Blenner and the effect his loss has on his family. I totally
understand that.

David also pointed out his accomplishments while in prison and
his plans upon release. Reading it even now produces a sadness in
me, considering the reception it was given.

My prison experience has been a difficult yet rewarding journey . . . I am a Paralegal Assistant . . . I earned my Legal Certificate to become a law clerk. Therapeutically, I earned a Certificate in Aggression Replacement Training (A.R.T.), Alternative to Violence Project (A.V.P.) and Peer Counseling. I received Inmate Program Assistance training that will enable me to become a certified teacher in fields of therapeutic and social education. Currently, I am law library clerk for the disabled.

. . . Given the opportunity at parole, I am extremely confident that I will do what is required and necessary for me to live and remain at liberty without violating the law . . . I plan to seek employment as a social worker geared towards helping people make good choices in order to avoid the pitfalls that are prevalent in society.

Before the hearing took place, Oscar phoned Ruth Ross, the ADA who had written all the opposing motions to David's numerous appeals dating back to the 1990s. For Ross, who always used her previous arguments as a boilerplate, making small adjustments depending on the nature of the appeal, it must have amounted to a dreary exercise. Her initial opposition to DNA testing had likely been an automatic response. However, Oscar wrote to tell me of a sudden change of heart on her part:

On the DNA issue, here is what is happening. Frustrated that I was getting nowhere with the Court, I had placed several calls to ADA Ruth Ross to see if I could get her to join me in a conference call to Judge Firetog. When she finally called me back, after I told her the purpose of my call, she said that when she had not gotten the order to Firetog back signed by him, she decided that she did not need the order because it was on consent and the Medical Examiner would do it for the DA if requested, so she did so and they agreed to start the process. This was some time in late January. She then explained to me that the first part of the process is eliminating Blenner's DNA. They are now trying to see if they can get a sample from any of the clothing recovered that had blood on it. If not, they will go to Mrs. Blenner to get a sample from her (should she consent). It is only after they have either gotten a sample or exhausted every avenue of getting Blenner's DNA that they will move forward to the next step. Once a sample is obtained, they will then upload a sample from the cigarette butts. . . . Once Blenner has been eliminated as the source of any DNA on the cigarettes, they will try to eliminate David and Willie. Once they eliminate David and Willie, they will try to eliminate Prince and Howard; once they eliminate Prince and Howard, they will try to eliminate the entire DNA database. She said the process can take 4–6 months ONCE they obtain a Blenner sample. She had no idea how long it might take to try to get the Blenner sample. She says she has been through this before and the process usually takes between 6–9 months in total, "but every case is different" as most have some victim DNA at the ready. I asked (actually begged, really grovelled) if she could just ask the Medical Examiner to test it against David, Willie and the two other suspects asap and do everything else later as the case is from 1986 and it is unlikely that there will be any repercussions against the Blenner family from having their DNA put on the database. She said the ME will never change its protocol and the guidelines for the process are very strict. I gave this explanation to David when I saw him a few days ago and he seemed excited about the prospect that at least it had begun.

Since we would have to await the test results for the better part of the year, we needed to move ahead on other fronts, especially interviewing possible witnesses. The key person at this point was Jake Prince, our prime suspect in the killing. Ray discovered through a records check that he was in prison. He and Marc wanted to arrange an on-camera interview. Much to-ing and fro-ing took place about how to win his cooperation. They proposed approaching Prince with a story that they were doing a film on the corrupt and violent inter-rogation techniques utilized back in the 1980s and '90s by a group of Brooklyn detectives. "We would say that we are interviewing people that gave statements to Butta when they were 18 or under and that we could really use his help in documenting if the techniques Butta used were effective."

Rubin disagreed with this strategy. He saw it as a risky diversion from the progress of the legal case, insistent as he was that we take Firetog's ruling to the federal level. Ray felt that we had nothing to lose and that Jake Prince might inadvertently slip us a valuable piece of information.

When I first saw his proposal, my immediate reaction was that of a parent. How could he be so unrealistic as to think a couple of young film directors could bring a resolution to this case? But my perception changed during several online exchanges among David's team. When Steve, Laura, and Oscar treated Ray's idea seriously, I suddenly saw him as an adult. His relationship and commitment to David was every bit as strong as mine. Oscar weighed in on the visiting strategy since he would have to conduct the interview:

I do not believe that Prince will admit being involved in the Blenner murder no matter how I phrase the questions. Of course, he may try to deflect from himself by giving us other information or other names to pursue.

At the same time, Oscar felt that we should not pass on the opportunity to take advantage of the suspect's incarceration. His question was whether to write a letter first, seeking consent, or to spring a visit on him, which he could easily refuse.

Steve suggested a different strategy:

> If the team feels that a letter has to precede a visit, I do not think the Butta angle is a good one—Prince probably does not recall Detective Butta and even if he does he will likely be unwilling to talk once he feels like he was deceived. I think you should be more straightforward. I think you should tell him that you are working with an organization that seeks to free innocent people from prison and that our investigation has led us to believe that he may have information that could help free an innocent person from prison.
>
> We have had great success with such an approach.

Looking back on this debate, I can see the benefits of having such a wide diversity of perspectives. Rather than becoming divided, we respected competing points of view. Although my experience in innocence cases is limited, I cannot imagine how a group of amateurs and highly regarded professionals could have done a better job working together cooperatively. I decided not to tell them about Rubin's skepticism, which even extended to the long, drawn-out DNA testing. No need for a rift. Steve urged Oscar to interview Prince before Ray did the on-camera interview. Another person would need to accompany Oscar as a "prover"— that is, a witness with legal expertise—and Oscar would have to take along an affidavit in case Prince "says something helpful," Steve instructed. Unfortunately, after all the strategizing, Jake Prince refused to meet with us. Another hope quashed, but hey, there was still parole.

David did well in his hearing with the parole board, but in their collective wisdom, they denied him. When confronted by the unreasoning and pro forma judgment, I didn't know whether to scream or cry.

Parole denied. Hold 12 months. Next appearance 4-2011.
Parole is denied. After a careful review of your record, your personal interview and due deliberation, it is the determination of this panel that if released at this time, there is reasonable possibility that you would not live at liberty without violating the law, your release at this time is incompatible with the welfare and safety of the community and will so deprecate the seriousness of the crime as to undermine respect for the law.

To think, despite every positive letter and evaluation, that the parole board could even say these things confirmed the mechanical nature of the exercise. After describing the crime that David did not commit and how it showed "a complete lack of concern for the welfare of others," the board went on to giveth and taketh away:

Note has been made, and although compelling, of the documentation submitted regarding the efforts being made to prove your innocence. However, at this time nothing has been substantiated. Consideration has been given to your program completion and satisfactory behavior. However, your release at this time is denied. (Commissioners concur.)

I was literally sick for days after. I was just as devastated by this rejection as I was by Firetog's.

David felt as if he were letting his family down. He asked me to give them the bad news, which Ernestine took stoically. I then contacted the team: "David did not get parole. They told him to come back in a year. Hard to find solace in this process. Nothing more to be said." But solace is what I got. David had been given one year until the next hearing; he would go through this process again in the spring of 2011. First Oscar weighed in: "Well, we knew it was a long shot Ken. I think coming back in one year is a positive sign. It's usually two years. Then Laura: "I'm so sorry for David but agree with Oscar that the one year re-hearing date is a good sign. I will try to talk to David at some point this week about the appeal process. How is he doing, Ken?"

A prisoner can appeal the denial of parole, but the absurdity of the process is mind-boggling. It takes more than a year to get an appeal decision, during which time David would come up for his next parole hearing. So, in effect, he would have to delay the next hearing if he wanted to conclude the appeal. Even more ridiculous is that the only result of a successful appeal would be another parole hearing! So why bother? I guess because it gives the prisoner something else to focus on before the next hearing comes up.

Steve's take on the one-year wait made it three for three. I had to believe in this reassurance coming from three respected pros:

> This is disappointing but it is progress. It is rare that someone gets paroled the first time up. The parole process can be very taxing on an inmate's well-being. Each year, the inmate gets his hopes up that he will be released and oftentimes these hopes are dashed. In my experience, the Boards often deny parole as a test to see how the inmate reacts to adversity. Whoever speaks with David needs to tell him that he must not act out, he must stay the course, he must not give the Board any excuses to deny him again next year. If he is not exonerated by the DNA testing before his next parole hearing, he needs to reappear next year without any blemishes.

We were in a holding pattern regarding parole, but enough other news was emanating from the city and the state that David could always feel the big break coming around the bend. Sometimes he would focus on media coverage. He held out hope that one big block-buster story would blow the lid off the case, expose the cover-up and the corrupt investigation.

Rubin's objective view of media never changed: it will not work unless it becomes part of a larger campaign. While wrongful con-victions are a rich source of stories, prisoners generally face disap-pointment if they think that a story in the newspapers or on TV will suddenly focus attention on their cases and make their release imminent. Coverage in the *New York Times* is an exception, in that no district attorney or assistant district attorney can afford to ignore what they write or the opinions of their readership. If a particular columnist from the *Times* continues to follow the case, one's chances increase dramatically. David was aware of this.

> There is an excellent journalist (Jim Dwyer) from the New York Times who has written several articles on wrongful convictions. What is the point of waiting for a judge who obviously does not care? The public needs to be aware of the injustice that is being perpetrated against me and Willie Stuckey. I don't see another recourse.

None of us understood the long-term implications of major media stories around wrongful convictions in general that gradually began to surface in 2010. In May, Cyrus Vance Jr., the New York County district attorney, started a program to prevent future wrong-ful convictions and to investigate previous ones. Most of these older cases stemmed from the crime spree era of the 1980s and '90s, when more than a thousand New Yorkers were being murdered every year and, as we now know, police and courts routinely disregarded constitutional norms. Vance called his new unit the Conviction Integrity Program and appointed ADA Bonnie Sard to head the program. Joshua Marquis, then an Oregon district attorney, set the tone in a newspaper interview for these units that were cropping up around the country: "The worst nightmare of a prosecutor is not losing a case; it's convicting an innocent person. I think a prosecutor has always got to be willing to look back and say, 'Hey, did we do the right thing?'" It sounded so much like music to every innocence project in the country, but people awaited deeds to match the words.

These initiatives received a boost because of an increasing roster of cases. DNA evidence, beginning with the pioneering efforts of the Innocence Project, led by Barry Scheck and Peter Neufeld in New York, forced district attorneys to become proactive. The exonerations coming from DNA samples, especially in cases in which defendants falsely confessed, were causing public embarrassment and resulting in large financial settlements.

Barry Gibbs, wrongly convicted of killing a prostitute and represented by Scheck, was awarded $9.9 million by New York City, along with $1.9 million by the state. At the time, it represented the largest personal settlement in New York City history. Back in 2005 a Brooklyn judge overturned Gibbs's conviction, which one of the infamous and amoral Mafia cops, Louis Eppolito, had garnered. Eppolito himself was jailed for life for taking part in Mob killings, an interesting way to moonlight. The *Times* reported that "Mr. Eppolito focused the investigation on Mr. Gibbs because he was trying to protect the real killer, who might have had mob ties." Because the case came out of Brooklyn, David emphasized its similarities with his own. Eppolito produced false witness statements, withheld exculpatory evidence from prosecutors, intentionally failed to conduct an adequate investigation, and beat Mr. Gibbs into a false confession. Right in front of us was the entire modus operandi Brooklyn police had utilized in David's and Willie's convictions. Our theory that police substituted McCallum and Stuckey for the actual killers was now completely credible.

Another case from Brooklyn, that of Jabbar Collins, then in the fifteenth year of a thirty-four-to-life sentence, was further cause for encouragement. Hynes's office on Jay Street was slowly becoming ground zero for wrongful convictions. Collins, a skilled jailhouse lawyer, uncovered the dealings of his prosecutor, Michael Vecchione, through Freedom of Information requests. Even in the face of egregious behavior in manufacturing Collins's wrongful conviction, the Brooklyn DA and his office stood behind the prosecutor. The appeals court judge in the Collins case, Dora Irizarry, excoriated Hynes and ADA Kevin Richardson for their lack of contrition, using words like "shameful" and "beyond disappointing." She was referring, in a wider sense, to the DA's office meting out rough justice to African American defendants by using coercion, making deals with fraudulent witnesses, concealing evidence, and lying. At the time of the Collins hearing, Vecchione was overseeing the office's rackets division!

The DA's office refused to investigate the case or attend a hearing. They simply stopped opposing Collins's release but claimed that they still thought he was guilty, the same tactic Suffolk County employed against Marty Tankleff. "We lack sufficient evidence to retry the case," they claimed. At first, they made the same unconscionable offer to Collins that they made to Emel McDowell: to release him based on time served, thereby allowing them to preserve the conviction. He refused.

Another significant development for us occurred in 2010 when the cold case of Sam Quentzel's murder in Nassau County, New York, was finally solved. Back in 1986 Quentzel had been accosted and murdered in his car. Four cigarette butts found at the crime scene were tested for DNA against the state's data bank, and a match was discovered. It tangibly demonstrated that DNA can be readily accessed from very old evidence. I now understood Steve's urgency about the cigarette butts in Blenner's car.

The similarities between the Quentzel case and David's case were obvious, but one big difference stood out: a cold case is not a wrongful conviction. Everyone welcomed veteran detective Tom Goodwin's success in finding the killer after two decades of dogged police work. In a wrongful conviction case like David's, the system goes into protective mode.

Referencing Quentzel, Oscar petitioned Ruth Ross to expand the DNA search on the cigarettes in Blenner's car and apply it to the state's database. Although we knew that David's and Willie's DNA were not on the cigarettes and we hoped that Howard's and/or Prince's were, we still needed to get beyond the limited scope of the investigation. What did the Brooklyn DA's Office have to lose?

Rubin's commitment to David's release never faltered, but his health issues resulted in less active involvement with the work of David's defense team. Finishing our book, which he repeatedly called his legacy, became his priority. He identified so completely with *Eye of the Hurricane* that he became the book, memorizing every word!

Sometimes he wouldn't answer the phone. Given his questionable physical condition and his constant smoking, I worried that he was lying dead on the floor. I asked people to check in on him. Other times I wondered if he refused to answer because of something I had done or said, one of my constant fears. Once, after a two-week absence, Rubin called and told me to stop being a worrier. He explained that he would go inside himself for extended periods. I was just relieved to hear his voice.

By the summer, the final version of *Eye of the Hurricane* was ready for our approval. Rubin and I pored over it separately. One of the editors at Chicago Review Press suggested some minor word and phrasing changes that were, at least to me, insignificant. I put them in the text because they came from the publisher, and unlike the snafu with Key Porter, the changes did not involve legal issues or changes in meaning and intent. Regrettably, I had forgotten an earlier e-mail Rubin had sent me:

Hi Ken,

It is now 11:55am. I've been up all night working with this. And, quite frankly, I'm becoming more and more "pissed off" every time I go through this and find that you did not include my "markings" in the text! I keep going over this and each time it's the same thing. I can't trust you. You are too easily swayed by everyone else but me, and that is why I have to keep reading this word for word, sentence for sentence, every time. You are not taking what I do with the manuscript seriously. In fact you are not paying any attention to me at all!

Listen to what I am saying to you, now, because you and I are heading for a "showdown" if you are not careful. I have not been going through this manuscript, time after time, for the fun of it! Look at my "markings"—check them out—and then put them in the text as I intended even if you don't like it, still, put my "markings" in the text where I say they should go.

Also, this is the last time I hope to be going through this manuscript. So, when you are finished going through what I have sent you today—DON'T TOUCH IT AGAIN!!! After you finish going through it today, the only "somebody" who can touch it is the Publishing House. Now I told you this before, but you aren't paying any attention to what I said— Enough is enough! I'm through!

This tirade was in response to my eliminating hundreds of exclamation marks. It took me a long time to persuade Rubin that he was overusing a punctuation mark that was designed to draw attention to something particular; the more he used them, the less likely that people would pay attention. Rubin saw his writing as an extension of his public speaking but eventually agreed to most of the deletions.

My phone rang one afternoon in early July. I could see it was from Rubin, but his voice was strange.

"Is this Ken?"

"Of course, Rubin."

"No, no it's not. It's not Ken. What's happened to Ken?"

"Are you OK, Rubin?"

"I'm talking to a poltergeist. I want to talk to Ken."

There was such controlled ferocity in the voice that I knew he wasn't joking. Even from over two thousand miles away, he frightened me.

"Rubin, what's wrong?"

"I don't want to talk to a poltergeist; I want to talk to Ken. The Ken I know and love. The Ken who worked with me for all these years."

"This is Ken, Rubin."

"If this is Ken, you can't be the poltergeist who changed our book."

By this time, I was on the speakerphone, and Mary Ellen was listening as well. The attack went on for over an hour, but the theme never changed. Every so often I would get in a word or two, asking him what changes to the manuscript he found so important. He did not understand that we were reviewing the copy and that everything was still subject to further alteration. But I had forgotten that angry e-mail. I failed to realize the full implications of being his mouthpiece. The changes to the manuscript seared him body and soul.

Sometime after hanging up, I got a call from Gary. Rubin asked him to find "the real Ken" and to have the real Ken call him back. Gary, completely dumbfounded, insisted to him that I was not a "poltergeist" and that my loyalty to Rubin could not be questioned.

Soon thereafter, I got a call from Sam Leslie, Rubin's closest friend. Loyal Sam took Rubin's part, letting me know what a terrible thing I had done. The most punishing part of all of this was that I started to believe what both of them were saying. What saved me from losing myself was David McCallum's reassuring voice. Speaking to him on the phone reaffirmed my priority: getting this man out of prison.

Over the next two days, Rubin called back numerous times and started in again. At some point, I refused to answer the phone. It was liberating. I decided that our friendship would have to end, the book be damned, and that future contact with him be about the wrongful conviction business and nothing else.

A friend in Vancouver, a seer, told me something she could not have known in any conventional way: "He's dying, Ken." Not only was she right—the process had already begun back in 2009—but his frequently repeated words took on their full significance. "This book is my legacy to the world." He said it would win the Nobel Prize. I felt a terrible sadness, because in treating me as he had and in his overblown assessment of *Eye of the Hurricane*, my second father was showing weakness and vulnerability.

Days later he calmed down and left a message of apology, asking me to call him. Of course I did so. Although he continued to blame me, the manic Rubin was gone. Without asking if I was ready, he started right in on the manuscript, reading back every single word. After two hours, when we had made it through only fifteen pages, I told him I couldn't take anymore. Sue Betz at Chicago Review Press did the final edit with him, working with him on the phone from Chicago as he continued to read and test out every last word of the book.

David sent a letter that restored my balance. He was now mentoring both father and son.

> I am still saddened by Rubin's behavior toward you. I happened to agree with you that you should be hurt and disappointed by what he did. I thought you said it best when you said his behavior might be that of a man who had done twenty years in prison. First of all, he is a principled man, and sometimes that could be a bad thing in terms of failing to look at one's self. I was not trying to downplay Rubin's actions when we spoke, but clearly, he was out of character. I was more interested in helping you feel better so that you could go to bed with peace of mind. . . . In some way, I believe Rubin should reattach himself with his children. He would probably be surprised how much fulfillment that experience may have for him. . . . Sometimes when people make hurtful comments, they retract them after they have had time to digest what they have said.

At the end of this ordeal, I had to acknowledge that Rubin and I were still joined at the hip. Although I would now protect my core, my soul, I had to maintain the relationship for David's sake and for the sake of another prisoner we were representing in the state of Washington. The book itself, while a land mine, still remained a joint contractual venture; Rubin had even insisted that I be credited as the coauthor. Going on a book tour with Rubin Carter still appealed to my vanity. And I still loved the man, just as all the other people he mistreated still loved him. David sensed the change in me:

> It seems as though you are feeling much better than you were a few weeks ago. I think that by coming to terms with the relationship that you and Rubin once shared, it really allowed

you to free yourself from a situation that you truly never had control of. It saddens me that it had to come to that, but the reality is what choice did you have? There was no sense allowing yourself to be put in virtual prison. This is not a place where any rational thinking man with principles should be. You are a fine man, Ken, and no one can take that away from you.

David kept up his work with Ray, who had come to him with an ethical problem. He wanted to join his future wife, Robbie, who had gotten a sales position in a small fashion house in New York. While he had American citizenship, she was the one with the job. He was offered work in New York but decided that he couldn't leave his friends to deal with the problems of a budding takeout restaurant venture in Montreal. David was proud of his decision:

I don't think I can respect him any more than I already do. After you told me that he is going to stay committed to his partners and see things through, what more can I say about him? It is something that I would expect of him. He did not run for cover. . . . For that I think he is going to be a better person. I am big on integrity. I don't think there is a more important way to live. . . . Being true to yourself is very important to surviving in a world that is full of corrupted and unethical people. He will be rewarded for standing on truth.

And so, I hoped, would David McCallum.

9

MR. DNA

The Suspect

DAVID BEGAN A COURSE in European history focused on Communism in the Soviet Union and Fascism in Italy, Germany, and other parts of Europe. He was suffering through a situation that was worthy of the bureaucratic absurdities of these states. While not dealing with the Stasi or the SS or the KGB nor facing physical brutality from the guards, the subtle tortures of his imprisonment could result in the numbing of the mind and the resultant loss of the will to resist. While Oscar said that most long-term prisoners are released after thirty-five years, there was no absolute guarantee that would happen. The sentence was twenty-five years to life; some are carried out in a box. Even thirty-five years meant that David would not be out until 2020. None of us relished the prospect of providing unending emotional support to a man with no hope.

My personal take on the parole decision was pessimistic with respect to future hearings. The impersonality of the words and the refusal of the board to even consider innocence told me that they, like the DA's office, could only see David as a criminal Beyond an admission of guilt and remorse that would validate the system, his humanity meant nothing to them. I was no longer sure that David could be paroled without giving them the satisfaction they craved.

Then, like an answer to prayer, we received the results of the DNA tests. We learned that the residues on the cigarette butts excluded Nathan Blenner, Prince, Howard, David, and Willie. But DNA matching a felon in the data bank was found on two of the eight cigarettes, proving he had been inside the Blenner car for some period of time. While the DA's office was unwilling to share the identity of this individual, Steve was in high spirits:

> Their refusal to identify the hit is frustrating but this is nonetheless very exciting news for David. David is excluded as the source of the DNA on the butts and so is Blenner. The mere fact of exclusion is powerful evidence that David is innocent. . . . A match to a criminal should be enough to allow us to move for the conviction to be vacated, especially if the criminal has a history of car jacking or auto theft and is unconnected to David. . . . Given that David's case is mentioned prominently in Rubin's (and your) new book, the press might also be interested in these results.

With this background of renewed hope, I came to Toronto in February 2011 for the book tour. Rubin spoke in front of hundreds of people at the Ontario Institute for Studies in Education, where you could feel the love. Alonzo was there, and Rubin spoke warmly to him and even introduced him to the audience. It was another welcome example of relenting.

Although I was born in New York and live in Vancouver, Toronto will always be home. I came of age along with the city itself. When I moved there in 1967, Toronto was staid and Victorian, even boring.

Perhaps three non-Chinese restaurants in the entire city were open on Sunday. Good Friday was a lockdown! There were ample reasons for its moniker "Toronto, the Good," positive (its civility) and negative (its squareness). Every year thereafter, Toronto became increasingly cosmopolitan and vibrant but also a little ruder.

My graduate education at the University of Toronto was no more instructive than the people I met from all over Canada and the United States. Thousands of Americans in Toronto were draft dodgers, the majority of whom would eventually return home. We had all suffered disillusionment and shock, especially at the Martin Luther King Jr. and Robert Kennedy assassinations in 1968, and yet, with not a little pride, we gathered to watch the moon landing. The friendships we made during that intense time have endured.

Ray was brought up in Toronto and so absorbed many of the values of its open and mixed society. The community that nurtured us was supportive and close-knit. The educational system was progressive and experimental, the schools a meeting ground for a generation of involved parents. When Rubin and I looked out at the audience for the launch of *Eye of the Hurricane*, the culmination of our years of work together, I knew many more people personally than he did.

It had taken five years, but the book had been reborn. While David's name and the details of his case were finally made public to a wider audience, its appearance was even more a symbol that anything now was possible, most important our client's release. The logjam of delays in every aspect of our endeavors to free David McCallum was now broken.

In New York City, the publisher set up two separate launches, one in Fort Greene, Brooklyn, at Greenlight Bookstore, a happening place, and one in Upper Manhattan at Barnes & Noble. Rubin had numerous opportunities to speak to the media, notably during an interview by William Finnegan of the *New Yorker*. While any author might see this tour as a dream come true, the truth is that the experience was filled with physical pain and unbelievable stress.

Rubin's condition had deteriorated. He scuttled morning media appointments the publisher set up. They were furious when he failed to appear at Radio City for a series of interviews. I pleaded with him to honor his commitment, but he was adamant: his mind was willing, but his body was not.

The weather was extremely cold in February 2011, more than a foot of snow on the curbs for the full stay. It was difficult to walk anywhere, especially for a man in pain. Whether by coincidence or synchronicity, Mary Ellen was also suffering extreme pain in her back, to the point where she had difficulty sitting.

Ray, Marc, Mary Ellen, and I took the subway out to Brooklyn for the Greenlight launch. When New York is really cold and windy, you may as well be at the base camp of Mount Everest—at least you would be properly dressed. We met Rubin, who had sensibly come by cab. The highlight of the night was to be the presence of Ernestine McCallum and her daughter Mattie. What I hadn't appreciated was the immensity of Brooklyn, the sixth-largest city in the United States. Although I grew up in the New York area, I had been to downtown Brooklyn only one time before: to go to a Dodgers-Phillies game at Ebbets Field in the early 1950s. The McCallums, as well, knew little of its neighborhoods outside their own little area in Bushwick.

On my urging and his journalistic instincts, William Finnegan came to Greenlight rather than Barnes & Noble so that he could meet David's mother and sister. How could I not be thrilled and anxious at the same time? One of the *New Yorker*'s lead contributors was waiting with us for mother and daughter to arrive. The store proprietors wanted to get the presentation underway, so I had to begin speaking. This was to be David McCallum's night, and I was going to make the most of it, with or without Ernestine and Mattie.

Eye of the Hurricane is the work of Rubin "Hurricane" Carter, in particular his advocacy on behalf of wrongly convicted prisoners like himself. It is to one of those cases, the case highlighted in this book, that we dedicate this evening: David McCallum of Bushwick, number 86-B-2336, currently residing at Arthur Kill Correctional Institute on Staten Island.

Fully cognizant of the fact that the Jay Street offices of the Brooklyn district attorney and the courts were a few blocks from the store, I proceeded to criticize the work of Hynes's office. Just that morning, they had been hammered in the *New York Law Review*, who revealed that six of Brooklyn's ADAs were being sued for concealment of documents in the Jabbar Collins case. According to the article, the ADAs "allegedly prepared affirmations in response to state Freedom of Information Law (FOIL) requests from Mr. Collins, which stated that the documents Collins was seeking were not in the office files [when they were]." Joel Rudin, attorney for Jabbar Collins, "sought to demonstrate that prosecutorial misconduct has been pervasive since Mr. Hynes became district attorney in 1990." Rudin attached a list of fifty-six cases in which judges found that Brooklyn prosecutors failed to turn over required exculpatory material to the defense or otherwise engaged in misleading tactics. The complaint also asserted that the office "has never disciplined a prosecutor for misconduct." I continued piling on:

Three days after Judge Firetog's ruling against David, the material evidence, buried for twenty-five years, suddenly appeared at the DA's office. I'll say nothing about intent here; maybe it was an unfortunate coincidence. They did allow us to test the cigarette butts found in the car for DNA, albeit with restrictions. A year later, we were still awaiting the results when our pro bono attorney, Oscar Michelen, reached an assistant DA in the Kings County Office. "Didn't I tell you that the DNA testing came in some time ago? The test may have excluded your client and the victim, and oh, by the way, it matched someone else's DNA in the databank. Call me next Friday, I'll have his name for you." Four Fridays and four calls later, and she still hasn't told us.

Rubin also had to begin without the no-shows. He was in full throttle preacher form, running on adrenaline: "The light shines in the darkness, and the darkness has not overcome it. . . . Ladies and gentlemen, I stand before you here as a survivor of the so-called American criminal justice system!" Partway through his speech, mom and daughter entered the store, looking lost. With great charm, he stopped and said, "This must be Ernestine and Mattie McCallum. I am so pleased you could make it on this cold night." He hugged them both. At the conclusion of the presentation and the Q-and-A, Finnegan spent a long time interviewing Ernestine and Mattie. The entire event and the interview were featured in the *New Yorker*'s "Talk of the Town" section.

Just as Rubin had done for Sarokin's presentation in San Francisco, he signed autographs, shook hands, and smiled for everyone, Marc and Ray filming every moment. No one, aside from our circle, knew of the pain he was in.

The following evening, Rubin was wincing in his hotel room. Because he had to wait for a dose of Tylenol to take effect, we were late finding a cab to get us up to Barnes & Noble. When I came outside, the taxis passing by the hotel were all busy, the doorman's whistle futile. He advised us to ask the guy across the street. Who did he mean? He pointed to a driver sitting at the wheel of a white stretch limo, waiting for an upcoming appointment. We offered him twenty-five dollars.

As we rode west on Eighty-Third Street, approaching Broadway, I told Rubin that we shouldn't be seen getting out of a stretch limo in front of Barnes & Noble. That might not be the image he wanted to convey. The driver left us off on Eighty-Third Street, and we made our way, laughing in the cold, to the front door.

The presentation area in the store was stuffed with people, many of them sitting behind bookshelves. As a writer, launching a book at Barnes & Noble in New York City seemed the ultimate moment, like an opera singer performing at the Met. I had my first face-to-face meeting with Laura Cohen. She had come to the launch with Alona Katz, a highly regarded future prosecutor who was leading the investigation into the McCallum case run by Cohen's Rutgers clinic.

After Rubin spoke, dozens of people lingered to ask questions about his boxing career and had him sign books and memorabilia, no doubt for future sale on eBay. Rubin told me on many occasions that he was no longer interested in talking about boxing, but boxing to a large extent still defined him to segments of the American public. Someone even had him sign a pair of boxing gloves! I think he was genuinely happy that people remembered him, but his feelings about being in the city were mixed, colored as they were by the physical pain.

Upon his return to Toronto, Rubin consented to see a medical doctor, a decision brought on by a sudden inability to walk. The advanced prostate cancer diagnosis was confirmed, the size of the tumor enormous, his prostate-specific antigen count off the charts (over a thousand, he said). He consented to a massive dose of radiation therapy. It left a burn mark on his skin but was effective in shrinking the tumor. Still, he needed rehab therapy just to get on his feet and move from one room to another.

I visited Rubin at St. John's Rehab, north of Toronto. It was a bright, sunny day, and his room was empty. After several useless inquiries, I finally found a nurse who was able to direct me to the parking lot at the rear of the hospital. When I got there, I found him in a wheelchair, looking dramatically thinner and smoking contentedly. He was confident that he'd be up and about fairly soon. The pain had gone, and he was able to use a walker in the hospital hallways. He complained about everything, from the food to the way the nurses looked, so I knew the old Rubin was still alive and kicking. "They ain't letting me on the treadmill yet, but I told them they didn't know Rubin Carter."

I wheeled him back up to his room for lunch. He ate skimpily and with noticeable distaste. Of course the food was awful and, with that set of false teeth, eating was never a particular delight for him. He loved the chocolate pudding, however, and had several containers lined up on the radiator. A nurse came in with a doctor and drew the curtain, examining the radiation burn to make sure it was healing properly. The doctor came out from behind the curtain, so I asked her about the prognosis.

"In the short term, he's got to start walking again."

"Long term?"

"The cancer has spread into his bones. He knows it's a matter of time."

"How much?"

At this question, she shrugged. "There's no timetable."

Short term or long, everyone on the team knew what losing Rubin would mean to us. The other problem was that as long as Rubin was in rehab, he could not earn a living as a public speaker. The longer he was out of circulation, the fewer engagements he would be able to get, even if he was able to return to public life. The fewer the gigs, the harder it would be to pay the rent. Eventually, when he started to walk steadily, he would have to go home and fend for himself. The other option was a palliative facility, but Rubin was not ready to die.

When I got home, Joan Schafer, a Toronto filmmaker who, along with her husband, Peter Thurling, was making a movie about Rubin's final years, took on the huge responsibility of setting up Rubin's support system. She sent me an e-mail indicating he might be around much longer than anyone might believe:

> Dear Ken
>
> Peter and I visited Rubin yesterday at St. John's. We took him to the NPR show and he loved it. He was grinning from ear to ear. He's still very thin . . . has not gained the weight he was hoping for and is tired but the Spirit . . . oh . . . the spirit. Such a guy!
>
> We got him 3 hot dogs. We had intended to eat with him but he dove into the first one and put the rest away for later.
>
> His exercise regime is his life line. He's graduating to a HI Teck walker soon and he's pleased about that.
>
> He hopes to stay in until the end of August to get the physio he needs but then wants to return home.

Joan and Peter paid Rubin for his work on the documentary. Unfortunately, no one had the money for all the meals and the rent, to say nothing about finding a caregiver, who would need to be paid as well. Joan and I beat the bushes and got some generous donations from our legal team and from individuals who were part of the extensive North American innocence network. Everyone knew Rubin, although not everyone helped, regardless of the fundraising that he had done for so many of them. We could only gather enough for three months. Rubin had always been saved from the brink by others, but now we feared that he would be evicted and forced to live in supportive housing or palliative care against his will.

Desperate for assistance, he called his old friend from Georgia, Sam Leslie, and asked him to come to Toronto. Sam was having difficulties renewing his passport. After two months of waiting for Sam, Rubin concluded that his friend—a fellow inmate at Trenton

State whom he helped free from prison—was unwilling to make a long-term commitment. Feeling betrayed and abandoned, he stopped taking telephone calls from Sam and severed the relationship. I was shocked, just as I was with Alonzo, by the brutality and finality with which Rubin was able to drop close friends. Rubin told me two months later, without apparent sorrow, that Sam had died. I believe it was from a broken heart.

Late that fall, John Artis, Rubin's coconvicted, came to live at the High Park house and would remain with him until the moment of his death. Artis's presence over these last years provided comfort to Rubin and to those of us who could not be on the scene. But money remained a grave concern, and to this end, Rubin had to continue doing speaking engagements, traveling as far as Australia again, where the people were more generous than those anywhere else.

A day after the New York book tour ended, the DA's office announced the creation of a new Conviction Integrity Unit (CIU), designed to uncover wrongful convictions in Brooklyn. David's case was among the first chosen, likely a result of enmeshing Rubin's name with the case and, for me, a confirmation that the book's appearance harbingered a miracle. On a mundane level, we were encouraged to believe that they had succumbed to the pressure of public opinion and the negative press. Unfortunately, they had only assigned three people to run the unit. We already knew that the length of time for a single investigation and exoneration could stretch out for years. The other problem, at least for David and me, was that ADA John O'Mara was appointed to head the unit. The CIU had the appearance of window dressing.

After our initial euphoria over the DNA hit, we were surprised to find that the DA's office tightened up on our requests for further evidence testing. Since we now had proof from the DNA profiles on the cigarettes and a fingerprint on a business card that at least four other people—two of them known felons—had been inside that car, we thought that the investigation should widen. The second known felon was Kevin Brewer, a suspect we referred to as Mr. Fingerprint because it was his print on the business card found inside the car. The DA's office had given us his name, but he had been killed in a police car chase. We knew from the police reports that some of the fingerprints on the outside of the car belonged to two of the boys who set it on fire. We hoped the DA's office might be able to get at least one of them to talk about who paid them or directed them to burn Blenner's car. Even if O'Mara's team failed to identify the actual killer, the stolen car would be linked to someone other than our client.

We wondered why they would be reluctant to pursue a thorough investigation if the goal was to right a wrong and find justice. If that was not the goal, then they were deliberately obstructing their own investigation. In response to a motion for more DNA testing, David and I thought that the DA's office tipped its hand,:

Detective investigators from this office contacted male donor C and interviewed him. This person, who was fourteen years old at the time of the events in this case, denied having any contact or knowledge of the case but admitted that he walked to school in the neighborhood where the victim's car was found, abandoned in a parking lot, at some time after the murder and that he might have passed the car. This person was asked if he would consent to speaking to defense counsel; he stated that he did not wish to do so. In view of this private citizen's expressed wishes not to be contacted by the defense, the People have thus far not turned over this person's contact information. . . . At the court's request, the People will provide the Court with the individual's contact information and will provide the defense with the information if ordered by this court to do so. . . . The mere presence of someone else's DNA on cigarette butts in a car that had been abandoned in a parking lot for some unknown period of time—possibly for as long as several days after it had been stolen does nothing to establish defendant's innocence of the crime to which he confessed and for which he was convicted.

The car, found on the twenty-second, had not been abandoned for several days, and the kerosene can had come from a place where one of the original suspects worked. Did the DA's office believe that kids walk around the streets with heavy kerosene cans looking for cars to burn? Wouldn't the can have come along inside the car, where it was found in the back seat? And how could Mr. DNA's feeble explanation for the presence of the cigarettes be taken at face value? When Laura Cohen contacted O'Mara and asked him to elaborate about the cigarettes, he said that Mr. DNA claimed to have flipped a butt through the car window. "How then," she asked, "could two cigarettes bearing his DNA end up inside the ashtray?" O'Mara ignored this impossibility and said that Mr. DNA, though "criminally savvy," had turned his life around and deserved to be left in peace. The significance of this double-dealing was not lost on David. From the start, he never believed that Hynes's office would help us.

I think too much is made of someone deciding to give up or quit at something. My perspective is that walking away can be justified and necessary in order to preserve one's sanity. I have set a deadline for myself. If the motion for [further] testing is denied, I am moving in another direction. I refuse to continue taking this punishment. Eventually, my frustration is going to work against me. . . . I see myself as being realistic. I know O'Mara is obstructing and spoon-feeding us information. . . . I know we have been sent in a direction away from the science while we are spoon-fed information that does not carry significance. They expect us to keep our mouths shut while they continue to contaminate the case.

David also picked up on the Ping-Pong game the DA's office was playing by referring our requests for further evidence testing and the name of Mr. DNA back to Judge Firetog. He felt that ADAs Ross and O'Mara were simply waiting for the judge to deny the motion, a decision that would allow them to say, "We tried to help, but the judge refused."

The stalling continued to the point where I was forced to rehire Jay Salpeter to find the people who burned the car. We debated whether using our uncommunicative previous investigator was a wise move but decided that bringing a new investigator up to date at this crucial point would be too time consuming.

The one person from the car-burning group who Jay was able to find was incarcerated, and when Jay visited the prison, he was unwilling to give us any useful information. Jay believed he was making headway with the witness, but his follow-up produced nothing as well. At that point, Jay once again dropped out of sight.

Laura, in a lengthy e-mail, kept finding reasons to trust the DA's investigation. She related how the detective from the DA's office, Patrick Lanigan, was also unable get through all the resistance from potential witnesses. Were they feeding Laura information to mollify us, as David believed? Laura did not think so:

I asked O'Mara again about the other physical evidence. They still don't have it, but Lanigan is trying to track down the latent prints from the kerosene can. Because the conversation was quite productive, I did not push him on why this had not yet been done but certainly will follow up on both the latents and the evidence itself.

Laura and her students had a sit-down with O'Mara. Was this willingness to meet face-to-face a show of good faith on the part of the ADA? During the meeting, O'Mara let slip a name that seemed to refer to Mr. DNA. No one was certain they heard it correctly, and no one asked him to clarify. Later attempts by Steve to zero in on the name they heard proved inconclusive.

Patrick Lanigan visited Wallkill prison to interview Jake Prince. Everything he told the investigator, beginning with Willie Stuckey receiving a gun from someone named Jaime, was remarkably similar in detail to what he and James Johnson told police a quarter of a century ago. Of greater interest was Prince's insistence that David McCallum had nothing to do with the killing but that Stuckey was nicknamed "Supreme," the name Prince had given to the police. I asked David in a phone conversation if he could explain why both he and Willie were referred to as "Supreme" in police reports of witness statements. The confusion was understandable since David, bulky from childhood, was known as "Big Supreme" and his friend Willie as "Little Supreme." He added that the name became a hot potato during the interrogation since neither of them wanted to be tied to a name that had been associated with the crime. Following up on a question from Steve, we asked David if Willie Stuckey could have done the carjacking with some other person. Despite being given an out, he always insisted that Willie was with him that day, the entire day, in the park. He would never betray his deceased and innocent friend, although he had selfish reasons for doing so. We still don't know why Jake Prince would have accused David or Willie.

The CIU was given a mandate (just how broad I'll never know), and O'Mara was, at least partially, trying to adhere to that mandate. He told Oscar that he'd read the analysis of David's case in *Eye of the Hurricane*. Yet he said that they needed "a body for a body"; that is, before David could be cleared, we had to find the real killer to take his place. To be charitable, they may have been concerned about the Blenner family's reaction to the loss of closure. Finding absolute proof of the real killer's identity in a sea of uncooperative witnesses was extremely difficult. The CIU had many more resources than we did, but at this stage they let the case founder. It was frustrating for sure, but the process once begun had its own momentum.

───────────

The 2011 parole hearing wound up just like the 2010 hearing. Despite the psychological assessment we provided in 2010 and their own psychological assessment placing David at very low risk, David was said to represent a significant threat to reoffend, once again tied to his refusal to acknowledge his guilt and show remorse. They gave him another year to stew. Although Laura and Steve felt that there was always value in the process and that each succeeding year established a record of David's integrity, the pain of his family's suffering was unbearable. With respect to getting parole, I now understood with finality that being guilty of a crime was far easier than being wrongly convicted.

Reacting to his frustration with parole and the lack of progress in his case, David sent a disturbing letter to Oscar. In effect, he found Oscar's and Jay's work to be careless and wanting in almost every aspect. Out of nowhere, it appeared as if he was on the verge of firing our attorney. After reading the letter, I knew that it had been written not by David but by a skilled jailhouse lawyer, Derek Adams, who had been advising David at Arthur Kill for years. The letter, entitled "The Oscar-Salpeter Errors," lays out a litany of "failure," a word repeated more than a dozen times. The excerpt quoted here provides the unremitting tone:

Oscar failed to adequately investigate the FACTS of this case. Examples of this inadequacy are set forth in the facts contained in the memorandum from me to the defense team dated 11/12/09 . . .

Salpeter failed to conduct an adequate investigation and produce a formal written investigation report relating to his first investigation assignment.

. . . This memo raises some important questions, demands honest answers and enjoins a collective agreement of responsibility and accountability in moving forward.

After his release, David reflected on this letter: "I began to doubt. My case was grinding to a halt. I fell under the spell of a sharp and angry guy. He was going through his own personal crisis, and I agreed to send an offensive letter to Oscar. Derek edited it, but I took responsibility and still do."

Oscar read the letter with sadness and did not respond until after the Memorial Day weekend. He accepted responsibility for not communicating frequently enough with David. He also offered to resign if that was what David wanted:

In conclusion, David, I have considered it an honor and privilege to be working on your case with Rubin, Ken, Steve, Laura and her team, and of course Ray and Marc on the film piece. I think I have always done what has been asked of me and have been a faithful member of the team. But you are the most important member of the team and I can certainly understand your frustration at the lack of success I have achieved in getting your freedom, so if you want me to step away from it I will. Please let me know. I will continue working on the case until I hear from you.

This was a crisis that had to be handled in the most delicate way. I called Oscar and told him that David did not write the letter, but since he approved its contents, we had to see it as an expression of frustration. What David and Derek failed to see was that Oscar had a busy legal practice, nor could they have known that he was working out the details of an amalgamation with another legal firm.

Even though I knew Rubin was ill, I e-mailed him David's letter. When he phoned, Rubin became so furious that his words were incoherent. Finally he strung a sentence together: "Tell that . . . that fatty that I'm going down to that prison to kick his ass . . . even though I'm sick as hell. Here he's got a great lawyer working for nothing, and he thinks he can fire him!"

I relayed the message to David and let him know that I was not prepared to find another lawyer for the case and that if Oscar left, he might lose everyone else's support. Of course David did the right thing and drew back from the precipice. But the letter also had a positive effect: Oscar sent a fax to ADA Ruth Ross outlining our concerns about the limitations of their investigation and the lack of transparency. He told her that David was not interested in prioritizing pieces of evidence to be tested for fingerprints or DNA. "The items are not numerous so the request to do all the requested testing is not onerous." He then pointed out the most serious problem with respect to mutual trust:

> Additionally, I remain troubled that your office will not even release the name of "Mr. DNA," the individual whose DNA was found on the cigarette butts in the murder vehicle, even though he gave untruthful responses about how his DNA came to be in the vehicle. If we had to "prioritize" our requests, certainly that is our top priority.
>
> In conclusion, while these are our priorities, I feel all of our requests should be honored. ADA O'Mara's investigation has only strengthened our claim of David's innocence.

From this point on, David never doubted Oscar again. "He became more than a lawyer. He became a friend. I knew he was there for me and would continue to be there for me however long it took to get me out," he said later.

Experiencing my own extreme frustration, I decided to send an e-mail to O'Mara:

> We are puzzled by your reluctance to release the identity of the individual whose DNA was detected on cigarette butts in the automobile belonging to the victim. He did not know the victim and he lied about how the cigarettes got into the ashtray. In the Sam Quentzel case, a cold case was broken by the presence of 24 year old cigarette butts.
>
> The purpose of the DNA data bank is to identify felons who may have committed another crime, no? The very existence of this data bank is to deny privacy in such cases. Otherwise, this data bank would not exist.
>
> I ask you to consider if your son or daughter were in prison for this crime they did not commit, how long it would take for you to turn this guy upside down to find out what he was doing in that automobile.

Looking back, I can see the dangers of amateurs like myself getting involved in legal cases. Steve was angry with me because he feared that my e-mail might bring retribution from the people he hoped were trying to help us. O'Mara answered me impulsively, copying Steve:

> As a member of Mr. McCallum's "team," you are aware that we notified other members months ago that while the DNA tests we voluntarily performed on the cigarette butts produced results which did not match the profiles of the individuals we were asked to compare the results to, but did correspond to the DNA of another individual when run through CODIS.

We also advised members of your team that not only had we identified that individual, but also had spoken to him. When interviewed, that individual indicated that he did not want his identity or contact information disclosed. The information used to identify and locate the individual was obtained through confidential law enforcement data sources subject to agreements restricting access and public disclosure. While no direct exculpatory information was produced, I recognized that the defendant's representatives have a legitimate interest in speaking to the individual as this might lead to further evidence or information which could be of value. We therefore advised attorneys for Mr. McCallum to seek the information through a Court Order, and that while we would advise the Court of the individual's preference, we would not oppose disclosure. We finally received a copy of such a motion last week and the matter should be resolved in Court in the near future.

Murders, rapes, and other crimes by their nature can elicit strong emotions. To attempt a just result however, it is essential that investigations of such cases are handled without decisions or actions being clouded by emotions. You may wish to consider whether you really would instead want such cases handled by prosecutors or others who would affect an emotional transference to the position of a parent of a victim or suspect and handle a possible witness or suspect in the manner you urge I proceed. Be assured that this office will continue to handle the investigation of any reasonable claims made on behalf of Mr. McCallum in a professional, thorough and ethical fashion. However, please direct any future communications to me through one of the attorneys on your team.

I have to acknowledge, from my present vantage point, that the gist of his response was correct and reasonable, and yet the e-mail, with the quotation marks around "team," was contemptuous. When I asked if he would turn this witness upside down, I did not mean physical assault but rather questioning him to the hilt. I thought his real goal was to stoke Steve's anger at me. However, in forwarding my e-mail to Steve, O'Mara attached another document, a previous letter he sent to Mr. DNA with the name of our suspect right at the top. It was the same name that he had accidentally mentioned to Laura and her students. We now had the name and address of someone who might have murdered Nathan Blenner or been there when it occurred. Was forwarding this information a fortuitous accident or a sign of O'Mara's inner conflict?

Firetog denied us further evidence testing, but he did agree to release the name of the DNA hit. It was the only ruling he made in our favor throughout the long struggle. I think the judge may have given us the name because he knew we already had it. Firetog's ruling on all the other evidence parroted Ruth Ross's opposition to our motion almost word for word. He denied us, as he said, because the discovery of new DNA would not necessarily exonerate David and Willie. Even in a normal appeal, the ruling was unreasonable, but in a situation where the Conviction Integrity Unit in the DA's office had launched an investigation into a possible wrongful conviction, the judge's denial was unconscionable. His supposed concession was highlighted at the end: "There being no legal basis for granting the relief sought, *except as to the contact information for Male Donor C*, the motion is denied" (italics mine).

David decided to stop "playing games" with the DA's office, whom he believed was colluding with the judge. Ruth Ross then agreed to test "one or two other items." Despite Steve's insistence that "any DNA testing is better than none at all," David would accept no further limitations. If Hynes, O'Mara, Ross, and company were not full partners in the investigation, he wanted us to break away from them. We had no choice but to accede to his wishes. A new and assertive David McCallum was emerging, as evidenced in a letter he wrote to me:

> I know there are people out there who believe in me. I know people are working for me. I truly appreciate everything that is being done on my behalf. I am not ungrateful to anyone who are sacrificing a part of their lives to help me regain my life. . . . I am not sure if I was born to experience this trauma, but I believe that something is preventing me from stepping into this society that I never should have left. . . . I know you are tired of this process. The machine known as the District Attorney's Office is adept at wearing people down. I will not stop thanking you, Rubin and Gary for coming into my life. If not for you three men, I would have self-destructed a long time ago.
>
> Please let Rubin know that I am thinking about him and wishing him a speedy recovery. Of course I am looking forward to hanging out with him in Toronto.

The closing of Arthur Kill prison, as part of a statewide attempt to save money in the criminal justice system, presented us with a new unknown. We worried that David might be shipped to some inaccessible prison far upstate. At a new prison, he might just as easily find himself mopping floors again or be confronted with daily violence.

Otisville Correctional Institute, to which David was transferred, is northwest of New York City. It is a difficult location to get to, although the trip never deterred Ray and Marc, who continued to make friendly visits and do film interviews. I took a harrowing trip there with Oscar one morning during a tropical storm. When we sat down with David that day, we both had the impression that our client was aging before our eyes. He was enervated by the length of the ordeal, the dashed hopes, the continual stalling. He found it difficult to smile. He told us something we had both inferred from phone calls. Otisville, even more than Arthur Kill, was filled with people who had given up. When we drove through the gates, a score of prisoners in plastic raincoats were descending from the unit at the top of the facility. The prison had at one time been a sanatorium, but no one now was being healed. No programs were being offered. The prisoners housed at the top level of the grounds had to walk a mile and a half to get down to the cafeteria, three miles round-trip three times a day, if they wanted to eat. The image of that listless, slouching group of men dragging themselves forward in the hard rain has stayed inside me ever since. David was now in prison hell, not the kind of violent hell one sees on prison reality TV programs, but the hell of unremitting boredom.

The one redeeming factor at Otisville was the guards. Unlike those at Arthur Kill, they maintained a semblance of respect. With all the filming and the visits from Laura and the Rutgers students, Ray and Marc, as well as from Robbie and her family and friends, they understood that David had dedicated support. Did the guards, seeing this love, believe in David's innocence? I would like to think so.

In December 2011 Jabbar Collins and attorney Joel Rudin filed a massive $150 million dollar civil rights action lawsuit against the Kings County District Attorney's Office. An article by Andrew Keshner in the *New York Law Journal* reported again that Collins "cited 56 decisions to argue that Brooklyn District Attorney Charles J. Hynes and his office were intentionally indifferent to Brady violations, the use of false or misleading evidence and other prosecutorial misconduct." While the city opposed the lawsuit, there was much consternation behind the scenes. With each new case and each new story that had to be covered up or explained away, the DA's office was losing its credibility. With more shocking revelations to come in 2012 and new candidates from his own party vying for district attorney, the good ship Hynes had begun to list.

10

MARVIN SCHECHTER

The Gadfly

LAURA'S ARTICLING STUDENTS contacted David's support team for the next round of parole recommendation letters. After two failed attempts at parole, I resisted writing another letter that focused solely on David's accomplishments. I wanted to blast the board for its intransigence and its refusal to face reality and, getting it off my chest, wrote something completely unacceptable for Laura to include. This time I decided to write it like a motion one might submit to a union or other democratic structure for a membership vote. My motion was an attempt to avoid emotional involvement:

> **Whereas** David McCallum, from the age of sixteen, has spent twenty-seven years in the New York State correctional system and has never committed a serious infraction as a prisoner at Eastern Correctional, Arthur Kill or Otisville and has, to the contrary, sought to educate himself and assist other inmates;

Whereas David McCallum is supported in his claim of innocence by three separate innocence projects;

Whereas not a single piece of hard evidence ties him to the murder of Nathan Blenner or even indicates that he was in the borough of Queens on the day of the crime;

Whereas DNA testing on cigarettes and fingerprint evidence from inside the victim's auto has, during the past year, revealed the presence of two offenders;

And whereas David McCallum is a caring, intelligent and sensitive individual from a large family, whose father has died during his time in prison and whose mother is seventy-four, we ask you to please release David for parole and allow him the chance to live a productive life outside the prison.

I think this format was original, if nothing else. How could I be a supplicant to people who were at best unconscious and at worst malicious?

Many fine and heartfelt letters were written as well. The parole package put together by the Rutgers clinic was a thing of beauty. I look back on all that work with a sense of sadness. To write such letters presupposes that the recipients, the parole board members, are caring and concerned individuals, susceptible to reason. Steve went through the details of the case and finished his letter with a plea:

David's innocence and his desire to prove it has sustained him throughout all of these years—it has endured the death of loved ones; it has endured despite the death of his co-convicted Willie Stuckey. Please do not penalize him for not giving up the one thing that has helped to sustain him. Please judge him based on his behavior in the institution, his parole plan, the way he has educated himself in prison, and all the other factors that speak to his low risk for reoffending.

My sister, Joan, laid out the steps David had taken to prepare for life on the outside and concluded respectfully: "It is abundantly clear to me that, if released from prison, David McCallum will be a productive and respected member of the community. Knowing him has enriched my own life."

And Gary: "Mr. McCallum is a wonderful example of how in the face of adversity one's spirit can triumph. . . . David has learned the meaning of empathy and he continues to teach it by example to others."

And Ray:

Another important life lesson David has taught me is to be thankful for my blessings, my two incredible parents, the roof over my head, and the freedom to be able to make choices that will affect my future. This may seem obvious, but I was not always aware of how fortunate I am.

A month prior to the hearing, a prison counselor informed us that Ken Taub, the head of homicide in Hynes's office, had placed a letter into David's parole file. Once again, the tea leaves were being read. Might he be recommending David's release? Alas, most of the prognostications, including Laura's, were negative. The majority assumption—and it was to prove correct—was that Taub had gone to the Blenner family asking what they thought about David's possible release. Taub had multiple ways of asking the question. He might have asked, "Since David has been in prison for twenty-seven years, would you consent to his being released on parole?" Or he could have put it in a way they would almost certainly refuse: "David McCallum, the murderer of your son, Nathan, wants to be granted parole. How do you feel about that?" (Of course, the Blenners may have objected either way.)

At the time, a group of highly motivated people had formed an advocacy association, the National Organization of Parents of

Murdered Children (POMC), to block parole for convicted killers. For $250, they would launch a campaign on behalf of a bereaved family. They had already blocked thirteen hundred releases and had won praise and appreciation from people across the country, such as this Brooklyn parent, who said, "Parole informed me they received approximately 100,000 signatures from all across the United States. Our deepest thanks to the Parole Block Program and all those who continue to make it successful." For me, the work of this organization smacked of vigilantism. People who had superficial knowledge about a particular case would nonetheless sign petitions to keep prisoners, some perhaps innocent, perennially incarcerated. Many parents of murdered children, maybe the majority, feel that way with ample justification, which is why victims' rights should not include making decisions on parole eligibility. The fact that the POMC was profiting off this exercise made their motivation questionable.

When in 2012 David was refused parole, the decision notice indicated that he had spent a breathtaking 307 months, or 9,396 days, in prison. While recognizing David's disciplinary record inside prison, the rationale for denying parole had become mind numbing:

> Parole is denied for the following reasons: after a careful review of your record and this interview, it is the determination of this panel that if released at this time there is a reasonable probability that you would not live and remain at liberty without violating the law and your release at this time is incompatible with the welfare of the community. . . . During interview, you deny any involvement or culpability for this heinous act against another human being.

It was the same boilerplate stuff but a test for Ernestine's faith. We worried when she said, "I don't think I can take it anymore." Her son, innocent and yet presumed guilty, was trapped inside a world with its own distorted logic. We also noticed that a board official named James Ferguson seemed to insert himself into every one of David's hearings. The choice of particular parole boards should be random, but Ferguson was now three for three and, according to the transcript, was the individual who carried on the questioning. Laura launched another appeal.

For David, the parole process is still the most difficult aspect of his imprisonment to talk about: "They wanted to keep me in there; they took the case personally. They wanted me to admit guilt. . . . The hearings became an interrogation, rather than question-and-answer. They were retrying my case when they were supposed to be evaluating my suitability to leave prison.

Having to tell my mom I'd been denied was so painful. I had to let her know I was fine and would continue to fight. I faced another long year in prison with no end in sight. She tried to make me feel better. She was religious, so she thought there was some kind of purpose in it."

I tried to boost David's morale after this third parole denial:

Weak men hate what they cannot control. If you don't grovel, they will stick it to you again and again . . .

So while we continue to work on your freedom from prison, I want you to do me another favor. I want you to walk through that place with even more dignity than before. . . . I want you to show them what freedom really looks like because they need to see it. . . . You are freer than any guard or official at that prison. You are freer than that parole board. Never let them take your dignity.

At this increasingly desperate time, Steve enlisted the help of Centurion Ministries, whose titular head, Jim McCloskey, was a good friend of Rubin's. Steve cautioned us not to get David's hopes up, as they might decide to pass on his case. We would also have to cede control:

> Centurion Ministries does not often collaborate with lawyers and investigators outside of a small inner circle of people whom they carefully vet. When they get involved in a case, they "run" the case and those who work with CM need to have thick skin, especially the lawyers.

We agreed to this option because Centurion had the resources to do a full investigation of a case that was proving to be more complex than any of us had originally thought. David was initially opposed to Centurion, especially to being kept in the dark, but he eventually consented. They assigned their major case worker Kate Germond.

About two months in with no word, I sent Kate a succinct e-mail, asking only, "Any news on the McCallum case?" Her reply caught me off guard:

> While we have great respect and affection for Rubin and recognize that there are special circumstances attached we still cannot rush in and abandon our commitments. I am sure you can respect this; nor do we just take people's word that this is a great case for innocence. We have to come to our own assessment. We are slow and plodding. We are up to our eyeballs in a case load.
>
> Added to this is my concern about all the hands that have been in this case talking to witnesses. I generally as a rule don't get involved in cases where someone has already talked to witnesses. It makes my job all the harder in an already difficult world to navigate.

Weeks later, David made the same inquiry and got the same discouraging answer. As Steve had indicated, we were being told to step aside and avoid doing anything further that could ruin the investigation. That spoke to a lack of trust and understanding and to a probability that future problems would arise. David's response was apt: "In truth, we have lost control over this process."

While I supplied all the materials they asked for, Centurion had not spent the past eight years poring over the documents and combing the streets of Brooklyn and Queens. I could not get comfortable with the passive choice we made, especially waiting for them to catch up. When would they visit Mr. DNA? Had he already been spooked by the DA's office? The less we had to do on David's case, the more Gary, Mary Ellen, Joan, and I had to keep David from depression. He, in turn, tried to keep up our spirits:

> I hope you are feeling better then when I spoke to you last week. I have this tendency to not focus enough on other people's issues. . . . After all, people like you have done that for me, without asking for anything in return. I can, and will, be more cognizant of that moving forward.
>
> Please let Mary Ellen know that I said hello, and that it is always a pleasure to talk with her. Not to mention that your sister is a wonderful human being. I have so much respect for her. I am curious to know if you and Joan had a competitive battle educationally, growing up? The purpose of asking you this is because in some aspects, she actually reminds me of you. . . . When I speak to you and Joan, the both of you have the same spirit and wonderful soul, always teaching me something, even if you don't always intend to.

David's continual compliments were our sole payment for the work. They kept us going. In thanking David, I told him that Joan and I were not competitive in the least. There was no contest. Joan was the brilliant and hardworking kind of student who few people—especially me—could match. What struck me about his letter was the growth in his language—a word like "cognizant"—for example. What a student *he* was!

David was now taking a business course. The practicality seemed to suit him more than the purely academic work. His recollection now is that the course opened his eyes to reality: "I thought I would start a business. I learned how difficult it was. You don't just open up a business and see the profits start rolling in. What I learned about investing, credit, location gave me a respect for businessmen. And I also learned that my math skills were almost nonexistent."

He admired Ray's work with business, especially the takeout restaurant in Montreal. Speaking to Ray about the restaurant was "part of living outside the prison before I actually got out of there," he told me later. "I got off the phone feeling uplifted." At this time, though, it was the film that did the most to boost morale. David remembers now how "[Marc and Ray] were being perfectionists, but I wanted the film out—even if it was not professionally finished—as soon as possible. I was in no position to understand how limited [the use of] the film would be if it looked like an amateur production."

The situation around funding began to look better when rights to the film were bought by a Toronto film company, Markham Street Films. Aaron Hancox, one of Markham Street's directors, had been an acquaintance of Ray and Marc at Concordia University. Markham's first step was to get a small media grant from Hot Docs (in full the Shaw Media–Hot Docs Fund), the largest documentary festival in North America. More than the money, the grant established instant credibility. The people at Hot Docs had seen the early takes of the film and were convinced that the project was viable.

The next step was finding a way to get a broadcast license from TV Ontario (TVO). Documentaries are difficult to fund because they are generally unprofitable. Young filmmakers like Marc and Ray, motivated by a powerful belief in their projects and the people they are helping, have to rely on friends and family. Funding from public sources or wealthy donors are two ways to get around this problem. TVO gave Markham Street a significant sum, an incomprehensible sum, when so many directors, even established ones, were scrounging money for equally important projects. Maybe some force—might it be called justice or karma—was beginning to turn in David's direction. Ray said simply, "Now the film will be finished." For Rubin, it was an example of higher laws acting on a lower level. He spoke of the process as "irresistible."

With their new budget, Ray and Marc redid large sections of *David & Me*. I learned that the film was going to focus not only on Ray's relationship with David but also on my relationship with both of them. The three of them did a full-day interview together at Otisville, which David wrote to me about after:

> The filming went great. Although, at times, it was an emo-
> tionally charged interview, I was really grateful to have shared
> with the future viewing audience the wonderful support I
> have received, especially from you. The fact that you trusted
> me with your son says a lot. I am sure you are going to love
> the film, but I believe you will find the topic of conversation
> about you and Ray rewarding and highly emotional.

An encouraging article then appeared in the *New York Times*. New York State attorney general Eric Schneiderman created a bureau to investigate "questionable convictions." Words from high-ranking politicians that sound promising and idealistic can engender hope in the previously hopeless, especially the wrongly convicted. Schneiderman was quoted:

There is only one person who wins when the wrong person is convicted of a crime: the real perpetrator who remains free to commit more crimes. For victims, their families and any of us who could suffer the nightmare of being wrongly accused, it is imperative that we do everything possible to maximize accuracy, justice and reliability in our justice system.

The *New York Times* went on to describe the mandate of the bureau and then threw in a stipulation that I, in my hopeful excitement, minimized: "If a district attorney's office chooses to refer the case to the attorney general, then the attorney general's office will have jurisdiction to reinvestigate the case and subsequent legal proceedings." If the devil is in the details, the word "chooses" turned the state's offer on its head. While some DAs might be happy for extra resources to investigate wrongful convictions, others would be free to refuse it. Why would Charles Hynes ask for help if such help would reveal a plethora of corrupt practices? Conversely, nothing was explicitly stated to make one believe that the attorney general's office would intervene without that referral.

Still, the need—and it was a need—to respond to wrongful convictions also had residual effects. DNA would now be routinely collected and compared to a more sophisticated database; ways of determining compensation would be standardized. Words of praise for the governor and the attorney general would be rung out. But always there were caveats. While compensation would now be routinely awarded to people who falsely confessed—people such as David and Willie who had been fed details by detectives—a bill coming before the legislature left out key components, such as videotaping interrogations and double-blind photo arrays for witnesses.

It didn't take David a day to start firing off letters to Schneiderman and to Thomas Schellhammer, the new bureau chief. He thanked the attorney general "for taking steps to resolve one of the biggest travesties of the criminal justice system." An official form letter followed in less than a week: "I appreciate your views on this important issue. I will certainly keep these comments in mind as I continue to fight for your rights, and policies that benefit all New Yorkers. . . . I welcome your continued input."

David decided to take the letter literally, continuing to offer his "input" while attempting to be more specific:

Dear Mr. Schneiderman,

Thank you for responding to my letter dated April 16, 2012. It was necessary to express my views on the issue because of the prevalence of wrongful convictions and the lack of transparency among local prosecutors. . . . I am optimistic that wrongful convictions claims will be reviewed vigorously as opposed to glossing over and ignoring these claims. In announcing the formation of this bureau, you said "For victims, their families and any of us who could suffer the nightmare of being wrongly accused, it is imperative that we do everything possible to maximize accuracy, justice and reliability in our justice system." I respectfully ask that you consider reviewing my case.

Faced with expectations like David's, the faceless bureaucracy got into high gear. David's letter was referred to Schellhammer, who was now delegated to send out discouragement:

Please be advised that in most situations, jurisdiction with your case resides with the District Attorney who prosecuted it. Generally, the Attorney General does not possess the jurisdiction to intervene in criminal matters prosecuted by other agencies. In some cases, this Office may have or may acquire jurisdiction over a specific criminal case.

After our preliminary review, the Attorney General may
or may not have jurisdiction to investigate your case further.
We may require more information from you as part of this
review. If so, we will contact you in writing.

I actually laughed out loud at seeing the *may or may nots*, and
were that not bad enough, the strategic *if* that ended the letter. *Don't
call us; we'll call you.* Marty Tankleff's lawyer, Bruce Barket, spoke
to the media. Reported by the *New York Law Journal,* "He said the
willingness of district attorneys to conduct state-aided reviews may
become a function of how invested the prosecutors are in the convictions. Downstate district attorneys tend to remain in office for a
decade or longer. 'Are they going to invite people in to say that their
office made an error?'" But then Barket said something prophetic:
"With the shorter tenured ones, it may not have been that person's
prosecution to begin with."

David kept after Schellhammer, notwithstanding, writing five
futile letters in all. David wrote to me in the summer with increasing desperation:

> I am contemplating my next big decision in my quest to prove
> my innocence, but I realize that I don't have many options. I
> have no doubt in my mind that Centurion Ministries is a cred-
> ible and reliable organization, but I am in a bit of a quandary.
> I reached out to the New York Attorney General . . . because
> I believe we must get this case away from the Brooklyn DA's
> office, who obviously has a conflict of interest.

Both Oscar and Steve felt that David was better off with Hynes's
office than the attorney general. For them, the referral problem was
insurmountable. David continued to believe that the AG's office could
acquire jurisdiction and that they would investigate his case, but we

saw Schellhammer's offer as disingenuous. Although he sent them a long summary of his case, David's goal of getting them to take over jurisdiction was never realized. Schellhammer wrote back yet again assuring David that his submission would be kept on file but saying that the jurisdiction of his case resided with Kings County—from which they needed a referral. With their continued refusal to take over cases without referrals, even where DA's offices had backed off investigations such as David's, our fear was confirmed: the new investigations bureau was as much window dressing as the Brooklyn one.

We also worried that Centurion's investigation might prove to be too long term for David. Oscar had an inside contact with another well-to-do organization, the Jeffrey Deskovic Foundation for Justice. Deskovic, strong-minded and intelligent, was wrongfully convicted at the age of seventeen. He took an $8 million settlement and committed $1.5 million of it to the new foundation. Oscar's contact reported that Deskovic saw David's case as similar to his own, since Deskovic also made a false confession at a very young age. After Oscar was guaranteed that Deskovic would take over the case, David wrote to Centurion, thanking them for their help but indicating that he was ready to go with another foundation. Two other aspects of Deskovic's potential involvement were encouraging. First, he was very familiar with the Brooklyn DA's Office. Second, Governor Andrew Cuomo referenced Deskovic in a *New York Times* article. Oscar's new law firm was Cuomo LLD, giving us a link with a relative of the governor.

Strangely, nothing happened—not short term, not long term. No further communication came to us from Deskovic or his office. David had now given up on Centurion, a bird in the hand, but the one in the bush had disappeared. I thought things could not get any worse. But was there a message in all of this? I remembered standing outside Eastern Correctional Facility with Rubin, wondering who was going to get David out of that massive and forbidding place, and Rubin answering, "You are, Ken, you are." Those words now sounded like

a challenge to me and the entire team. Don't expect help from else-
where; the work was ours to complete and no one else's. In asking
for help, we had surrendered our faith in the miraculous process
that began with the appearance of *Eye of the Hurricane*. It was time
to start believing again.

Then a bomb named Marvin Schechter, chair of the criminal
justice section of the New York State Bar, dropped on the New York
City legal world. Schechter had the courage, one might say the gall, to
write in his "Message from the Chair" that the spate of exonerations
due to DNA evidence showed that Brady violations by prosecutors
had become routine. In the drive for convictions, prosecutors were
not sharing exculpatory evidence with defense attorneys. Even more
explosive, he wrote, "Assistant district attorneys do not emerge from
law school with a genetic disposition to hiding Brady material. Instead
this is something that is learned and taught."

The op-ed was reported in the *New York Law Journal*, a periodi-
cal that is little read by the public but functions as an in-house paper
for the various legal offices in New York State. The reaction to this
allegation—that DA's offices are breeding grounds for Brady violations—was swift. Schechter struck a nerve because he was, like many
whistle-blowers, speaking truth to power. Letter after self-righteous
letter condemning Schechter came in from all over.

Under the title "'Brady' Comments Are Inaccurate and Below the
Belt" in the *New York Law Journal*, Bronx County district attorney
Robert T. Johnson wrote:

> Finally, Schechter's suggestion that hiding Brady material is
> something that is "learned and taught" is indeed outrageous,
> and slanders an entire group of dedicated attorneys. . . . Like
> my colleagues, my career has been spent seeking to do justice
> and teaching others to do the same. I wish Schechter had
> opened his eyes to that.

Kathleen Rice, the district attorney from Nassau County, using words like "reckless," "flippant," and "offensive" to describe Schechter, weighed in similarly:

> I would have told him that I became a prosecutor to seek justice and the truth, not to merely get convictions. By suggesting that every Brady violation is intentional, Mr. Schechter refuses to acknowledge the role of human error in a criminal justice system that is very much human.

In a phone conversation, Rubin reminded me of how difficult it was to get prosecutors to acknowledge the role of human error in many wrongful convictions. Prosecutors are loath to take responsibility when the consequences have already taken a toll on the innocent victim. When deliberate malfeasance is discovered, prosecutors attempt to minimize the damage. "They say they want to 'put this behind us. Let's move on.' But what they did is a crime. You hearing this, Ken? A crime! Imagine a burglar coming into the courtroom and saying to the judge, 'I didn't mean to steal that jewelry, Your Honor. Let's just put this behind us and move on.'" He laughed hoarsely and began to cough. I imagined the cigarette burning in the ashtray. I waited, and he spoke again: "Hey, Ken. You tell our friend I'm in a little bit of pain. But tell him I won't be leaving this Earth till he gets out of Otisville. So you better get his ass out soon, Ken. Know what I mean, my brother?"

———

Charles Hynes wrote to the *New York Law Journal* as well. David and I laughed at the irony.

> It should be pointed out that Brady violations are prohibited by our Rules of Professional Conduct and where identified by

a lawyer must be promptly reported to an appropriate griev-
ance committee. The failure to do so is a separate violation
of the rules.

   . . . After 22 years as Kings County District Attorney and
as a member and former president of the New York District Attorneys Association there is absolutely no doubt in
my mind that my practice of making disclosure of evidence
favorable to defendants, which is both an ethical and moral
obligation, is practiced by my 61 colleagues in New York State.

With Rubin's assistance, I wrote Hynes a letter and cc'd Thomas
Schellhammer. I also sent the letter via e-mail to a *Daily News* reporter,
who initially professed sympathy for David but proved unreliable.

Dear Mr. Hynes,

Your quoted words: ". . . disclosure is not only an ethical obligation, it is a moral obligation," in a letter to the New York
Law Journal, caused us to ponder the distinction in the law
between ethics and morals. Even where the letter of the law
allows for a particular action, the truth for which all must
aim (the basis of legal morality) is a higher principle, and
must therefore take precedence. . . . In the case of wrongful
convictions, however rare they might be, it behooves officers
of the court to make certain that the individual who is serving
a sentence is the guilty party.

   It was in this spirit of moral obligation, we hope, that the
Conviction Integrity Unit in Kings County was established.

The purpose in writing the letter was to keep Hynes and his office
on the defensive. Rubin encouraged me with a familiar analogy from
the boxing ring, something to the effect that if you get your opponent

backpedaling or on the ropes, you'd better take advantage while you can, and never, ever give him time to catch his breath.

Hynes gave the letter to John O'Mara, who, in turn, replied to Oscar; he had already made it plain that he would only respond to attorneys.

> As we discussed over the phone today, I am forwarding copies of two letters. The first is a letter from Ken Klonsky. While the letter is dated December 14 [2012] and notes that it is addressed to District Attorney Hynes, our incoming mail log does not reflect receipt of such letter as of this date. The copy provided is from a Daily News reporter, who received the letter electronically from Mr. Klonsky, as well as a call from Mr. Klonsky apparently alleging in part that there was a "conspiracy" to keep Mr. McCallum in jail.

Using the word "conspiracy" may have been a way for the *Daily News* reporter to ingratiate himself with the DA's office, perhaps for future favors like early tip-offs for crime scene investigations. It was naive of me to trust a media person who had his own agenda.

Yet O'Mara agreed to make "one further effort to locate items of evidence for DNA testing." He told us, however, that the DA's office was not conducting any active field investigation, "as no further productive areas appears immediately apparent," but they would, he said, "consider any request for additional investigative steps if they appear of sufficient promise to warrant the use of resources." In other words, they had dropped David's case. To be charitable, they lacked the manpower to do a thorough investigation. But O'Mara threw Oscar a bone:

> You also briefly mentioned that you had identified a particular area of the statement from co-defendant Stuckey that you

believe merits further analysis, and that you would amplify
that argument in an email. Upon receipt of the particulars, I
will again review the confession and relevant sections of the
trial transcript.

In the meantime, have a good Holiday and Happy
New Year.

His newfound interest in Stuckey's statement came as a surprise.
He was responding to a challenge that Oscar had thrown down and
none of us had known about. Oscar explained it to me:

I told [O'Mara] that no one has ever explained satisfac-
torily how Stuckey in his DD5 confessed to the Chrissie
Owens incident and then the main theme of the DA's case
was that that the incident with Owens was unrelated to
the Blenner incident. I asked him to further explain why
Bjorneby and Butta went to great lengths to distance the
incident from Blenner at trial. I told him Judge Firetog
plainly did not understand that argument and its significance. I said it is the absolute objective proof of the men's
innocence. I told O'Mara that if he could explain those
two points to my satisfaction in a way that does not lead
to innocence, I and the whole team will forever leave him
and his office alone. I told him not to rush, to read it
carefully and that we would touch base about it the first
week of January or so.

Offering to drop the case was a risky tactic of which we were
unaware, but we need not have worried; rather than answer the challenge, O'Mara stalled.

If ever anyone deserved his fate, it was Charles Hynes, whose office kept trying to deny and cover up a long series of startling allegations against him and his prosecutors. Ken Thompson and Abe George, both untested as political candidates, decided to run against Hynes in the Democratic primary. A godsend came their way when Judge Frederic Block publicly chastised Hynes for praising and promoting a prosecutor in his office, Michael Vecchione, whose tactics sent Jabbar Collins to prison for fifteen years. Mr. Hynes's office, according to the judge, "relied on false testimony, coerced witnesses and suppressed evidence [Brady violations] in the case." In a pretrial hearing over Collins's lawsuit against the city, the judge lashed out at Hynes: "I'm disturbed that Hynes praises Vecchione after what happened. Hynes hasn't treated this seriously, has he? Name one thing that he has done in light of Mr. Vecchione's aberration."

Equally important was the public revelation of tactics used to bring about false confessions. A film documenting the Central Park Five case from 1989 showed how a group of frightened teenagers falsely confessed and were wrongly convicted of the beating and rape of a young female jogger. In a *New York Times* op-ed about the film, Brent Staples described the modus operandi:

> By the time the videotaped confessions were taken, the defendants, their lawyers say, had endured lengthy interrogations and been subjected to coercive and deceptive interrogation techniques, including force and trickery, sleep deprivation and isolation from their families. The complaint further asserts that *the boys were told that they could go home if they provided statements placing themselves at the scene and incriminating others* [italics mine].

Marty Tankleff and David McCallum were both teens when falsely confessing to murder; both were fearful and, therefore, easily

susceptible to tactics of seasoned interrogators. Both were isolated during interrogation. Where did the police learn these techniques if not
from each other, whether in formal or informal meetings? Winning
the "legal game," as Rubin called it, was more important than seeking
out the truth. Marvin Schechter's accusations, instead of disappearing,
were echoing throughout the system.

Despite the frustrations David had suffered and was still suffering, these media stories were laying the groundwork for his future
exoneration. He was disappointed by the insistence of the attorney
general's office that it lacked jurisdiction in his case and was upset
with Oscar yet again for not pressing the issue, but Oscar never saw
Schneiderman's office as the way forward. The way forward was right
in front of us, in Brooklyn, and if we took a bit of time, things would
eventually break in our favor. Being inside the process of an exoneration, we often got sidetracked by the frustrations.

In the short term, we needed to keep Rubin engaged as long as
he was alive. That would involve assuring his financial security. He
had to provide for John Artis as well as himself, but further speaking
engagements were not coming his way. Over the past year, he would
not leave his house unless he got paid. With his corporate gigs dried up,
he was reduced to signings. For three thousand dollars, he would even
go to New Jersey to sign boxing gloves, books, and other memorabilia.

Joan Schafer and Judge Sarokin then pulled a rabbit out of a
hat. Through an agent, Joan got the contact information for Denzel
Washington. The judge called him on a movie set in a desert location, and the actor promised to take up the issue upon his return.
True to his word, and unknown to anyone but us, he provided the
long-term solution for Rubin's financial woes. Washington gave Rubin
fifty thousand dollars and promised him that as long as he was alive,
he would continue to support him in the same way. Unbeknown to
the actor, keeping Rubin solvent was supporting the effort to free
David McCallum.

Rubin was then invited to speak on December 14 at the Bring Leonard Peltier Home concert at the Beacon Theatre in New York. Although it was an unpaid gig, he was moved to make an exception. Who better to speak for Peltier, wrongly convicted of the killings of two FBI agents on the Pine Ridge Reservation in South Dakota? Since Peltier was seriously ill and his next parole hearing was scheduled for 2024, the only hope, and the purpose of the concert, was to persuade President Obama to issue a pardon before he left office. John Artis drove Carter to New York, where they were put up at the Beacon Hotel, adjacent to the theater.

The concert was a final milestone for some of its participants. Pete Seeger, at ninety-three, had a short time left to live, yet he managed to sing a couple of his songs, one of them "Bring 'Em Home," an antiwar anthem converted to a plea for Peltier's freedom. Jackson Browne, Bruce Cockburn, Harry Belafonte (who could no longer sing but whose presence was the single greatest motivator for Rubin), and Yasiin Bey (Mos Def) were on hand as well. Michael Moore called out, "If not you, Obama, who?" Oscar and Ray reported that, even with all that star power at the concert, Rubin was the man who lit up the evening.

"Oscar," I asked, "did he tell the Denzel Washington story again?"

"Yes, and I can tell you they ate it up!"

Yet again, Rubin pulled out his writ of habeas corpus, saying, "Our freedom account is being looted!" Rubin "Hurricane" Carter was good for a round or two more.

Obama never did issue that pardon for Leonard, despite an editorial from the *New York Times* pleading with him to do just that.

11

VAN PADGETT

The PI

THANKSGIVING AND CHRISTMAS were the worst times for David, because the pain of his deprivation was greatest during family holidays. Mary Ellen and I make a large Christmas Eve dinner at our apartment for friends in Vancouver and relatives who live out of town, including Ray of course. David phoned as always to talk to everyone. We could feel some sadness, but we were happy to have him with us, even if only on the speakerphone. He wrote later:

Thank you for helping me enjoy one of the better holiday seasons that I can recall by allowing me to speak with everyone. I probably talked too much but I was very excited and was appreciative of the opportunity. It was gratifying talking to Robbie and hearing the excitement in her voice at being at her in-laws home for Christmas. As for Ray, I can't recall ever meeting a young man who is attacking life in the manner that he does. From the very beginning of our relationship, Ray seems to have a plan, especially when it comes to starting a family. He thought it would be irresponsible to do so without first having his own life in order.

David was forty-four years old when he wrote this, and while achieving a certain wisdom in prison, he was forced to live his life vicariously. Part of his compelling interest in my son was that Ray was in the process of becoming a full adult. David had missed out on all those precious formative years; now he was middle-aged.

Time was constricting all of us, no one more than Rubin. I was unable to reach either John or him for a week and, in my typical way, began to worry. I called every day, only to hear Alonzo's recorded voice still answering the phone. The outgoing message would play— "You have reached the offices of Innocence International and the home of Dr. Rubin Carter, founder and CEO. Please leave a message and we'll return your call as soon as possible"—and Rubin would wait to hear who the caller was. Finally, I sensed someone on the other end.

"Rubin, it's Ken."

"What's up, brother man?"

"How are you?"

"I am perfect, my brother." Anyone who knew Rubin more than casually will recognize this salutation, which indicated, I am certain, that you were speaking to the fourth, or conscious, Rubin Carter.

"Where have you been?"

"John and I went down to Virginia to take care of some business."

"Virginia? How can you travel to Virginia? I mean a couple of weeks ago you were at death's door."

"Death's door. Yeah. I knocked on that door, Ken. Old Man Death came out and looked at me. He was pissed off. Know what I mean? 'You woke me up, Carter, got me outta bed. Now get the fuck outta here! I ain't ready for you yet." He laughed hoarsely.

I laughed as well, trying to imagine the encounter. This Old Man Death spoke without the solemnity that legend had led me to believe. After a pause, Rubin continued.

"I've been meaning to call you, Ken. I'm dropping out. Dropping out of the picture. No more signings. No speaking engagements."

I thought about how Rubin's leaving the stage would be a great loss to the innocence community and an even greater loss to those innocent people languishing in prison. The publicity he generated would be irreplaceable. But he was not quite finished with the work.

"I'm asking you to keep me up to date with David's case. It's all I got energy for."

"I promise I will."

"I believe you, my brother. I know I've told you this before, but thank you for everything you've done."

"Thanks for making me feel useful, Rubin. I promise we'll get him out soon."

I so much wanted David free before Rubin's death. I envisioned a meeting between the two of them. To experience that moment, we had to abandon anything and anyone not leading us forward, or hindering David's release. Since the DA's investigation had ended and Jay had left the scene, I hired Van Padgett, a private investigator from Brooklyn who David read about in the *New York Times*. When I called Van and mentioned Rubin, he called David's case "the one I have been waiting for." As a plus, he was eager to take part in Ray's film:

Hey Ken

I spoke with Ray and it was a pleasure. I have noticed so far the great chemistry among all the parties involved in this campaign to free David. I am honored to be part of such a magnificent undertaking. I really do feel that we can make a difference in a system (Brooklyn, NY) that's prone to business as usual attitude when dealing with wrongful convictions, not to mention lackadaisical defense teams.

Laura, Oscar, and I met Van on the second level of a large New York cafeteria prior to going to the *New York Times* building for an interview with Michael Powell. With Van's engaging manner and fresh perspective, we were newly energized. He was the investigator *we* had been waiting for. We regretted not having found him sooner, but hindsight is futile in the field of wrongful convictions. What came before his arrival was all a necessary part of the process. While we may have been put out by Jay Salpeter's style, it was important not to lose sight of what he had given us: Chrissie Owens's location and, through his inside contacts, the evidence voucher leading to the DNA. With Van, who was African American, we had someone with credibility in the community. We asked him to focus on people in Bushwick close to David's age or those who had known him as a teenager.

In January, Van located the sister of Murray Howard. He also found a mug shot of Howard dating from a sexual assault charge in the 1980s, his hair unmistakably braided. His height was five foot four, a further alignment with Owens's description. Laura's students and Jay had made previous attempts to find Howard; the information they got from the street was that he lived in a crack house and was dying of AIDS. Now, two years later, Van discovered he was still very much alive:

Hey Ken

I visited the crime scene. The purpose of the visit was an attempt to locate any witnesses and to get a backdrop on the park.

I also interviewed the sister of Murray Howard via the telephone. She agreed to an interview at my convenience. Murray Howard is currently on Rikers Island serving out a sentence for petty larceny. I will interview him tomorrow. The sister stated she was interviewed along with Murray Howard in 2011 by a white male and female who she believed was from the District Attorney's office. Ms Howard has given me the impression that she possesses intimate knowledge of the events surrounding Mr. Blenner's death. I will keep you guys updated.

Thanks guys.

We were delighted at both the contact and the level of communication. The DA office's interview with Howard in 2011 was news. While both Prince and Howard had been in custody in 1985, before David's arrest, only Prince's interview had been reported. While he may not have been willing to speak to Jay, Howard agreed to speak to Van.

"What luck!" I exclaimed on the phone.

"Luck is for nonbelievers," Van replied.

His subsequent interview with Howard on Rikers Island resulted in a startling discovery:

Murray Howard was not much of a conversationalist. He was evasive and reluctant to speak. I did appreciate his reservations to discuss a homicide case while in jail within a day of being released. What I got from the interview is as follows:

Murray Howard stated he had visited the crime scene the night in question. He had been riding his bicycle approximately two (city) blocks from the crime scene. He explained he was just being "nosey" and the police vehicles flashing lights had drawn his attention to the area. What he did not explain is why he immediately became a person of interest by the police. He was taken from his home (no dates or times given) on three occasions to the precinct to be interviewed. According to Murray Howard, during his second visit to the precinct he had been placed in a room with a two way mirror. The detective informed Murray Howard he had not been identified and would be released.

Murray Howard denied knowing anything regarding the homicide of Nathan Blenner. Murray Howard was aware of David and Willie (knew David went by the name of Supreme).

Murray Howard did comment on his Queens (after I read off the info on DD5) arrest with Jake Prince. Murray Howard stated he was once again riding his bike in Queens and inadvertently came across Jake Prince. The two were arrested and taken to 104 pct. and placed in separate rooms. A police officer did question Murray Howard briefly regarding Aberdeen Park. Murray Howard stated he informed the officer that he did not have any information on the homicide. Murray Howard stated the Queens case was later dismissed.

Murray Howard agreed to a secondary interview.

Howard was being untruthful about his "inadvertent" contact with Prince. Police and court records indicate they had both been arrested in Queens for stealing a chain off a woman's neck on the subway. Prince was eventually convicted of the crime, while the charge against Howard was dropped. The chain snatch on the subway was another detail that Butta fed to Stuckey to make his confession sound authentic. While Howard may not have been the most credible witness, his story about being taken in for questioning was backed up by his sister. Why weren't the three police interviews and the interview with the sister written up as part of the police investigation? Were these reports also suppressed in the same way that some New York detectives and prosecutors, according to Marvin Schechter, suppressed potentially exculpatory information? We thought so.

One write-up we did have was a police report from Butta dated Monday, October 21, 1985. Butta came to the area of Aberdeen Park, Brooklyn, where Blenner's body was discovered. In a small box on the DD-5 report marked "suspect," Butta had typed in "corn rows." We concluded that Butta came to the park with Chrissie Owens's description of braided hair. At the time, Howard was the prime suspect. Van told me he guessed that Howard "came by the park on his bicycle, maybe not because he was nosy but because he was returning to the scene of the crime." The police obviously thought so too.

Howard would not confess, though. His sister said he would rather die than snitch on someone. He and Prince were four years older than David and Willie, and both had extensive criminal records. Far easier for the police to intimidate two younger African Americans who served their purposes just as well. In fact, since Howard's sister told us that her brother had "dirty dealings with the police," David and Willie may have served their purposes a lot better.

Van speculated that the prosecutor and the police detective created the case against David and Willie to satisfy the Blenner family and the community in Ozone Park, Queens. "Butta stopped building a case and started to create one," he said. I was reminded of Rubin and John Artis being pulled over by the New Jersey police, who told them that they were looking for a pair of black males in a white car. Rubin answered with a pregnant question: "Any two will do?" If we could get Howard to sign an affidavit about his three failed interrogations, we would have a potential ace in the hole.

Keeping the momentum going as Rubin urged, Van accompanied Oscar for a visit to Mr. DNA at his home in an out-of-the-way spot near Kingston. Finally! Ray and Marc parked nearby, and our PI wore a hidden camera. The scene, with the face of the witness obscured, is played out in *David & Me.* Mr. DNA repeats the story he told the DA's office about flicking the cigarette into the car on the way to school. Oscar then confronts him: "We have a problem here. Your DNA is on two cigarettes found inside the car's ashtray." At first he denies that they are his cigarettes. Then, conceding that the cigarettes have his DNA, he insists that he has no idea how they got there. The longer they question him, the more adamant he becomes. Afterward in a consultation with Van, Ray, and Marc, Oscar said, "What are we going to do? Tase him? Waterboard him?" Having thought that Mr. DNA would answer questions about the killing of Blenner and the burning of the victim's car, we were disappointed, but at least we had him on camera caught in a lie.

Weeks later Van and Oscar returned to Rikers, where Howard was still on remand. When Howard came into the visiting room and found out that Oscar was a lawyer, he became verbally abusive. Oscar assured him that they were not there to implicate him in the crime, only to show the gaps in the police investigation that might help get David out of prison. Howard relented. He willingly signed an affidavit, insisting on writing it out himself and attesting to everything that he told Van in the previous interview.

Van and Oscar had successfully gained the trust of a suspect in Blenner's killing. That he might have signed the affidavit to help David McCallum, just as Jake Prince had tried to help David in ruling him out as the perpetrator, showed perhaps that even hardened criminals have consciences. What we had in hand was evidence that the police had suppressed information favorable to the defendant. Had the jury been aware that Howard had been brought to the precinct three separate times to be interrogated, they might well have concluded that David and Willie were an afterthought. They might also have reasoned that two sixteen-year-old kids from Bushwick would have been far less likely to have committed the kidnap and murder than a couple of car thieves on a spree in Queens were. Even if David had capable legal representation, his attorney could not have known about the interviews. The due diligence argument would be moot.

———————

Upstate, Governor Andrew Cuomo finally announced his promised justice initiatives. The first of these was making the recording of interrogations for serious crimes, like murder and kidnapping, mandatory. Recording would be part of what Cuomo called "innocence protections.'" Physical and legal threats, which often caused false confessions, would be banned. He also asked for double-blind safeguards in lineup identifications to combat eyewitness errors. Cuomo did very little in the way of pardons, but this reform was far better than none. The formal recognition of coercive interrogation techniques and the injustices accruing from them would make it easier for David if we got a hearing.

The list of wrongful convictions, recanting witnesses, and unscrupulous police and prosecutors in Brooklyn kept growing. William Lopez spent twenty-three years in prison for what Michael Powell of the *New York Times* variously described as a "car wreck" and a "busted valise of a case." David knew Lopez from Eastern Correctional, where they worked together in the law library. Lopez was released by a federal judge who held that the conviction was based entirely on the subornation of witnesses. Hynes claimed that the federal court ruling—which also lambasted his office—was the result of "second-guessing." While recognizing Hynes's previous contributions to restorative justice, Powell nonetheless wrote about "the occupational hazard of the long-serving public official who develops an immunity to doubt." When Powell quizzed Hynes about the Jabbar Collins case, Hynes said, "We believe he did it," despite there being no evidence of his guilt. Another case, that of Ronald Bozeman, fell apart on closer scrutiny, but in this instance, Hynes took what credit there was to be had in the exoneration: "It was our investigation that revealed the problems." The end of Powell's op-ed was punctuated by Hynes's unintended irony:

> Why, I ask Mr. Hynes, appeal this busted valise of a case? Mr. Lopez had an impeccable behavior record in prison. There is a strong chance he's innocent and a stronger chance still that no jury will convict him again.
>
> Mr. Hynes shrugs. "Because you're supposed to uphold the rule of law," he says.

Nothing came of Hynes's supposed appeal against the Lopez ruling, because it was clear that he would lose. Otherwise, he was increasingly out of touch with reality.

In examining these cases and the Conviction Integrity Unit's one major exoneration, of David Ranta, we saw that the greatest weakness in our case was the absence of evidence against David. It may seem counterintuitive to believe that little to no evidence and no witnesses would actually hurt a wrongly convicted man. But the requirements in cases without DNA often entails the recanting of a witness or the discovery of other kinds of forensic evidence implicating someone else. The case against McCallum and Stuckey was based almost entirely on the false confessions. Ranta's conviction was easier to overturn because his legal team had so much more to work with. With David, we had to prove negatives: he had never been in Queens; his lawyer did not prepare a case; he couldn't drive a car; he never had a gun. All these assertions are true but not provable, as in *Prove to us that he never had a gun and shot an innocent man*. Since there was nothing substantive to overturn, we knew we needed goodwill in the district attorney's office to free him. We had to make the case that there *was no case*. Our hopes rested on those Brady violations—the more the better—and electing a new district attorney who might be inclined to recognize them.

Having lived in Canada since 1967, my knowledge of local New York politics was superficial. What I feared was that people were indifferent to races for district attorney or would reelect district attorneys as long as crime was perceived to be under control. Hynes could claim that a large reduction of crime in Brooklyn took place under his watch, although experts questioned whether it had anything to do with him. But experts don't determine voting patterns. For Hynes to be defeated, people had to care about *justice* issues, specifically wrongful convictions and unequal enforcement.

David spent the greater part of 2013 following the progress of Hynes's two challengers: Ken Thompson and Abe George. Yet he indulged in negative thinking or placating the evil eye:

> I think DA Hynes' bid for re-election has taken some hits— not just because of the wrongful convictions coming out of his office—but also because of accusations of a cover-up in his office regarding sexual abuse in the ultra-Orthodox Jewish community. Politics are funny—DA Hynes will likely be re-elected.
>
> . . . Although I suspect that Hynes will win a closely contested election, I give the challengers credit because I don't think it's good politics to allow Hynes to run unopposed, as he has done in the past.

In reality, David and the entire team feared that unless Hynes was defeated, our chances were slim at best. Having suffered so many disappointments, David began writing to Ken Thompson. If Thompson was elected, David wanted him to remember his case and place it near the top of his list. The more than fifty Louis Scarcella cases would overwhelm any conviction integrity unit.

Through Gary Dolin, David made contact with John O'Hara, an attorney who had worked in Hynes's office but whose legal career had been sidetracked and nearly destroyed as payback for political disloyalty. O'Hara was charged with and convicted of voter fraud, for voting in the precinct where he was living with his girlfriend and not at his primary residence, the first person convicted of such a crime since Susan B. Anthony! As a result, he temporarily lost his license to practice law. Helping us was a way for O'Hara to get back at Hynes and revive his own career.

Rubin, sensing a confluence of events, recommended that we now turn to the media. Chris Glorioso did an invaluable, spot-on I-Team (NBC New York) segment about David's false confession. A writer for the *New York Law Journal*, John Caher, wrote a long piece on David's case that appeared in early March. Caher focused on the upcoming parole hearing, the fourth kick at the can. He interviewed James Ferguson, the parole commissioner, who continued to follow David from one hearing to another like a modern-day Javert. He wrote, "Ferguson observed that McCallum's claims of coercion were considered and rejected by the court. He also noted that prosecutors are trained to look for signs of abuse, and there is no indication that the assistant district attorney in this case detected anything amiss." While the article as a whole was favorable to David, and the story was now in front of the entire legal community, the chilling implication in Ferguson's statement was that David would be turned down again, especially if Ferguson were to appear at the next hearing. Caher ended the article with an interview with Mattie McCallum, David's sister, who proved time and again to be an effective advocate for her brother:

McCallum's sister, Mattie McCallum, said she has nothing but sympathy for the family of Nathan Blenner and could not fault them for opposing her brother's parole release.

"I feel for the family," she said in an interview, "If that was my brother or my child, I would want the person who did it to pay. I can't imagine what it would be like to lose a brother or child that way. But you need to make sure you have the right person."

Mattie McCallum said the last 28 years have taken a terrible toll on her 75 year old mother, and said the repeated parole denials are exceptionally difficult for her brother, who is now 44. "I am afraid he will lose hope and do something to himself. I keep telling him, 'Your day is coming, your day is coming.' I just don't want him to give up hope."

Our overall media strategy, designed to pique the interest of what we hoped would be a new district attorney, was well served by the Caher piece. David weighed in with typical ambivalence:

Commissioner Ferguson clearly does not believe me, so I think the article neutralized the Board of Parole to some extent, and hopefully made it difficult for Ferguson to sit on the panel. My expectation is to be released next month. . . . I understand that parole is not guaranteed. My main priority is for Willie and I to be exonerated and I will fight for our innocence to the very end.

The David Ranta case was, as previously mentioned, the first significant breakthrough for Hynes's Conviction Integrity Unit. There were parallels between David's case and Ranta's, including the same presiding judge, but two major differences: (1) Evidence existed to initially implicate Ranta. That evidence was discredited by the discovery of coached and heavily incentivized witnesses, recanting witnesses, a phony police lineup, and the failure of the detective to take or keep notes. (2) Ranta was white. Since an overwhelming majority of questionable cases involved African American defendants, Hynes may have feared a potential flood of claims if he were to recommend the exoneration of a person of color. In all probability, he and

O'Mara pushed Ranta forward as a way to demonstrate that the CIU, despite its lack of staff, was actually functioning. Since the primary was approaching, Hynes would now be seen as righting wrongs in the one area where he was most vulnerable. But the number of Scarcella's unsafe convictions—and Ranta's was only one—multiplied. The media sensed an epidemic of malfeasance and were now in competition with each other to root out Hynes's stories.

In an unusual move during its investigation, the CIU brought Ranta in to be questioned. David wondered why they would take so much trouble with this one wrongly convicted man and exclude so many others. The CIU's conclusion, written by O'Mara, were words any innocent defendant would hope to hear:

> Based on this information, there is cause to believe that a probability exists that had such evidence been received at trial, the jury may not have convicted the defendant in this case. This affirmation is therefore prepared in support of an application on behalf of defendant David Ranta to vacate the judgment of conviction pursuant to [his 440 motion].

In Denis Hamill's *Daily News* column, O'Mara admitted to mixed feelings:

> "I don't have the unadulterated feeling that this is an actual innocent person that got let out," he says. "There's still some doubt over that. But Ranta is certainly a legally innocent person. We did the right thing. That's what we do." At the Do-Over Squad.

Hence Hynes's office recommended the release of another prisoner who they thought might still be guilty. The press painted Scarcella, previously hailed as a model for cracking difficult cases, as an unscrupulous and shameless self-promoter. Scarcella, in turn, accused the Brooklyn DA of throwing him under the bus. An ugly internecine squabble was taking place in the public eye between a sitting DA and a retired detective. Scarcella branded himself a scapegoat, claiming, "I never framed anyone in my life."

Further stories undermined Hynes's credibility. One of these involved a hotel where witnesses were placed under virtual house arrest until they were needed to testify. In another, the *New York Post* reported, "Five of Brooklyn's top prosecutors—including the head of a politically sensitive conviction integrity unit—knowingly flout[ed] state and city laws by living in New Jersey." Even from childhood, I noticed that Americans have a taste for Mark Twain–type anarchic satire when confronted with ludicrous, corrupt, and self-serving behavior. The *Post* went on:

> "All Kings County assistant district attorneys must live within the state of New York," Brooklyn DA spokesman Jerry Schmetterer confirmed. Schmetterer said Hynes gave his "permission" to the Garden State Five but declined to say what authority the DA had to grant his employees immunity from residency laws.

Given the hits to his reputation, it turned out that Hynes needed David Ranta as much as Ranta needed him. Ranta suffered a heart attack soon after leaving prison. Rubin always said that prison is the unhealthiest of environments, both from a physical and a psychological standpoint—"the lowest level of human existence aside from being dead." Twenty-three years behind bars had destroyed Ranta's health; the proof of his suffering outweighed the good publicity over his release.

Hynes then made a calculated gamble to pump up his image. CBS announced that DA Hynes was getting his own reality show. The chutzpah was breathtaking. The *Daily News* exposed him to ridicule:

The show—and the potential free time for Hynes—infuriated his two challengers, lawyers Kenneth Thompson and
Abe George. "Charles Hynes doesn't want to be DA; he just
wants to play one on TV," said George, a former Manhattan
prosecutor. Thompson, a former federal prosecutor, said if
Hynes "spent less time worrying about getting on TV and
more about his job, Brooklyn wouldn't have the lowest fel-
ony conviction rate in the city." Hynes campaign spokesman,
George Arzt, tried to mock Thompson. "Jealousy is not a
positive for political figures."

The discredited Michael Vecchione was to have some of his less
questionable cases featured. We were apprehensive that the people
of Brooklyn would be taken in by this advertising charade. Someone
inside the media had done Hynes an awfully large favor, allowing
him to fight media with media. Any time I spoke to Rubin, and it
was now down to one time per month, he reminded me that our
media campaign had to be sustained and that I need not worry about
anything issuing from the Brooklyn DA. I then received a rare e-mail
from him: "It's happening, Ken. They can't hold back the tide. The
people of Brooklyn are smarter than you think."
    We then received a letter from O'Mara, who had finally dealt
with the Chrissie Owens issue:

> I was initially interested in your argument regarding the
> portion of co-defendant Stuckey's confession that may have
> related to Owens's observations, as it was new to me. How-
> ever, you did not inform me that the same point had been
> raised before. Upon re-reading the transcripts and files, it
> became obvious that this was an issue not only previously
> raised through defense post-conviction motions, but also at
> the trial itself.

What O'Mara established here is that his Conviction Integrity Unit was no such thing, since the supposed purpose of its creation was to reexamine evidence that may have been overlooked or misinterpreted without reference to previous court decisions. He went on in the same paragraph:

> Your apparent claim that the prosecution failed to disclose that Detective Butta showed photographs of the defendants to Ms. Owens, if true, would present not only a likely Brady violation but also that Detective Butta committed perjury at the trial. However, I have uncovered no evidence to support this. Ordinarily, we would seek to interview both Detective Butta and Mr. Stuckey regarding the interrogation; unfortunately, both were dead before any post-conviction motions were made.

Here he was disregarding the Owens affidavit in which she states unequivocally that she was shown photos by the lead detective. That her account of the visit was backed up by both her mother and boyfriend was obviously of no importance to him. He never dealt with Owens's appearance in Willie's confession. Oscar replied to O'Mara:

> Chrissie Owens's observations were also what you said "initially interested" you in taking another look at the case. So I was rather dismayed and disappointed when your letter revealed you did not in fact look into the issues I raised. Your statement that the issue was raised by David and me in our 440 motions is accurate; your statement that the issue was raised at trial was inaccurate. But either way—isn't the whole purpose of your unit to take a second look at things that may have been raised before either inartfully, incompletely, or without the hindsight that new evidence presents?

O'Mara was exercising willful blindness, choosing to see only what might sustain the conviction. Had he wanted to recommend David's exoneration, he had ample reasons to do so. He wasn't just too tied to the people in the DA's office; he was one of them. Fresh eyes and objectivity were all that were required.

That September, Abe George dropped out of the race for district attorney. We soon had reason to celebrate. Thompson beat Hynes in the primary with fifty-five percent of the vote. Rubin had been right. I thanked the people of Brooklyn in my blog and my heart. My faith in an educated electorate, indeed my faith in democracy itself, was reborn.

Right after this resounding and unprecedented primary victory over a sitting New York district attorney, Hynes decided to run as a Republican despite previous assurances that he would never do such a thing. His campaign, such as it was, claimed that Thompson was too inexperienced for the job and that only he, Charles Hynes, could keep Brooklyn from a descent into another crime wave. That his bid had racial overtones is speculation on my part, but, in any event, Hynes was obliterated in November. Thompson garnered seventy-five percent of the vote, more than the entire Democratic electorate.

Soon after, it was alleged that Hynes financed his campaign through the proceeds of criminal activity—money recovered from sales of stolen cars, drug dealers, and organized crime. The now former district attorney of Brooklyn had, according to reports, pilfered a sum in excess of $200,000. David and I envisioned Hynes on Rikers Island in an orange jumpsuit. Ten years of frustration deserved a bit of vindication, unlikely as it was to happen. The last vestige of Charles Hynes's good reputation had been destroyed.

Oscar, encouraged by the new atmosphere, redoubled his efforts. He found an unexpected break when he contacted David Rappaport, the ADA who took David's taped confession in 1985. He was now working in an unrelated field and more forthcoming than anyone could have expected. On the confession tape, he spends a minimal amount of time with each suspect. David and Willie are keen to blame each other for the shooting. Beyond requesting that they speak louder, the ADA makes little attempt to get either of them to clarify their statements.

Rappaport told Oscar that Eric Bjorneby, David's prosecutor, stormed into his office and scolded him, describing the confessions as "worthless." Yet taped confessions, even supposedly worthless ones, were so powerful for the jury that these sufficed. This revelation about Bjorneby suggested a high level of cynicism within the office of Elizabeth Holtzman, the DA before Charles Hynes.

We then found ourselves at the spring parole hearing, number four and counting. All parole hearings, in an attempt to save on travel expenses, now took place via video conference. As in the past, James Ferguson was in charge, asking ninety-five percent of the questions. While David reported being treated with respect, the transcript showed Ferguson playing his previous role as prosecutor, boasting of his ability to recognize if a young person was lying or telling the truth. He had even watched the confession tapes, supplied by Hynes's office. He said it was obvious that David was telling the truth about the murder, whereas in 2012 he was sure that Willie was the truthful one. I was moved to write in my blog, "Where did this parole commissioner attain this level of clairvoyance? Even with the use of MRIs, which chart brainwaves and have 70% accuracy, no forensic scientist has claimed sufficient reliability for any method used to decipher truth and lying."

David was turned down again, in the cruelest possible way. Beneath the prison time served at the top of the decision page—now 317 months—was the same boilerplate language. Ferguson went on to describe the kidnapping and killing of Nathan Blenner and outlined

David's prior juvenile record. He then noted David's accomplishments and the numerous assessments describing him as "lowest possible risk, clean disciplinary record, positive presentation," and his "assertion of innocence." At this point he revealed his animus against David. Laura believed that he was exceeding his authority as a parole commissioner both by retrying the case and assigning motive to the crime. Ferguson had written:

> The helpless unarmed victim was shot in the back of the head to prevent him from identifying you. Despite your corroborated and detailed confession, you deny your guilt. . . . You clearly failed to benefit from prior attempts at rehabilitation.

When the date was once again set to the next year, the timing felt less like a concession to David and his numerous supporters and more like what it was: torture.

David phoned me with the bad news. He struggled to make the best of it, saying that being released on parole was trading one prison for another. "Rubin was right," I told him. "Parole is not your way out of there. If I were you, I would never say another word to them." Laura found the denial heartbreaking, but she believed that we still had to build the case for David year after year. She and her students put together a brilliantly written appeal attacking Ferguson's impartiality.

Ferguson made a serious error, according to the transcript. He recognized that Steve Drizin was a noted expert on false confessions but said that his opinion, as a "hired gun," carried less weight. Steve was infuriated:

> Should I write to Commissioner Ferguson and tell him that I have never taken a dime in this case, that I resent being called a "hired gun" and that I only weighed in after my own investigation raised serious questions about the reliability of the

confession? I would also point out that not only do the new test results buttress David's claims of innocence but David's consistent claims of innocence coupled with his insistence on doing DNA and fingerprint testing are also telling. This is not some "Johnnie come lately" who is just now claiming his innocence looking for a murky DNA result to get back in court. He has taken his case all the way through the state and federal systems and been seeking DNA testing for years, testing that if he were truly guilty could confirm his guilt.

A week after the parole hearing, O'Mara wrote to Oscar about Steve, questioning Steve's impartiality in similar fashion and once more revealing his hostility to us as a group:

> While Steve Drizin has apparently written a report (which I have not seen) "opining" that the confessions shared elements of proven false confessions given in unrelated cases, any opinion he may have expressed must be considered in the context of his continued association as an attorney/advocate on Mr. McCallum's self-described "defense team."

We were shocked that he never read Steve's report despite having it in his possession for years and despite being head of the CIU. His accusation of partiality on Steve's part, coupled with Ferguson calling him a "hired gun," pointed to collusion between the two offices.

Referencing McCallum, Marty Tankleff published a letter, titled "When Admitting Guilt Is Not an Option," in the *New York Law Journal* about the problems innocent people face when applying for parole:

> As an exoneree who served over 17 years in prison, I had the opportunity to work with many men who were appearing before the parole board and who were denied parole release.

These men were consistently told that they had to admit their guilt to obtain parole release. For those that were innocent, this was not an option.

The position of Parole Commissioner James Ferguson ("Inmate Cannot Clear His Name Without Evidence of Guilty Party," NYLJ, March 6) regarding the claim that David McCallum falsely confessed to the crimes for which he is incarcerated establishes Ferguson's lack of insight and understanding of youthful suspects falsely confessing to crimes they did not commit. Empirical evidence demonstrates that youthful suspects, similar to McCallum, falsely confess to crimes they did not commit at a higher rate than adults. As of this date, the Innocence Project in New York City has obtained the exoneration of 303 people, and more than 25 percent of those exonerations were caused by false confessions.

Has Ferguson obtained any expert training in analyzing false confessions? Has he reviewed the record? There is no way that he, or any parole commissioner, has the time to review a prisoner's entire case file and make the determination that he made in McCallum's case. Further, Ferguson's claim that "McCallum's claims of coercion were considered and rejected by the court" is disingenuous as hundreds of innocent men had their claims rejected and were eventually exonerated.

How many more innocent men will be denied parole and then be exonerated, having to endure more years in prison than if parole had released them at their initial appearance? Proclaiming one's innocence should not be a factor in denying a prisoner parole.

Unfortunately, it is clear with the McCallum decision that is exactly what the parole board is saying.

Martin H. Tankleff

John Caher reported on the parole hearing. He mentioned "the other youth who died" (Willie Stuckey), which suggested a further reason for the intransigence of the DA's office and its collusion with the parole board. If David were to be released without acknowledging his guilt, the city and the state would be directly implicated in Willie Stuckey's death.

Ernestine and David's nephew and niece, Aaron and Mia, were being filmed (a scene that features prominently in *David & Me*) when the bad news came. Back in 2012 all Ernestine had said was, "I don't think I can take it anymore." That it might have been literal truth was not lost on any of us. At the fourth refusal, she showed equal amounts of religious faith and inner strength. Her granddaughter asked David how he was able to go on after moments like this. "That's a tough one, sweetie," he answered, swallowing a sea of emotion. "The love and support of my family and all the people out there helping, give me the strength to go on. I just want you to know that I love you all and I won't give up until I walk out of here a free man."

Another falsehood from Ferguson's decision was the phrase "corroborated and detailed confession." Ferguson, O'Mara, and Hynes are intelligent people, yet a child could see that those confessions were not corroborated. I went back to the confessions from Butta's interrogation notes. Damned if I wasn't going to throw this lack of corroboration in their faces! I produced a word-by-word comparison of David's and Willie's confessions (see appendix), and sent it to each member of the innocence team. It was eventually seen by Ken Thompson.

In making one last effort to review the body of evidence, I came across a document that David had attained through a Freedom of Information request. One of the oddities of police and court documents and trial transcripts is that when you go back through them, and this is true of professionals and amateurs alike, you always find things you missed. This document was a letter from Anthony Cordero, a professional investigator from Westbury, Long Island, whom Peter Mirto, David's inept trial lawyer, hired. While this letter was in our possession for years, we never looked at it closely nor made use of it in our 440 petitions. Cordero interviewed a group of alibi witnesses, kids who had been at Halsey Park on the day David and Willie were there playing handball, the same day Blenner was kidnapped. Cordero also interviewed James Johnson a week before the trial, but Mirto never made use of these statements during cross-examination. Was Mirto, who was under investigation by the Bar at the time, too distracted to utilize them?

Cordero's investigation initially focused on alibi witnesses. After visiting David on Rikers Island, Cordero sought out those people who had been with him in Brooklyn on the afternoon of October 20, 1985, when Blenner was kidnapped in Queens.

Dear Mr. Mirto,

Concerning the case of David McCallum. In connection with the alibi he offered I have identified and interviewed the following persons:

Cordero listed four names and their home addresses.

They all stated that on October 20, 1985, the date of occurance [*sic*], from approximately 11 a.m. to 6:30 p.m., the client was playing handball at Halsey Park.

These witnesses also stated that a Willie Stuckey and his sister Regina were present at the park during that time.

Then he wrote up his interview with Johnson. What Johnson said to the investigator to some degree obviated the need to find this elusive character. Here was a state witness who back in 1986 was trying to help out the two people he was about to betray in the courtroom. While Johnson faced serious charges in the bodega robbery, he would also have had to deal with being a snitch in his home neighborhood. In speaking to the investigator, he appeared to be playing both sides. Cordero's report read:

> In my interview with James Johnson, DOB 06/07/66 of 564 Central Avenue, Brooklyn, (top floor) he stated that shortly after the crime that he heard on the street that David and Willie had been down on [i.e., arrested for] this murder. He said that he had also heard that Jake Prince had been the driver of the car. He said that he had also heard that Willie and David had not done it. James said that the police had picked him up and brought him to the stationhouse. When he was there he said that he told them about the rumors. He said that he had also learned that Jake Prince had also been picked up by the police, and that Jake had been arrested for robbing a chain from a woman.

From our vantage point twenty-eight years in the future, we surmised that Johnson was telling Cordero the truth. First, the account about the chain snatching was confirmed by Howard. Also, according to David, Johnson was indeed at the stationhouse when David was arrested. But Johnson also said that Jake Prince, our main suspect, was said to have been driving Blenner's car. How could anyone have missed this? The key here was not the hearsay evidence itself but the fact that Johnson was disavowing his court testimony. The sad and almost unbelievable fact was that Mirto failed to use any of Cordero's work in cross-examination or to elicit information from his own client with regard to the report. His first interview with David was on the eve of the trial! These revelations would have weight, not in a courtroom but for a conviction review unit that was not bound by the technicalities of an appeals court.

After David's release, Oscar made contact with Cordero for the purpose of the compensation hearing. Cordero told him that he drove Mirto to the courtroom every day of the weeklong trial. Every morning he was offered a glass of vodka by the attorney, who himself was never sober.

———————

When David phoned after Ken Thompson's victory, I told him that I would never again use the word "hope" with regard to his release. "You are getting out within the year, David. This will be your final Christmas in prison." I knew in my soul that the last miracle of Rubin Carter had begun in earnest.

As the year ended, David wrote a letter reflecting the newfound optimism among all of us:

> It is hard for me to put into words how I felt yesterday talking to everyone at your home. As I said on the telephone, this particular Christmas was unlike any I have had. After receiving the clothing yesterday, I was reminded of my childhood. The joy and appreciation of receiving those gifts was almost child-like. After trying on those clothes, I tucked them away in a duffel bag under my bed, with the hope of wearing them someplace else. I am aware that I won't have much clothing when I am eventually released, so taking clothes home with me is necessary.
>
> I'll be doing a lot of reading and writing. It will be a good thing because it is hard for me to watch television in here because those guys watch the same movies and TV shows over and over. It's kind of sad. . . . I think all one needs to do is take a look inside of these prisons and one would learn that a large

segment of the prison population is not interested in long term planning or success. I do take into account that some or most are not fortunate to have the kind of support that I have so I'm not necessarily passing judgment on these guys; but still, I can say with confidence that there is something to be said about self-motivation and self-awareness.

12

KEN THOMPSON

The District Attorney

And when great souls die,
after a period peace blooms,
slowly and always
irregularly. Spaces fill
with a kind of
soothing electric vibration.
Our senses, restored, never
to be the same, whisper to us.
They existed. They existed.
We can be. Be and be
better. For they existed.

—Maya Angelou

KEN THOMPSON'S ELECTION in November 2013 marked the beginning of the series of events that would, almost a year later, result in David's release. The election made David's release possible, but even then freedom was not assured. The problem for our friend and client was the competing cries for help from Brooklyn's wrongly convicted, victims of an epidemic in the 1980s. When those who enforce laws violate the Constitution for the sake of expediency, the results are predictable. When wrongful convictions are laid bare, people come to understand why citizens have the right to be safe-guarded from unlawful arrests and rigged trials. That those accused of criminal acts have these rights is our most formidable bulwark against the breakdown of a civil society.

Thompson, to his everlasting credit, immediately set up a new unit—the Conviction Review Unit (CRU), distinguishing it from the defunct Conviction Integrity Unit—to look at the slew of potential wrongful convictions. The new DA was walking the walk, not hand-ing out excuses about why this was no time to do such and such or that money was unavailable. He had said investigating wrong-ful convictions was going to be his first priority, and he delivered, staffing the CRU with a dozen high-ranking people and putting a substantial amount of money into the endeavor. He appointed Ron Sullivan, a renowned Harvard Law professor, to supervise the legal work of the unit. As an outsider, Sullivan would not be subject to the potential cronyism of the old guard in the DA's office. Mark Hale, a straight-shooting Brooklyn ADA and thirty-year veteran prosecutor, along with an independent review panel staffed by attorneys Bernard Nussbaum, Jennifer Rodgers, and Gary Villanueva, rounded out the top echelon of the unit. The independent panel was to function as a fail-safe mechanism, sending cases back to the CRU if the members found irregularities in the CRU recommendations.

Reform and renewal were not limited to Brooklyn. The election of Bill de Blasio as mayor of New York indicated that New Yorkers were seeing the limitations of the big-money politics Mayor Michael Bloomberg represented. While Bloomberg was a visionary who got things done, and while he was able to embody the bigness of vision that characterizes New York City, the real estate prices and the swollen corporate salaries made large areas of New York unaffordable for the middle and working classes. De Blasio, with talk of social justice, economic inequality, and an end to racist stop-and-frisk police policies, was the anti-Bloomberg. David felt these changes:

> Today seems like a different day to me. Perhaps some of it might have to do with watching the inauguration of the new mayor, Bill de Blasio. . . . As I said on the telephone, I don't get caught up in the message. I tend to be a wait and see, show and prove person. Yes, I have expectations, but they are grounded in reality because I have been down that road before and won't allow myself to go back there.

In January we learned from John O'Hara, who still had sources inside the DA's office, that Ken Thompson was aware of David's wrongful conviction and saw indications that made him think the case was worthy of investigation.

David continued to envision life on the outside, emphasizing simple pleasures: walking down the street, going to work every day. Even in terms of travel, his ambitions were close to home:

> I hope Ray wasn't rubbing it in with the pictures of him in Thailand. Sometimes I can't wrap my head around the many places Ray has visited. Enjoying nice food on a boat in Thailand. Wow! I'll just be happy going to Coney Island, and possibly enjoying a boat ride and a hot dog.

That David McCallum was still in prison was Rubin Carter's one regret. At some point near the end of *David & Me*, Ray and I were interviewing Rubin over the phone from my Vancouver apartment. Between long bouts of coughing, he allowed that he was not "up to snuff" in David's case. He would have pushed even harder for a federal appeal had he been fully focused, not slowed by his health and fretting about his poverty. After a bad coughing fit, he cut the phone conversation short, saying he didn't want to talk anymore.

In February I got a call from Joan Schafer: "If you want to see him while he's still alive, I'd advise you to come soon. The doctors say he may not last the month." Two days later, I was on a plane.

I stayed with my dear friends, Rob and Eleanor, at their west side Toronto house, a place of love and hospitality that meant so much to Mary Ellen, Ray, and me. Rob, a graduate of Cambridge University and an outspoken York University professor and playwright, asked me years ago in reference to Rubin, "Why do you let that man abuse you?" I couldn't answer him then, only to say that what he alleged was true. Somehow it didn't feel that way now.

I was in Toronto for two separate but related reasons: the first, to say good-bye to this controversial and heroic friend; the second, to fulfill a mission from Ray, who would soon be on his way with Marc to Toronto. They had wanted to film Rubin on his deathbed, but given Rubin's deterioration and his need for privacy, he wouldn't agree to it. Ray then suggested that Rubin and I write an op-ed piece telling the world about Rubin's cancer and making a plea to the DA to review David's case. If Rubin was willing to tell the world that he was dying, "that type of drama," Ray wrote, "could be something the *Times* would publish." He went on, "If you titled it something like 'my dying wish' and introduce Rubin's story quickly and then go into the case I think it could get quite a bit of attention. It just might give us the extra push we need." John O'Hara loved the idea and was able to get a commitment to publish from Harry Siegel of the *Daily News*. I had no doubt at all that Rubin would agree.

John Artis answered the door. He indicated that Rubin was upstairs and had just awakened but would not be coming down. Rubin being upstairs suited me, because I had brought over a gift of money for John to recognize the work he had done on Rubin's behalf. The gift was symbolic; paying him for time and labor was impossible. "You don't have to do this, Ken," he said. But I felt immense gratitude.

Rubin called out that it was OK for me to come upstairs. Inside the bedroom, he was propped up in a hospital bed. The windows were closed, and the heat was cranked up. His thinness—he was now down to one hundred pounds—made it difficult for him to stay warm. No longer the elegantly dressed and polished Rubin Carter, this Rubin Carter was devoid of vanity. His hair was longer and uncolored, his bald spot no longer hidden beneath an Akubra, and a gray beard had grown in full. His face without the concealing Akubra was radiant. His energy level was lower than usual, and the violently frightening cough took hold at regular intervals. At his peak as a fighter, Rubin, a small five-foot-eight man, had weighed close to 160 pounds. To look at old photos, one might believe that he was perhaps the buffest fighter in ring history, frightening to look at if you were his opponent. Now a frail man with full acceptance of his approaching death, he was down but not quite out. With the help of Joan Schafer, Peter Thurling, Judge Sarokin, and John Artis, along with Denzel Washington's financial support, he was at least comfortable.

It was easier for me to tell him that we would write an op-ed about David rather than "I'm coming to say good-bye forever." But both of us knew the subtext. As much as Rubin loved living, his death was never a great concern for him. In losing his body, he believed that he was casting off a shell—a worn-out and now useless part of him—and releasing his spirit, the yolk, into the universe. He wanted his corpse burned with no ceremony or celebration of life, a fierce and emphatic demand, like Shakespeare's curse against anyone with the temerity to disturb his grave. "Throw my ashes wherever the hell you want," he told John. John would take them to Kentucky and scatter them on a horse farm, a tribute, he said, to Rubin's love of horses.

He laughed at my foolish gawking. During our twelve years of on-and-off friendship I had rarely seen the person behind the slick facade. It was vindicating to see evidence of a genuine and loving interior. Though I had indeed suffered abuse from him, his mistreatment did not stem from malice but reflected the pain he carried deep within. Now, having experienced physical pain as he never had before, the soul-disfiguring pain appeared to have gone. I knew that I loved this man.

"You're looking . . . good, Rubin."

He sat back and smiled at me. "Shit."

"You know I don't make up stuff."

He nodded.

"I think about you every day. Mary Ellen, Gary, and I talk about you every day. Our lives won't be the same without you."

"That's not true, my brother. I'm always with you. I was with you on that plane you flew in on. I made sure you landed safely."

"I don't doubt it."

"Don't you ever doubt it, Ken. I can't ever thank you enough for what you did."

"Right. What would my life have been without knowing you?"

"You had to know me, brother. No one gave you a choice. Every-thing is as it should be. Even this world of sleeping people. This world is just as it should be. It makes the work we do miraculous."

"And you've got one last miracle to perform."

"*We* do."

"We, yes."

"That young man. I let this get away from me."

"No, you're going to get David out. Ken Thompson will pay atten-tion to what you say. If there's one person he will pay attention to, it's Dr. Rubin Carter. Rubin 'Hurricane' Carter. He won't pay atten-tion to me."

Rubin shook his head. A noise issued from him, some stifled inner music.

"On this level of life . . . you hearing me, Ken? On this level of life, there are no straight lines. Straight lines only exist on a higher level. I live on this lower level where we all live, but sometimes I was able to see the straight line. I could see the end of our efforts and the steps in between. I knew the lower courts were not the way. I knew parole was not the way. I knew these things but somewhere I lost track. I let myself get sidetracked. Now I see it again. The straight line I lost sight of. You hearing this?"

"I hear you."

"Good."

"I hear you, but I don't understand. Isn't it all about trial and error?"

"Because you don't see it doesn't mean it isn't there."

I waited and then asked if he was OK, and he nodded. "Can we do this?" I asked.

"There was a line going directly out the door of the prison, but we couldn't see it." Rubin began to cough, a productive cough, and he expectorated into an improvised spittoon. "Let's get started. I ain't going anywhere. Not yet."

"Tell me something. What do you think you'll find? . . . I mean where do you think you'll be when you leave this place?"

"When I'm dead? I don't mind saying that, Ken. You don't need to be talking shit about 'leaving this place.' I was alive on this Earth, and I'll be off this Earth; the Rubin Carter you see here on this bed will be dead. It's a straight line! And if I find a heaven after this life, I'll be quite surprised. I wouldn't have the qualifications to be there! But I don't see death as a place at all. In my own lifetime, when I awakened to this world of infinite possibility, now that's heaven. I lived in hell for the first forty-nine years of my life and been in heaven for the past twenty-nine." Watching me take notes, he smiled and began to laugh that deep laugh of his, but then it turned into the deep and terrible cough.

Between fits, we composed the letter to Ken Thompson. We knew from John O'Hara that Thompson was media conscious and media savvy. He was also the only person with the authority to recommend David's release.

We finished midafternoon. Rubin was spent. When I left the house, I took the Bloor subway to Ossington and, despite the awful cold and the snow, walked up the hill to Rob and Eleanor's. I had taken as much Innocence International stationery from Rubin as I could carry. Between the smells of cigarette smoke on my clothes (Artis also smoked) and the cologne on the stationery, I needed the open air. Tears came down my face, and not just from the cold.

At the house, I began to assemble the op-ed from my notes. The plan was to finish the letter, go back to Rubin's house the next day, and have him sign it. Then I'd take it to be scanned and send it to Harry Siegel and John O'Hara. I must have eaten dinner but don't remember doing so. I didn't finish the work until midnight. This had to be the best collaborative document I could possibly produce; the stakes were too high for anything else.

After all the time spent composing from the notes, I laid in bed thinking that the ending lacked punch. The op-ed had to finish with something memorable, something that could sum up the twelve years I spent knowing this man, and something that would propel David to freedom. It was my job to channel Rubin, just as with *Eye of the Hurricane*. I was playing Cyrano de Bergerac, finishing a love letter to the world in someone else's name. While it was coming from me, it really had to come from Rubin himself.

I got up before dawn and sat down again at the computer. This line would be for David, for Ray, for Marc, for Gary, for Joan, Mary Ellen, Oscar, Steve, Laura, and all the wonderful people, each of them indispensable, who were behind this huge ten-year effort. All of us who had worked toward the same elusive goal. From all of us to the district attorney.

———————

I took the subway to Rubin's house sometime near midday. Rubin had agreed to see Ray as well, so I met my son at the Runnymede Station and we walked over. I knocked on the front door. No answer. I went to the side door and knocked again. No answer. I phoned. No answer. I phoned John's cell. No answer. I waited. It was 2002 all over again, and I was waiting for Rubin on the porch on Delaware Avenue.

I called Joan and Peter. They came and picked us up. They had no idea why Rubin and John were not answering. Maybe Rubin had been taken to the hospital. Maybe John's cell needed to be charged. Or was this just vintage Rubin—a reminder that even at the end he could still fuck with your mind? He had done the same thing to Joan and Peter only a week before.

Joan and Peter dropped Ray and me at a lunch place in Toronto's Little Italy. Marc was already there, and we ordered veal sandwiches. I had to get that letter signed and send it to the *Daily News* before I left the following afternoon for Vancouver. I was beside myself, but Ray, who had as great a stake in this op-ed as I did, remained calm. I picked up on his equanimity and began to pay attention to what I was eating. My mind cleared. I had the letter after all.

We parted company, and after promising Ray I'd get back to him if anything changed, I returned to Rob and Eleanor's. Rob suffers from crippling arthritis, but not if you were to judge his dexterity by the things he can still do. One particular talent in which he takes pride is forgery. Legitimate forgery, sort of. Rob and Eleanor had bought *Eye of the Hurricane* at the Toronto launch and had it autographed by Rubin. The search for the book took some time, but we found it on a densely packed shelf in a densely packed bookcase. Sure enough, on the title page was Rubin's very large and elegant signature. It took this Cambridge graduate an hour to get the handwriting perfect. It was slightly shaky, but that would be expected of a man in Rubin's condition. It would more than suffice.

As evening came, my cell phone rang. It was Rubin. "Ken, my brother, I didn't remember you were coming this morning. John took me out to Brampton for a haircut." *A haircut? On a freezing day after he was bedridden only yesterday?* The refusal to answer the door was terrible enough, the fib even worse. I tried to rationalize the behavior. Maybe he was so sick he didn't want to be seen. Maybe he just wanted to maintain a level of control before he parted this Earth. Maybe he really did get a haircut in Brampton. But hadn't I seen the Black Swan in the street? "Can you come by tomorrow?"

What the hell. Fuck it. What does your pride matter? "I have to come early, Rubin. About ten. I've got a flight back in the afternoon."

"I'll be here."

"You mind if Ray comes?"

"Ray? Of course. I insist he come."

"All right. See you in the morning."

"You OK, my brother?"

"I'm just fine, Rubin."

"Good. See you tomorrow."

Once again, Ray and I met at Runnymede Station. We walked up to Rubin's house. The Mercedes was still sitting out front, snow covering the windshield. *Fuck it. Fuck it. Let it go. This is for David.* John was already at the door, very friendly. I found his attempts at excuses embarrassing. Ray and I sat with John at Rubin's dining room table. He told us of his imprisonment in Glassboro, New Jersey, and how he had been allowed to pursue his education at Glassboro State College and to participate in athletics. His prison stories, told with animation, suggested that those years may have provided the highlights of his life.

I looked across the table at Ray. Living a continent apart, we had not seen as much of each other as I would have liked. I loved him utterly but had not really known him. He carried on with John, speaking incisively and intelligently. What had become of this grand experiment with David McCallum? What would the film be like? How would it help David achieve his freedom? I did not know the future any better than I knew my son. Nor, I realized, did my own father know me. I had to accept the wisdom of Kahlil Gibran:

You may house their bodies but not their souls
*   For their souls dwell in the house of tomorrow, which you*
cannot visit, not even in your dreams

I remembered one time when Rubin was talking admiringly about Ray. He spoke—I think, regretfully—of not having a relationship with a child of his own. But he did have two children he would not see because, as he said, "That's a life I can't go back to." That stance seemed obstinate, like his refusal to attend his mother's funeral.

"Here I come!" we heard. We left the table and came to the stairway, where Rubin had reached the landing. Wearing white pajamas with blue stripes, he slowly descended the rest of the stairway. The irony of his wearing stripes was jaw-dropping. He sat on the bottom stair, head in hands, as if the descent had exhausted him. Shortly, he got up and led us back to the table. Was his insistence on coming downstairs just his way of demonstrating that he had been capable of going for a haircut the previous day?

I took out the letter and placed it on the table. "I want to read this to you before you sign it." He looked at me quizzically, as if he didn't remember. I knew he was on painkillers, so maybe that explained it. "It's the Ken Thompson letter."

"Go ahead."

I read the letter aloud:

My name is Dr. Rubin "Hurricane" Carter and you may remember me from my other life as a middleweight boxer. Fate had other plans for me; I was wrongly convicted of a triple murder in Paterson, New Jersey, and spent nineteen years in prison trying, along with generous friends and good people from every walk of life, to right this wrong and gain my freedom. I am now quite literally on my deathbed and am making my final wish which those in authority have the power to grant.

My single regret in life is that David McCallum of Brooklyn, New York, a man incarcerated in 1985, the same year I was released, and a man represented by Innocence International since 2004, is still in prison on a wrongful conviction after twenty-eight years. I only request that McCallum be granted a full hearing by the Conviction Integrity Unit, now under the auspices of the new Brooklyn District Attorney, Ken Thompson. Knowing what I do, I have a certainty that when the facts are brought to light, Mr. Thompson will recommend the immediate release of my client.

A man like David McCallum who has been wrongly convicted and spent twenty-eight years (from the age of sixteen) behind bars needs an unprejudiced higher authority, a person with nothing to lose or gain by righting an injustice, to examine the evidence that people have refused to act on all these years. Is it willful blindness or self-interest that was to blame? Willie Stuckey, McCallum's co-convicted, has already died in prison. Do we need David to die as well to avoid an inconvenient truth?

The details of this case would be the subject of the hearing, but I can say unequivocally that McCallum and Stuckey are as innocent of the kidnapping and murder of twenty-year old Nathan Blenner in October of 1985 as anyone now reading this plea. Not a single piece of evidence ever implicated them in this crime nor placed them anywhere near the scene. Their two confessions, gained by force and trickery, are not corroborated even by each other; they read as if two different crimes were committed. The police, prosecutor, and judge jumped on those confessions like dogs on a bone, and the previous DA's office had been chewing on it ever since. New affidavits strongly indicate that potentially exculpatory police reports were lost, discarded or suppressed. DNA testing and fingerprint evidence all point in other directions. The Brooklyn DA's office has, as I said, a Conviction Integrity Unit and this conviction has no integrity.

Wonderful things have been given to me in my life, my freedom from a place of living hell granted by the brave Judge H. Lee Sarokin, awards I've received from every corner of the globe, and dedicated people who worked for no payment beyond the thanks I was able to give. David McCallum was incarcerated two weeks before my release. I was then reborn into the miracle of this wonderful world from which death is now waiting to claim me. I'm looking him straight in the eye. He's got me on the ropes but I won't go down yet. Now I ask Ken Thompson to look straight in the eye of Truth, a tougher customer than Death, and not back down either. Just as my own verdict was "predicated on racism rather than reason, on concealment rather than disclosure," so too was Mr. McCallum's. My aim in helping this fine man is to "pay it forward," to give the help that I received as a wrongly convicted man to him who needs it now.

If I find a heaven after this life, I'll be quite surprised. In my own lifetime, when I awakened to this world of infinite possibility, now that's heaven. I lived in hell for the first forty-nine years of my life and have been in heaven for the past twenty-nine.

At this juncture, filled with emotion, I could no longer speak. Ray, John, and Rubin looked at me. From their stares, I wasn't sure they knew what was going on inside me, although I thought it was obvious. I took a deep breath and then continued: "To live in a world where truth matters, and justice, however late, really happens, that world would be heaven enough for us all."

I pushed the op-ed in front of Rubin and gave him a pen to sign. Three copies. He passed them back to me, each with the famous signature. I thought that Rob had reproduced it unerringly, even down to the slightly shaky cursive. Then I felt compassion for this man whose heart, like the king of Siam in *The King and I*, was "not always wise." What if he hadn't answered the door the previous day because he didn't want to say good-bye? I'd like to think so, and it's best for me that I do.

I had the op-ed scanned at a copy shop and sent it to the *Daily News*. After a minor disagreement with Harry Siegel over some wording and a small edit that I allowed, it came out the following Friday. The impact was immediate, I think because few people had actually known that Rubin was dying. The op-ed was printed in its entirety. At least a score of reporters asked for deathbed interviews, not the kind of drama that Rubin would accede to. For David's team, the most noticeable result of the letter was the news media investigating the allegations of the wrongful conviction. For the next two months, behind the scenes, the media looked into the case, and simultaneously began a death watch. It wasn't until Rubin died on April 20, Easter Sunday, that the stories of "Hurricane Carter's dying wish" appeared nationally and internationally. On April 21, Stephanie Clifford of the *New York Times* wrote a long article, "Even with Dying Boxer's Appeal, a Tough Road Ahead for Convicted Man," accompanied by Marc Lamy's now iconic photograph of David staring out a window at Arthur Kill Correctional. The piece, as its title implies, injected a note of somber reality. We weren't quite home yet. Still, after almost twenty-nine years, David's case was now on the front burner, where all of us wanted it to be. Ray's idea had triumphed.

John Artis called on April 20 with the news about Rubin's quiet passing. He had been a long time dying, and while I was sad and bereft, I also felt with absolute certainty that he had not left us just yet. My conviction was based less on supernatural belief—although I admit to some of that—and more on fact. His spirit was still present in the minds of David's supporters and would be a motivating factor for those deciding on his release. I now saw the straight line emerge. It had taken me long enough.

Right before his death, Rubin called Judge Sarokin. Two years later, Sarokin e-mailed me about the conversation:

Ken

Entirely by accident, I have just finished watching *David & Me* on Netflix. Beautiful. I have to admit crying—not only for David but for Rubin. I am sending a copy of this e-mail to David so that he will know how often Rubin spoke to me about his case. The scene of Rubin being unable to talk on the phone also brought back the most emotional moment of my life. Rubin called right before he died and said: I want yours to be the last voice I hear because you gave me back my life. Some crying went on there—at both ends of the line.

The media published all the prepared obits of Rubin. Some journalists emphasized his boxing career, arrest, and incarceration, as if Rubin had done nothing since his release in 1985. Others could see that his life after prison as a motivational speaker and an advocate for wrongly convicted people was more significant in its long-term impact. Between incessant alerts that I had received yet another e-mail, my phone would not stop ringing for thirty-six hours with calls from media in Canada, Australia, New Zealand, Ireland, and all over the United States. Most gratifying was the constant mention of David McCallum. Now the story of Rubin's death would not be complete without David's release. When Amy Goodman interviewed John Artis and me on *Democracy Now!*, the last question she asked me was about David and the work done on his behalf. Right before I answered, part of the trailer for *David & Me* was played. The film, Rubin's death, and the investigation into David's wrongful conviction were now tied together inextricably. It was no longer a question of "hope" with respect to David's release. Higher laws were now operating on this lower level of unconscious human insanity. I was sure of it.

The *Democracy Now!* segment finished with footage of an old speech that Rubin gave at Queens University in Kingston, Ontario. I noticed that unlike some of his later commencement orations, he moved from himself to the students, in reference to his speech impediment:

> Being stuck in a state of silence with all that frustration was my first experience of being locked away in a prison. You see, there are prisons, and there are prisons. They may look different, but they're all the same. They're all confining. They all limit your freedom. They all lock you away, grind you down, and take a terrible toll on your self-esteem. There are prisons made of brick, steel, and mortar. And then there are prisons without visible walls, prisons of poverty, illiteracy, and racism. All too often, the people condemned to these metaphorical prisons—poverty, racism, and illiteracy—end up doing double time. That is, they wind up in the physical prisons, as well. Our task, as reasonable, healthy, intelligent human beings, is to recognize the interconnectedness and the

sameness of all these prisons and then do something about them, because any kind of prison is no friend of mine. It brings out the hurricane in me.

This is clearly a call to self-awareness, social awareness, and political action, the subject of speeches that students generally hear inside graduation tents but delivered with Rubin Carter's extraordinary sense of style.

How does one explain the coincidence of Rubin dying on Easter Sunday, the op-ed reappearing, and *David & Me* opening at Toronto's Hot Docs festival exactly one week later? Mere synchronicity or miracle? The film had taken eight years to complete. Had it appeared a year earlier, its effect would have been muted. Coming as it did, when it did, maximized the impact. Seeing Rubin on-screen produced an audible reaction from the Toronto audiences mourning his recent death. I was sitting next to John Artis, and both of us were weeping.

The film, eventually bought by Netflix in 2016 and renamed *Fight for Justice: David & Me,* was one of the audience favorites at the festival and a critical success. People were pulling for David and happy to know that his case was being heard. I received e-mails from strangers saying how deeply touched they were by the film and asking how to keep abreast of developments.

The time came around for parole hearing number five. Given where the case was at the time, David did something small yet momentous. He asked for a postponement of his hearing, and it was granted. For me it meant that David had had shifted his focus from controlling the details of his case to taking control of the legal process. Psychologically, it was a declaration of independence from the cruelties and absurdities of the system. He wrote to me about his decision:

I appreciate your understanding of how I am approaching the parole matter. On the surface, it may seem that I have taken

a leap of faith by postponing, but the reality is that I want to
be released with no strings attached and not be treated like a
criminal for the rest of my life. . . . I don't think I am hanging
Laura out to dry; if anything, the opposition letter from the
Blenner family is not going away. This is a chip the board
could always play against me.

In May, Oscar, Laura, and Steve met with Ron Sullivan, Mark
Hale, and Mina Malik at the Brooklyn DA's Office. We were given
official notice that the case would be thoroughly reinvestigated. Oscar
was disappointed that the meeting did not result in a promise of
David's imminent release, but I took the reinvestigation as a positive:
they needed to be able to justify David's release to the press, the public,
and, most important, the Blenner family. I also knew with certainty
that whichever way the investigators looked, they would only find
further proof of innocence. Indeed, that had always been the case.

In June, David's application for landscaping work outside the
prison was readily approved. I reported this to the team, seeing it as
an initial step to freedom. The outside work was akin to a decompres-
sion chamber, being out with a crew in a rural environment under
minimal supervision before having to cope with the difficulties of city
life. David was filled with wonder, talking to us on the phone about
birds, trees, deer, any number of other animals, the sky, the sun. He
reported that the world felt different and looked different outside the
gates of despondency.

David & Me appeared at the Manhattan Film Festival that June
and won Best Feature Documentary. I met John O'Hara in person
for the first time at the showing, and his certainty about the eventual
outcome of David's case confirmed what I was feeling. At a Q-and-A
after the showing, someone asked if they could help with the effort to
get David out. Surprised by my own public confidence, I said that we
would not be needing help, because I fully expected him to be out soon.

The CRU called another meeting with us, and we were asked to present our case. Oscar prepared an elaborate PowerPoint presentation demonstrating the strength of our arguments and the problems with our client's conviction. A photo of David smiling, again taken by Marc, appeared at the conclusion. Prior to this crucial meeting, Steve e-mailed his possible misgivings from a legal standpoint. He wanted to know the standard the DA was using to determine whether or not they would vacate a conviction. He wondered if David would have to prove his innocence and proposed to enlist the state's help to reinvestigate the case.

I remembered what Rubin said about the law putting him into prison but not being sufficient to get him out. While Steve was being ultracareful, I was convinced that our case was already beyond the snares of an intractable legal system. I was no longer interested in speaking to witnesses or combing through documents. Yes, it would be helpful to know the standard that would apply to vacate wrongful convictions, but unless Ron Sullivan or others from the CRU specifically requested it, going back anywhere near O'Mara, Ross, Taub, or any of that group would be counterproductive. If we got word from Sullivan that the terribly high standards and procedural roadblocks an appeals court would apply were not applicable here, then we would finally be assured that the case would be decided on its merits.

When Sullivan himself echoed David's decision by recommending that he postpone the next parole hearing, we knew David was almost home. All we had to do now was wait for the decision, and, with David now working outside the prison, the waiting was a little less painful.

In September, Oscar attended a speech Ron Sullivan gave at a wrongful convictions conference in New York. Oscar approached him afterward to get some news on the state of the investigation. Ron told him, in a noncommittal way, that a decision would be coming down soon. It was hard to be one hundred percent certain, but I focused on my late friend Rubin laughing and telling me that he made sure my plane arrived safely. *Everything is as it should be, my brother.*

I received a letter from David, bursting with energy and anticipation:

> Please forgive me for being all over the place in this letter,
> but I always love writing to you, and I always have much to
> say. Who knows, I could be texting and e-mailing you soon.
> Now that sounds great!!! So true!
>
> I will always love you, Mary Ellen and Ray. Nothing or
> no one will ever change that!!!

And then October came. Monday, October 13, 2014, while I rode a
bus in Vancouver with Mary Ellen, my cell phone rang. She answered.
It was Ray, who, in an unusually brusque manner, asked to speak to
me. Ray and Marc were supposed to fly that day to the Warsaw Film
Festival, so I feared something was amiss. Being on a bus midday is
not exactly the environment one would wish for when receiving an
important call on a wonky phone. Of course, as during all public cell
phone calls, my voice was too loud. From what I could hear, he was
telling me to phone Oscar. He was also saying something about a
decision coming down. I tried to get him to clarify every single word,
so precious did the moment suddenly feel. My emotions were, like
David's, "all over the place." Looking at me and listening, Mary Ellen
thought something terrible had happened. I couldn't allow myself to
be happy, knowing how quickly it could all be taken away.

When we returned to the apartment, I phoned Oscar.

"Wait a minute, Ken, I'm getting off a call."

A long minute passed. Oscar came back on and said, "I think
we did it." Life has so few moments when you can actually savor an
emotion because something ends in a way that is totally storybook,
when the words "happily ever after" are not followed by "however."
This was one of those moments when I knew that Oscar was still a
lawyer. *I think we did it.* Of course we did!

"When's it going to happen?"

"Wednesday. Thompson is going to recommend that the conviction be vacated."

"Wednesday? It's Monday afternoon! Can't they give us some time?"

"You want him to stay in jail an extra week so you can have time to make arrangements?"

"No, but why can't they wait one more day? We've been waiting all these years and we've only got thirty-six hours?"

"Ken, they're afraid he might get killed."

When you have no choice, you get it done. Somehow you get it done. Everyone was coming: Joan from South Carolina, Gary from Washington, Steve from Illinois, Laura from New Jersey, Oscar, Van, my brother, David—everyone, including Mary Ellen and me. We would all meet at Ken Thompson's press conference at the DA's office on 350 Jay Street, Brooklyn, at 11:00 AM Wednesday, then walk over to the Kings County Supreme Court at 320 Jay Street, only blocks from Greenlight Bookstore. What we didn't know was who the judge was going to be. Firetog? That seemed impossible. But if it was, would he accept Thompson's recommendation? That's the kind of habitual and irrational worrying you do when you have gone up against the legal system for ten years. That's also what Rubin meant about losing sight of the straight line.

As for Marc, that day he got the call from Ray while his Paris-bound plane (connecting to Warsaw for the film festival there) was on the tarmac in Montreal. They wouldn't let him off the plane, so he flew to Paris and immediately booked a homeward-bound flight. Marc was not going to miss the occasion, especially since he and Ray were about to change the ending of the film. Life meets art.

October 15, 2014. We arrived in New York on Tuesday at midnight and met Gary the following sunny morning at the hotel. After breakfast we got on a subway that took its time getting to Brooklyn. I was afraid we'd be shut out of the press conference, and practically ran to the office, exhausting Gary in the process. Too caught up in the moment, I wasn't paying sufficient attention to the health issues that had dogged him over the past two months. Mary Ellen cautioned me to slow down.

David was picked up at Otisville that morning and told he might not be returning. He stuffed all his important belongings into a duffle bag and left other items—food, clothing, books—with fellow prisoners he was leaving behind. Unusually, he rode in a car, not a police van, to the Brooklyn DA's Office. On the way there, one of the officers in the car slipped a CD into the player. Out came Dylan's voice: "Here comes the story of the Hurricane," a recognition of the true spirit behind this day. At that point, despite having to wear shackles, David knew for sure he would not be returning to Otisville as a prisoner again. From his vantage point, his escorts were proud of the role they were playing.

Steve Drizin wrote a piece for the *Huffington Post* describing those moments:

> Throughout my career, I have been searching for moments of grace (and mercy and forgiveness) in the criminal justice system but these moments have been few and far between. I never thought that it would be a prosecutor—King's County District Attorney Ken Thompson and his Conviction Review Unit (CRU)—that would show me the meaning of grace. . . . Paying attention to these smaller details matters. This is where grace lies. The humane way in which McCallum and Stuckey were exonerated will be an essential step in Mr. McCallum's healing process. It won't erase the pain and

the hurt of nearly three decades that were stolen from him, but it will send him back into the world with less bitterness, less anger, and more hope as he tackles the enormous challenges of life after exoneration.

We met Ray and Marc, both hefting cameras, in the hallway and entered a shoebox-shaped room jammed with media. Inside we greeted Oscar, Laura, and, for the first time, Steve. Incredibly, after all those years I had never even shaken his hand. These wrongful conviction releases are major good-news stories, but David's twenty-nine years and his association with Rubin Carter made this one special. One of the messages these events convey is that in the end the system works. Ironically, Rubin insisted in many public appearances that the system does not work. Were it not for extraordinary measures (especially the CRU's) and plain miracles, most wrongly convicted people lacking DNA evidence would never be released.

After fifteen minutes, Thompson strode into the room flanked by some of his new appointees, Ron Sullivan among them. To Thompson's left and below the raised platform, a board with twelve facial photos was set up. They were the recently exonerated, with David among them. Two of the squares were blank with a name beneath. One was Willie Stuckey. All of David's legal team stood behind Thompson. Although I wanted to be up there, I was told that my presence might be seen as a government endorsement of *David & Me*. (I found this odd until one of the press corps later asked Thompson if he had been influenced by the film, to which the DA replied that his interest in the case began back in January.)

Thompson read a statement:

In the interest of justice, I will ask the Court today to vacate the murder convictions of David McCallum and Willie Stuckey. After a thorough and fair review of the case by my

Conviction Review Unit and the independent review panel,
I have concluded that their convictions should not stand and
that Mr. McCallum should be released from prison . . .

From the totality of the circumstances, the CRU and the
independent review panel concluded that the jury's fact-find-
ing ability as to both defendants was significantly corrupted
and additionally finds clear reasonable doubt as to the truth
and accuracy of the confessions, which were the sole bases
of the defendants' convictions.

This was the first public declaration of something we had known
for ten years. It is impossible to describe the effect that statement
produced in me. We had been in search of the miraculous, and here
we were at the end. We had gone the distance.

One of the facts that emerged during the investigation resulted
in Thompson's words "sole bases." Oscar said that in murder investigations the police first look for the weapon—in David's case, the
gun used to shoot Nathan Blenner. This gun was never found. In
courtroom testimony outlined earlier, James Johnson said that he
gave the gun to his Aunt Lottie, who had passed this gun on to Jaime,
who then gave the gun to Willie Stuckey. We always thought the
transaction sounded made-up, giving Johnson the distance that he
needed to avoid being implicated, and we could never find Jaime.
However, none of us, not even Van, ever thought to look for Lottie
so many years later, especially without her last name. The CRU, with
a greater capacity for locating witnesses, went to Lottie first. When
she angrily insisted that she had never seen a gun, the link between
Johnson and Stuckey was broken. We know from Lottie that Butta
and Bjorneby had not sought her out to verify Johnson's statement.
Why risk ruining their case?

During questioning about the previous DA's office, Thompson
dropped a verbal bomb. Silence descended, cameras flashed, and

pens moved. We looked at each other: Did we hear that correctly? Did Ken Thompson really say, "I inherited a legacy of disgrace"? He answered a follow-up question from a stunned reporter who suggested he was guilty of overstatement. Thompson gestured down to the board. "What do you think this represents? I say it's a disgrace." These words confirmed to me that Rubin's uncompromising spirit was in that room. I was also convinced that Thompson was appalled by what had befallen so many young black defendants. The social and racial composition of the exonerees was unmistakable: all of them were poor, most had substandard legal representation at the trial phase, and most were African American. Thompson's attempt to right these wrongs will be remembered by many as an act of bravery. The releases offended scores of entrenched authorities and prosecutors.

Following the press conference, David's supporters were invited to the district attorney's offices. Walking into an anteroom, we saw David, shackles removed, sitting there in his familiar green prison garb, but outside a prison for the first time in twenty-nine years. Had I ever felt like this before? Once, one time only, when Ray was born. I like to think of David's release as a rebirth and us the midwives. One of the detectives brought in takeout jerk chicken that David could not finish.

When I talked to David later about the day of his release, he spoke about that chicken: "I was hungry, man. I hadn't eaten the whole morning. I really wanted to finish it, but I was nervous and overwhelmed. And I was still not convinced I'd be released. Disappointment had become a reflex. But seeing all of you together in that office was surreal. I knew that everything would be OK."

We then went inside the DA's office. In an unusual gesture, Thompson brought his wife along for the occasion. The photo of him shaking David's hand appeared in media and was also featured on his website. What was it about the case that had so moved him? I concluded that he had indeed seen *David & Me*, suffused with David's unmistakable humanity and decency. I also guessed that Rubin Carter was as much a hero to him as he was to us.

Then David, technically still a prisoner, was separated from us, and we were told to return in an hour for the court session. He remembers now in detail: "I went into a separate room and changed from my state greens into a beige jumpsuit. This was the first time in twenty-nine years I was out of prison clothes. I threw the green uniform in the garbage. The end of an era. I was sad, thinking about some of the guys I left behind. Good people at Otisville who had redeemed themselves. I was thinking of Willie. I never stopped thinking of him. It sounds crazy to say, but I have to admit I was also sad to leave. 'We're losing a good one,' one of the guards said. Otisville and other prisons was the world I knew. I was moving from the known to the unknown."

At 2:00 PM, a crush of people—reporters, cameramen, and supporters—entered the courtroom. David was seated at the defense table, wearing the beige jumpsuit, meant, I suppose, to be transitional. The seats quickly filled, so people stood along the walls. Oscar and I looked around and wondered why the McCallum family hadn't arrived. Given the momentousness of the occasion, the proceedings were delayed. Because of the horrendous Brooklyn traffic, my sister arrived in a taxi at the courthouse just minutes before the doors closed. We assumed that David's brother's van was in similar difficulty. Still, we couldn't believe that the family hadn't come early, given how important they were to David. The situation reminded me of the night at Greenlight Bookstore.

Eventually the court was called into session without them. Judge Matthew D'Emic presided. Oscar requested that the judge allow Willie Stuckey's mother, Rosia Nealy, to sit with him at the defense table. It was a magnanimous gesture but marred by the irony that she was present for her deceased son and Ernestine had not arrived for her living one. David described to me later how he met a crying

Mrs. Nealy on the elevator going up to the courtroom. "She took my hand and told me she now had a second son," he said.

Judge D'Emic asked Oscar to present first. This also represented a break with usual procedure, in that the motion to vacate convictions almost always comes from the district attorney. Oscar was able to lay out several grounds for dismissal, including the ineptitude of David's defense attorney, that might have been impossible for Thompson to mention.

Mark Hale represented the state, or "the people." It was then that twenty-nine years were swiftly annulled by one sentence: "The people do not oppose the motion." Hale went on to describe the multiple flaws in the case, the DNA evidence, and the confessions, with their conflicting accounts of what had happened on October 20, 1985. I heard two words near the end: "no evidence." All those years of insisting, all of these top-flight professionals, and we finally had a public admission by the DA's office that David McCallum had been wrongly convicted. The very simplicity of it confirmed for me that, as Rubin insisted, the system does not work. If the system worked, David would have been released years ago.

Judge D'Emic reviewed the troubling aspects of the case and ruled to dismiss the indictment. David collapsed at the table, and Mrs. Nealy placed her hand on his back in a gesture of support. The courtroom burst into spontaneous applause. Later, David described his reaction: "We did it. We didn't quit. People always telling me no, no, no, no, no. All that fighting. Times I thought I'd never get out."

The reporters, photographers, and cameramen were asked to leave the courtroom first. For Ray and Marc, this was fortuitous, because just as they got outside, David's niece and nephew ran down the hallway, followed by Ernestine and the rest of the family. The scene of David hugging his mother and crying with joy were caught on camera. I kept remembering Rubin's words: *Everything is as it should be.* They were late not only because of Brooklyn's traffic but also because

Ernestine wanted all of David's favorite foods to be ready upon his return. The McCallums were uncomplicated people who had rarely ventured beyond the confines of their Bushwick neighborhood.

David then faced a bank of reporters and cameras and began carrying on a press conference as if that was all he had been doing for the past twenty-nine years. He called the moment "bittersweet," mentioning that "another person should be here with me: Willie Stuckey." In this way, David was true to everything he had been saying to us for the ten years. His loyalty to his coconvicted was steadfast.

———————

The end of *Fight for Justice: David & Me* begins out on a street lined with well-wishers and strangers who have discovered what the occasion is all about. David climbs into his brother's van. As David fumbles with the seat belt, Mia, his niece, cries out, "This is a thousand years of happiness." He looks through the windshield out into the street.

Looking back, David remembers this incomparable moment: "So many people were outside there, even more than in a prison yard. I was seeing everyone but feeling lost at the same time. I was so much in shock, I couldn't hear anyone. I thought, *You have to control this joy.* I was still afraid to let my guard down. In prison, you could lose your life for that. But I knew that there was no real reason to control it. I was going home."

Back at home, in the film, David goes first to his disabled sister Ella's room. She has not seen her brother in twenty-nine years. He leans down to kiss her and tell her that he's come home. As you watch, you wonder if she's been awaiting his return. Back out on Cooper Street, Ray, who has shown a loving, loyal heart and the perseverance to go with it, embraces David, irresistible smiles on both their faces. Most of the support team, along with David, Mattie, and the rest of the McCallum family, pose on the front stoop of the Bushwick apartment. He has come home, and we have been a part of it. As Ray says near the film's closing, "And for one little moment in a little corner of Brooklyn, New York, all was right with the world."

Does life on this lower level allow for anything better than that?

The final scene shows Ray and David walking out on a pier in Williamsburg, Brooklyn. David says the word "pier" as if attempting to ground himself, to embrace the dream of his freedom. Then Ray asks if he has anything planned the next day. David says no. Ray asks if he wants to go to see a movie. David assents. It's so apt. All that's left is for David to live his life, future unknowable. To a person incarcerated for decades, the certainty of uncertainty, the knowledge that tomorrow will be different from today, may well be the greatest gift of all.

Welcome home, October 15, 2014. Standing, from left: Van Padgett, Oscar Michelen, Mary Ellen Belfiore, Ken Klonsky, Marc Lamy, Gary Dolin, Joan Ustin, Ray Klonsky. Seated, from left: Aaron Johnson (David's nephew), Mattie McCallum (sister), David McCallum, John Jones (brother), Ernestine McCallum (mother), Rufus Jones (brother), Mia Johnson (niece).

EPILOGUE

UPON HIS RELEASE, David McCallum hunkered down in his mother's Bushwick apartment. With the invaluable assistance of Laura Cohen, he got a job at the Manhattan Legal Aid Society, where he quickly earned the love and respect of his fellow employees. Seeking female companionship, he then ventured into the world of online dating and on his second try met Valerie, a single mother of two boys, and she soon offered to have another child with him. Their baby girl, Quinn, was born in May 2016. Late that summer David and Willie Stuckey's family received settlements from New York State and New York City. As of this writing, David, despite much urging and encouragement, has still not gotten a driver's license.

Tragically, Ken Thompson died of cancer on October 9, 2016, leaving behind a wife, two children, and our everlasting gratitude. His time in office, during which he accomplished more than most politicians do in much longer spans, lasted less than three years. On October 15, two years to the day of his release, David was asked to speak at Thompson's public funeral held at his church. "Mr. Thompson didn't only give me my freedom," David began. "Mr. Thompson gave me my five-month-old daughter, Quinn. If you did not do that for me, I don't know where I'd be."

I have an envelope in my storage room containing police documents from David's case. The envelope is addressed to Ken Klonsky, director, Innocence International, and postmarked October 2011. I failed to notice until recently that Rubin had conferred this title on me. I had looked but not seen. The envelope has a residual smell of smoke and cologne. Smoke and cologne. Still I remember the Hurricane, in no way more palpable than that.

ACKNOWLEDGMENTS

Deepest thanks to Jabbar Collins, Marty Tankleff, Everton Wagstaffe, Joel Rudin, Bruce Barket, Stephanie Clifford, William Finnegan, John Caher, and Marvin Schechter, who may not know how much they meant to us. And to the members of A Drift Collective, whose participation in the manuscript kept it moving in a forward direction.

APPENDIX

CONTRASTING FALSE CONFESSIONS

The brief videotaped confessions given to ADA David Rappaport were shown to the jury and lacked the details of the interrogation notes taken by Detective Joseph Butta. On the videotape, Rappaport made only minimal attempts to have the suspects clarify the confessions. The following confessions of David McCallum and Willie Stuckey were told to (or extracted by) police detective Joseph Butta during the interrogation on October 27, 1985, the night of the arrests. Their answers, along with an occasional aside from Butta, are reproduced here verbatim. My editorial clarifications appear in brackets, and my analysis appears in italics.

According to Butta's notes, both boys were brought down separately to the eighty-third precinct and separately asked if they "knew anything about the man who was shot in Aberdeen Park, off Bushwick Ave." Both of them were reported by Butta to have answered yes and proceeded to make the statements without prompting from the detective. Conversely, McCallum and Stuckey both claimed to have been slapped and threatened by the detective and to not have confessed of their own free wills.

Meeting on October 20, and the Time They Went to Queens

STUCKEY: "Last Sunday, early in the day" at Halsey Park

McCALLUM: "About twelve o'clock" (place not given)

Getting to Queens

STUCKEY: "We went to the train station at Halsey and Broadway, we got on the J train. He told me to stand by the door. He snatched a chain, and we got off the train. We got on a train going back to Queens. I don't know what stop we got off, but it was Queens." *Ozone Park is serviced by the A train and has no junction with the J. To get from the J to Ozone Park on foot, one would have to cross a parkway, Cypress Hills Cemetery, Highland Park (or Forest Park), and all of Woodhaven, Queens.*

McCALLUM: "We got on the train and went to Queens."

Possible Fed Fact

"He [David] snatched a chain." *According to James Johnson, as told to private investigator Anthony Cordero, Jake Prince "had been arrested for snatching a chain from a woman." Queens police said that Murray Howard and Jake Prince were together on the subway when Prince snatched the chain.*

After Getting Off the Train

STUCKEY: "We walked around, we passed a girl who was cleaning her car. A red car. David said to the girl 'That's a nice car.' We kept walking to the corner. He told me to stop there. He kept walking across the street. He came back to where I was. He was in the street."

McCALLUM: "Got off the train and walked around."

Fed Fact

The "girl" was Chrissie Owens, who at around 2:00 PM was accosted by two black males who were described as being about twenty years old, one five foot eleven and one five four to five six (Murray Howard was known as "shorty"), and one with braided hair. They in no way fit the description of David McCallum and Willie Stuckey; McCallum and Stuckey were both sixteen, five foot five, and neither had braided hair. She described a conversation in which one of the men said, "Nice car," and she answered, "If it's not here in the morning, I'll know where to look." In court, the prosecution tried to change the time of this meeting from 2:00 PM to noon. They knew that Owens's description did not fit the defendants, yet Chrissie Owens appears in Willie's confession. The source of the alleged meeting had to be Detective Butta, who had picked up the story from a neighborhood canvass and fed it to Willie.

Time of Kidnapping

STUCKEY: Not established

McCALLUM: Not established

ACTUAL: Never established by the two child witnesses.

MISSING EVIDENCE: 911 (sprint) call report

Description of Kidnapping

STUCKEY: "He was in the street. I walked on the sidewalk towards the back of the black car. It had a burgundy interior. David walked over to the driver's side door in the street. It was open and the white kid had one foot in the street and the other out. He was trying to crank it over. David showed the guy the gun from under his arm and said, "Get in the back seat." The guy jumped over the back seat. He told me to get in the car. I said, 'What you doing, man?' He told me to shut up and we drove off."

McCALLUM: "We saw a white boy sitting in the car. A black car with
    red velvet interior. Then Supreme [Willie Stuckey] put the gun
    to his head and told him to get out. We jumped in. Willie told
    him to get back in the car. He got in the back."

Fed Facts

*The scenario came from the descriptions of two boys in the neighborhood
who witnessed the event. In fact, Stuckey described details—the open
door, the foot out in the street—that could only be seen from the driver's
side, yet he claimed he was walking on the sidewalk. It is also doubtful
that Stuckey, at his age, would have used the phrase "it had a burgundy
interior"; rather, it would likely have been elicited or inserted by Butta to
coincide with police reports. The boy witnesses told ADA Bjorneby that
they saw Nathan Blenner jump over the front seat into the back (but in
court they said that they said they could not see Blenner at that distance).*

Inconsistencies

*Stuckey said McCallum ordered Blenner into the back seat at gunpoint.
McCallum said that Stuckey pointed the gun at Blenner's head and made
him get out of the car. Then he said that he and Willie got into the car and
ordered Nathan to get back in the car. Why didn't Blenner run off if he was
standing outside the car and Stuckey and McCallum were inside the car?*

*Stuckey said that McCallum was in control of the entire operation
and everything was being done against his (Stuckey's) will. In the taped
confession, Stuckey said that David was driving the car. If McCallum
had driven the car, then Stuckey had to be holding the gun.*

The Time Between the Kidnapping and the Murder

STUCKEY: "We drove off for a couple of hours. David said wait until it
    gets dark. I said why? Because I wanted to go home. It was starting
    to get dark, we drove to the park (Aberdeen) off Bushwick Ave."

McCALLUM: "We drove around for two and a half hours and came back to Brooklyn. We went to Bushwick and Aberdeen Park. It was starting to get dark."

Inconsistencies

There is no confirmation that the murder took place at night—in fact, the medical examiner's report lists the time of death at 3:15 PM. Shots were heard in the park in the afternoon.

Questions

How could the car be driven around town undetected right after the kidnapping was reported and police had received the make of car and the license plate number? Where did they go? Would it be possible for McCallum or Stuckey to know road routes in any neighborhood outside their own? Neither of them had a driver's license nor had ever driven a car.

The Murder of Nathan Blenner

STUCKEY: "David told me and the guy to get out of the car. I walked first, the dude in the middle, David in back of him with the gun in his back and his other hand on his neck. We all walked into the park. He told me to lead the way. I went to the hole in the fence in the back of the park. Then he told the dude to walk in front of him and they went first. They went down in the hold. David pushed, I stayed on top, I heard one shot, the dude said, 'Why are you doing this.' I started to walk away and heard 2 more shots. David ran up to me and put the gun inside his pants belt, and put the jacket over it. We went out of the park the same way."

McCALLUM: "We all got out of the car and went into the park. We went to the back in the weeds and trees. Willie told the White Boy, 'you know what time it is.' The white boy said 'you what are you doing.' He cocked the gun and the white boy tried to run. He pointed the gun at him and shot one time. The white boy dropped, and his arms was moving on the ground. We ran out of the park."

Inconsistencies

Almost nothing in the two confessions is corroborated except the time of day (seriously in question) and the place, the rear of Aberdeen Park, where Blenner's body was discovered. The rest are attempts by McCallum and Stuckey to blame the other guy and present himself as a helpless bystander/witness. Stuckey even distances himself from the killing and says he was walking away and heard two more shots.

Points of Contention

1. *Who had the gun and did the killing? Stuckey says McCallum, and McCallum says Stuckey.*

2. *Who was present at the murder? According to Stuckey, he was up the hill and didn't see McCallum kill Stuckey. According to McCallum, Stuckey accompanied him to the killing.*

3. *What was said? Stuckey relates that Blenner said, "Why are you doing this?" Could Stuckey have heard these words, given that he was standing on the hill and David was down "in the hold"? McCallum says that Stuckey screamed out, "You know what time it is." Then Blenner said, "You, what are you doing?"*

4. *How was the murder accomplished? According to Stuckey, he heard three shots and saw nothing. McCallum said that Blenner tried to run, Stuckey fired one bullet, and "the white boy dropped and his arms was moving on the ground." To believe McCallum, you'd be forced to believe that Stuckey was able to shoot this accurately in the dark and to put a bullet angling upward into the back of a flee-*

ing man's head. Blenner was found lying on his face, his arms at his sides. It would have been impossible for him to flail his arms.

The Trip Back to Bushwick

STUCKEY: "We went out of the park the same way. I was gonna go to Bushwick Ave. David said get in the car, he made a U-turn and we drove off. We got to a two way street (Cooper St.) parked the car and walked to the JHS 296 Halsey Park. I went home."

BUTTA: "David McCallum said that Willie Stuckey drove the car and shot the victim, and after that evening he never saw the car again."

McCALLUM: "We ran out of the park, we got in the car and drove it to Furman St. and we walked to Willie's house and chilled out for ½ to 1 hour. I went home."

Inconsistencies

Parking the car at Cooper Street would have meant that David parked a stolen car, which had been used in a kidnapping and murder, in front of his own apartment for two days. Furman Street, where David said they left the car, is a good distance from Bushwick. The car was found burned behind a warehouse on Fulton Avenue, close to Aberdeen Park.

The Following Days

STUCKEY: "For two days David keep looking for me, I told my mom to tell him I'm not there. My mom asked if I got in trouble or did I owe anybody money. I saw (David) the next day in the car. When I was in the park on Halsey. He wanted me to go for a ride. I said I wanted to play handball. He called me a "Sucker" and drove off. On Wednesday (10/23/85) afternoon, I was coming from the train, he was walking up my block. He told me to come in the hallway, he gave me the same gun and he left. I took the gun upstairs and hid it under my mattress; it's been there ever since."

McCallum: No account whatsoever

Butta: "A little later that evening, the assigned along with Detectives O'Keefe and Johnson 83PDU visited Mrs. Rosia Smith, 1057 Jefferson Ave. who is the mother of Mr. Stuckey. She gave me permission to look under the mattress for the weapon. It was not there. I called the youth at the station house via telephone, and he said that yesterday some of his friends came over the house [redacted] and another guy; he believes that one of them took the gun when he left the room."

Inconsistencies

At first Willie Stuckey sounded convincing here, but he provided details with the understanding that he was going home and wouldn't be held responsible for the crime. It was in his interest to maintain the story of being a helpless victim of David McCallum, just like Nathan Blenner. The dates were arranged to account for the discovery of the burned car on the twenty-second.

Problems and Questions

Stuckey said McCallum was driving around Brooklyn in the same stolen car for two days after the carjacking, kidnapping, and murder. Presumably the police, searching the city for this very car, never saw McCallum driving it nor identified the license plate and pulled him over nor noticed it sitting on Cooper Street. Also, in those two days McCallum had not gotten rid of the gun that killed Nathan Blenner. He gave the murder weapon to Stuckey, who put it under his mattress. The same Willie Stuckey who had portrayed himself as a helpless victim and refused to see David McCallum and ride around with him in the car was still willing to accept the murder weapon.

Explanation

Butta needed to account for James Johnson's story about Willie Stuckey offering him the gun. To close the circle, Stuckey had to have the gun after the murder. That either of these two "clever" sixteen-year-old boys could cover up any involvement in a murder and still pass the weapon back and forth three days after the killing is the single most ridiculous element in the whole confession. Stuckey gave Butta just what he wanted, but Butta couldn't find the gun beneath the mattress. The gun could not simply vanish into thin air, so Stuckey said some friends took it. Right to the end, he gave Butta a story that Butta could use. Stuckey still thought that he was going home. The gun was never located, nor was its caliber ever revealed. McCallum's confession lacked detail because all that Butta really needed was David's admission that he was with Willie during the kidnapping and murder. As an accomplice, David would be convicted of the same crime.

On the basis of these two confessions and not a single other piece of evidence tying McCallum or Stuckey to this crime, David McCallum was imprisoned for twenty-nine years. Willie Stuckey served fifteen years in prison for a murder he didn't commit but, unlike David, never lived to see his name cleared.

KEY FIGURES

Dr. Rubin "Hurricane" Carter (1937–2014), former middleweight boxer, imprisoned nineteen years on a wrongful conviction, renowned advocate for the wrongly convicted

David McCallum, wrongly convicted man who spent twenty-nine years in the New York State corrections system and whose courage, determination, and brilliance inspired us for ten long years

David's Legal Team

Oscar Michelen, attorney, Cuomo LLC, New York, New York

Steve Drizin, false confessions expert, Bluhm Legal Clinic, Northwestern University, Chicago, Illinois

Laura Cohen, director of Rutgers Law School clinic, Newark, New Jersey

John O'Hara, attorney, Brooklyn, New York

Jay Salpeter, private investigator, Garden City, New York

Van Padgett, private investigator, Brooklyn, New York

David's Support Team

Mary Ellen Belfiore, friend and supporter, Toronto, Ontario; Vancouver, British Columbia

Gary Dolin, psychiatric social worker, Innocence International, Bellingham, Washington

Ken Klonsky, director, Innocence International, Toronto, Ontario; Vancouver, British Columbia

Ray Klonsky, filmmaker and friend, Toronto and New York City

Marc Lamy, filmmaker and friend, Montreal

Andrei Schiller-Chan, friend and supporter, Melbourne, Australia.

Joan and Martin Ustin, friends and supporters, Charleston, South Carolina

Brooklyn District Attorney's Office, pre-2014

Charles "Joe" Hynes, district attorney

John O'Mara, assistant district attorney, head of Conviction Integrity Unit

Ken Taub, head of Homicide

Ruth Ross, assistant district attorney

Eric Bjorneby, assistant district attorney, prosecutor in the case against David McCallum and Willie Stuckey

David Rappaport, assistant district attorney who took both David and Willie's videotaped confessions

Brooklyn District Attorney's Office, After 2014

Ken Thompson, district attorney

Mark Hale, head of Conviction Review Unit

Ron Sullivan, legal counsel, Conviction Review Unit

Brooklyn Supreme Court Judges

Neil Firetog

Matthew D'Emic

INDEX